Baby Talk

Judith Keim

BOOKS BY JUDITH KEIM

THE HARTWELL WOMEN SERIES:
The Talking Tree – 1
Sweet Talk – 2
Straight Talk – 3
Baby Talk – 4
The Hartwell Women – Boxed Set

THE BEACH HOUSE HOTEL SERIES:
Breakfast at The Beach House Hotel – 1
Lunch at The Beach House Hotel – 2
Dinner at The Beach House Hotel – 3
Christmas at The Beach House Hotel – 4
Margaritas at The Beach House Hotel – 5 (2021)
Dessert at The Beach House Hotel – 6 (2022)

THE FAT FRIDAYS GROUP:
Fat Fridays – 1
Sassy Saturdays – 2
Secret Sundays – 3

SALTY KEY INN BOOKS:
Finding Me – 1
Finding My Way – 2
Finding Love – 3
Finding Family – 4

CHANDLER HILL INN BOOKS:
Going Home – 1
Coming Home – 2
Home at Last – 3

PRAISE FOR JUDITH KEIM'S NOVELS

THE BEACH HOUSE HOTEL SERIES

"Love the characters in this series. This series was my first introduction to Judith Keim. She is now one of my favorites. Looking forward to reading more of her books."

BREAKFAST AT THE BEACH HOUSE HOTEL *is an easy, delightful read that offers romance, family relationships, and strong women learning to be stronger. Real life situations filter through the pages. Enjoy!"*

LUNCH AT THE BEACH HOUSE HOTEL – *"This series is such a joy to read. You feel you are actually living with them. Can't wait to read the latest one."*

DINNER AT THE BEACH HOUSE HOTEL – *"A Terrific Read! As usual, Judith Keim did it again. Enjoyed immensely. Continue writing such pleasantly reading books for all of us readers."*

CHRISTMAS AT THE BEACH HOUSE HOTEL – *"Not Just Another Christmas Novel. This is book number four in the series and my introduction to Judith Keim's writing. I wasn't disappointed. The characters are dimensional and engaging. The plot is well crafted and advances at a pleasing pace. The Florida location is interesting and warming. It was a delight to read a romance novel with mature female protagonists. Ann and Rhoda have life experiences that enrich the story. It's a clever book about friends and extended family. Buy copies for your book group pals and enjoy this seasonal read."*

THE HARTWELL WOMEN SERIES – Books 1 – 4

"This was an EXCELLENT series. When I discovered Judith Keim, I read all of her books back to back. I thoroughly enjoyed the women Keim has written about. They are believable and you want to just jump into their lives and be their friends! I can't wait for any upcoming books!"

"I fell into Judith Keim's Hartwell Women series and have read & enjoyed all of her books in every series. Each centers around a strong & interesting woman character and their family interaction. Good reads that leave you wanting more."

THE FAT FRIDAYS GROUP – Books 1 – 3

"Excellent story line for each character, and an insightful representation of situations which deal with some of the contemporary issues women are faced with today."

"I love this author's books. Her characters and their lives are realistic. The power of women's friendships is a common and beautiful theme that is threaded throughout this story."

THE SALTY KEY INN SERIES

<u>FINDING ME</u> – *"I thoroughly enjoyed the first book in this series and cannot wait for the others! The characters are endearing with the same struggles we all encounter. The setting makes me feel like I am a guest at The Salty Key Inn...relaxed, happy & light-hearted! The men are yummy and the women strong. You can't get better than that! Happy Reading!"*

<u>FINDING MY WAY</u>- *"Loved the family dynamics as well as uncertain emotions of dating and falling in love.*

Appreciated the morals and strength of parenting throughout. Just couldn't put this book down."

FINDING LOVE – "I waited for this book because the first two was such good reads. This one didn't disappoint.... Judith Keim always puts substance into her books. This book was no different, I learned about PTSD, accepting oneself, there is always going to be problems but stick it out and make it work. Just the way life is. In some ways a lot like my life. Judith is right, it needs another book and I will definitely be reading it. Hope you choose to read this series, you will get so much out of it."

FINDING FAMILY – "Completing this series is like eating the last chip. Love Judith's writing, and her female characters are always smart, strong, vulnerable to life and love experiences."

"This was a refreshing book. Bringing the heart and soul of the family to us."

CHANDLER HILL INN SERIES

GOING HOME – "I absolutely could not put this book down. Started at night and read late into the middle of the night. As a child of the '60s, the Vietnam war was front and center so this resonated with me. All the characters in the book were so well developed that the reader felt like they were friends of the family."

"I was completely immersed in this book, with the beautiful descriptive writing, and the authors' way of bringing her characters to life. I felt like I was right inside her story."

COMING HOME – "*Coming Home is a winner. The characters are well-developed, nuanced and likable. Enjoyed the vineyard setting, learning about wine growing and seeing the challenges Cami faces in running and growing a business. I look forward to the next book in this series!*"

"*Coming Home was such a wonderful story. The author has a gift for getting the reader right to the heart of things.*"

HOME AT LAST – "*In this wonderful conclusion, to a heartfelt and emotional trilogy set in Oregon's stunning wine country, Judith Keim has tied up the Chandler Hill series with the perfect bow.*"

"*Overall, this is truly a wonderful addition to the Chandler Hill Inn series. Judith Keim definitely knows how to perfectly weave together a beautiful and heartfelt story.*"

"*The storyline has some beautiful scenes along with family drama. Judith Keim has created characters with interactions that are believable and some of the subjects the story deals with are poignant.*"

SEASHELL COTTAGE BOOKS

A CHRISTMAS STAR – "*Love, laughter, sadness, great food, and hope for the future, all in one book. It doesn't get any better than this stunning read.*"

"*A Christmas Star is a heartwarming Christmas story featuring endearing characters. So many Christmas books are set in snowbound places...it was a nice change to read a Christmas story that takes place on a warm sandy beach!*" Susan Peterson

CHANGE OF HEART – "_CHANGE OF HEART is the summer read we've all been waiting for. Judith Keim is a master at creating fascinating characters that are simply irresistible. Her stories leave you with a big smile on your face and a heart bursting with love._"

~Kellie Coates Gilbert, author of the popular Sun Valley Series

A SUMMER OF SURPRISES – "_The story is filled with a roller coaster of emotions and self-discovery. Finding love again and rebuilding family relationships._"

"_Ms. Keim uses this book as an amazing platform to show that with hard emotional work, belief in yourself and love, the scars of abuse can be conquered. It in no way preaches, it's a lovely story with a happy ending._"

"_The character development was excellent. I felt I knew these people my whole life. The story development was very well thought out I was drawn [in] from the beginning._"

DESERT SAGE INN BOOKS
THE DESERT FLOWERS – ROSE – "_The Desert Flowers - Rose, is the first book in the new series by Judith Keim. I always look forward to new books by Judith Keim, and this one is definitely a wonderful way to begin The Desert Sage Inn Series!_"

"_In this first of a series, we see each woman come into her own and view new beginnings even as they must take this tearful journey as they slowly lose a dear friend. This is a very well written book with well-developed and likable main characters. It was interesting and enlightening as the first_ *portion of this saga unfolded. I very much enjoyed this book and I do recommend it"*

"Judith Keim is one of those authors that you can always depend on to give you a great story with fantastic characters. I'm excited to know that she is writing a new series and after reading book 1 in the series, I can't wait to read the rest of the books."!

Baby Talk

The Hartwell Women Series – Book 4

Judith Keim

Wild Quail Publishing

Baby Talk is a work of fiction. Names, characters, places, public or private institutions, corporations, towns, and incidents are the product of the author's imagination or are used fictitiously. Any resemblance to actual events, locales, or persons, living or dead, is coincidental.

No part of this book may be reproduced or transmitted in any form or by any electronic or mechanical means, including information storage and retrieval systems, without permission in writing from the author, except by a reviewer who may quote brief passages in a review. This book may not be resold or uploaded for distribution to others. For permissions contact the author directly via electronic mail:

wildquail.pub@gmail.com

www.judithkeim.com,

Published in the United States of America by:

Wild Quail Publishing
PO Box 171332
Boise, ID 83717-1332

ISBN# 978-0-9968637-1-1

Dedication

With gratitude to foster parents everywhere, who give children a chance to find love, security and happiness.

I also wish to dedicate this story to my husband Peter. It's rare to have the kind of love and partnership we share.

Love you, man!

Foreword

A number of years ago, I served on a volunteer Foster Care Review Panel that was set up to hear various cases within the foster care system in lieu of the judge who would normally hear them. We were all carefully trained and vetted, and if there was any incongruity with the outcome, the case would be turned over to the judge to review the Panel's actions.

It was, without a doubt, one of the most difficult yet satisfying things I've done for the community. There were highs from the happy, easy decisions made within the law and lows for the horrendous situations in which some children were placed or from which they came. Those were the tough times, times in which I sometimes went home and went to bed to deal with it. Foster parents who take in children and give them a loving, safe environment under sometimes difficult situations are among those people I most admire. It's not an easy job even under the best of circumstances.

As I began to think about writing Marissa's story, more and more of those memories came back to me. I realized then what her journey would be.

Some interesting facts:

On any given day, there are approximately **402,000 children in foster care in the United States.**

In 2013, over **640,000 children spent time in** U.S. foster care.

Source: Children's Rights Organization

In the U.S. 397,122 children are living without permanent families in the foster care system. 101,666 of these children are eligible for adoption, but nearly 32% of these children will wait over three years in foster care before being adopted.

Source: AFCARS Report, No. 20

In 2012, 23,396 youth aged out of the U.S. foster care system without the emotional and financial support necessary to succeed. Nearly 40% had been homeless or couch surfed, nearly 60% of young men had been convicted of a crime, and only 48% were employed. 75% of women and 33% of men receive government benefits to meet basic needs. 50% of all youth who aged out were involved in substance use and 17% of the females were pregnant.

Source: AFCARS Report, No. 20, Jim Casey Youth

As of 2012, more than 58,000 children in the U.S. foster care system were placed in institutions or group homes, not in traditional foster homes.

Source: AFCARS Report, No. 20

Three years is the average length of time a child in foster care waits to be adopted. Roughly 55% of these children have had three or more placements. An earlier study found that 33% of children had changed elementary schools five or more times, losing relationships and falling behind educationally.

Source: AFCARS Report, No. 20

For the majority (55%) of children in foster care, the Case Plan Goal is reunification with Parent(s) or Principal Caretaker(s); the goal for 25% of the cases is Adoption, with the remainder divided relatively equally between Living with Other Relatives, Long-Term Foster Care, Emancipation, Guardianship or Goal Not Yet Established.

Source: AFCARS Report, No. 22 July 2015

States spent a mere 1.2-1.3% of available federal funds on parent recruitment and training services even though 22% of children in foster care had adoption as their goal.

Source: Adoption Advocate No. 6: Parent Recruitment and Training: A Crucial, Neglected Child

CHAPTER ONE

On a clear, warm June day, I stood on the front porch of the house I now owned, staring out at the Maine coastline with a sigh of gratitude. I did this as often as I could. For me, taking a moment to appreciate all I'd been given had become a morning ritual I treasured.

In front of me, the blue-gray water met the sandy shore with a moist kiss, reared back like a shy lover then, tempted for more, embraced the shore again. Seagulls cried out, swooped down, and lifted up in the air in unending musical acrobatics. A few large rocks, precursors of the rockier coastline down east, protruded from the water's surface like sea creatures wanting a peek at the world.

Almost two years ago, the sandy beach had hosted one of the most important events of my life. Even now, my pulse quickened at the memory of Brad saying "I do" and sweeping me into an embrace that drew applause. The simplicity of the ceremony had touched the hearts of everyone. What a wonderful day that had been! I still felt the thrill of belonging to his family and mine—the family I'd discovered after a lonely childhood. I thought of the group gathered there and knew how lucky I was and smiled up at the sun, letting its warmth wash over me.

The screen door opened and closed behind me. Brad stepped out onto the wide porch that swept the front of the seaside estate and wrapped his arms around me. "Good morning, Marissa Cole Crawford!" The sound of my married name on his lips sent a tingle of delight throughout my body.

I smiled and turned to him, inhaling the spicy aroma of his aftershave lotion. Snuggling into his strong embrace, I stared up at him, taking in the caramel-colored hair and toffee eyes that were his alone. I adored this man who'd given me so much love, so much confidence. I treasured our life together, very different from the background that had once been my life.

"You're off to Barnham?" I asked, hiding the emptiness I already felt at his upcoming departure.

He nodded. "Thank God this commuting back and forth will end in another year or so. I'm hoping Dad is fully retired by then, and we can finally sell the law practice to someone else." He gave me the lopsided grin I loved. "By then, we'll have started our family, and I can stay settled right here."

I didn't reply but rested my head against his chest. We'd been trying for a baby since the wedding. Brad was anxious to have children, but the thought scared me to death. I had so many doubts about myself as a mother. I'd been raised by one of the worst.

"Walk me out?" Brad slung his arm around my shoulders.

We headed through the elegant house I was slowly but surely making into a real home—safe and welcoming to us both. Lady, my golden retriever, followed at our heels. Like me, she hated to see Brad leave for his weekly trek to Barnham, New York.

Outside on the lawn, I gave Brad a lingering kiss, telling him in my own special way how much I'd miss him.

He pulled away and sighed. "See you on Friday. Have a good week. Love you, woman."

I smiled and played along. "Love you, man."

He laughed and climbed into his Jeep.

Watching him drive away, I wondered if I should confess my reluctance to have a baby. Each time another month went by without my getting pregnant, I was almost pleased about it ... until I saw his disappointment. But I was sure he'd be even more disappointed if I turned out to be anything like the cold, heartless mother I'd grown up with.

Moments later, Becky and Henry Cantwell drove their red truck down the driveway toward me, breaking into my disturbing thoughts. I waved and waited for them to park the truck by the garage and cross the lawn. They'd worked for my grandmother for years. I'd inherited them along with the large house I now miraculously owned. I smiled with pleasure. They were so much more than a handyman and a housekeeper; they were the people who'd kept my dysfunctional family spiritually alive with their goodness.

"Brad gone already?" Becky asked.

"Didn't see his car," said Henry.

"He'll be back on Friday."

"It'll be good when he can stay here permanently, don'tcha know," said Becky.

"And how," I quickly agreed. I looped my arm around Becky's, and we walked together toward the house as Henry headed back toward the garage. She and Brad's Aunt Doris were two of the women I loved most in the world, along with my newfound Hartwell cousins—Allison and Samantha.

We entered the house, and I sat at the long, cherry table in the kitchen to have a second cup of coffee with Becky. The comfortable kitchen was the heart of the house. It had been upgraded when the sunroom was added onto the house ten years ago. I'd left it pretty much the way it was when the house was given to me. The cherry cupboards, some with etched glass doors, suited the formality of the gray marble countertops. The Sub-Zero refrigerator, its doors covered with cherry wood veneer to match the cupboards, was unobtrusive among the cabinetry. But it was the six-burner Viking range that brought out the cook in me. It was Becky's pride and joy.

We finished our coffee, and when she rose to work in the kitchen, I left her. The kitchen was Becky's domain, which I respected.

I stopped in the front hallway to freshen the flower arrangement. After a sniff at the delicate roses, I decided to go outside, to the front of the house. Henry and I had talked about planting a variety of flowers and I wanted to see which of the ones he'd suggested would look best.

Lady rushed past me and went to the screen door, barking. Seeing no one, I frowned. It wasn't like her to bark unnecessarily.

I set aside the flower vase and went to take a look. I peered out and gasped, then forced back a scream. A wicker basket sat on the floor of the porch by the screen door—a basket that held a baby. And if the light pink blanket meant anything, the baby was a girl.

Heart pounding with alarm, I opened the door, stepped onto the porch, and searched for the person who might have left the little girl there. In the distance, a couple of men were jogging on the sand. In the opposite direction, a young woman was running along the shore, long blond hair flying behind her like an angel's wings.

I hurried out onto the lawn for a better look at her. Too far away to chase down or catch, I stared helplessly at the retreating figure. I turned in frantic circles to survey the plantings around the house and the lawn beyond, but I saw no sign of anyone lurking.

The baby began to wail. My pulse skipped in nervous beat as I raced back to the porch. Staring down at the baby's red face and flailing arms, shock continued to roar through me.

Becky appeared in the doorway. "My stars! What's this?"

"A baby." Panic sent my voice to a higher register.

"Someone left a baby here on my porch!. We have to find the mother! Why would she do this? I don't know anything about babies!"

"Okay, Marissa, let's see what this is all about," Becky said with a calmness I couldn't resurrect. She stepped out onto the porch and lifted the crying baby out of the basket. As she did, a note fell to the floor below.

I snatched it up, and read it aloud:

"Dear Mrs. Crawford, I've watched you and your husband for a while now. Seeing as you have no kids of your own, I thought this would be a perfect place for Summer Marie to live. Take care of her because I can't. Please, please don't put her in the foster care system. I know it too well."

I rocked back on my heels. My heart beat so fast I felt faint. This had to be a joke. Things like this didn't really happen, did they? I stared once more at the note, but the words on the page did a dance that blurred my vision. Sick to my stomach, I looked to Becky. "What are we going to do?"

Becky cooed softly to the little girl and checked her over. Thin strands of light brown hair lay atop the baby's head. Her dark-blue eyes were alert as she tried to focus. Dressed in pale green pajamas, she kicked her feet and howled, turning her fine-featured face a bright red. "She's beautiful," said Becky, "but she's hungry and wet. I'll send Henry down to the store for supplies while we figure this out."

Before I could protest, Becky wrapped the pink blanket around the baby and placed her in my arms. "Here. You take her while I make a list for Henry."

Summer stopped crying and studied me solemnly as if she was wondering what had happened to land her in an incompetent stranger's arms.

Becky nodded with satisfaction at the quietness. "See? That's a sign." She walked away, leaving me alone with the infant.

A sign of what? Numb from all that had happened and what it might mean, I paced the front porch holding the baby. She started to cry again. Crazy thoughts circled in my mind like the whirling wind of a summer storm. *Surely no one thought I should keep this abandoned child. Or was this some kind of fate thing to test me as a person? Or worse yet, was it someone's nasty joke?*

Summer made a face and it suddenly became quite clear she needed a new diaper. I gagged at the smell. Gasping with dismay at the mess, I called for Becky.

"Oh, my goodness!" Becky said when she saw what had happened. "It just might be time for a little bath for Summer Marie. Come along, Marissa. You can help me get her cleaned up."

I held Summer away from me while Becky ran a shallow amount of warm water in the kitchen sink and laid a soft towel on the bottom. She took the baby and removed the soiled clothes from her little body. "Ahhh, she's a beautiful little girl, just perfect," she murmured, setting her down carefully into the water. "Who would give up a darling like this?"

"Her mother wrote that she couldn't take care of her." I gazed at the baby I was now supposed to take care of and clasped my hands together feeling powerless. "How old do you think she is?"

The little girl cooed, and kicked her feet in the water. Drops of water splashed around her like sparkling diamonds.

Becky gently washed the baby with the mild soap she kept at the sink for herself. "Can't be sure, but I'm guessing she's just a few months old. She's a young one all right."

After rinsing her, Becky drained the water, patted the clean baby dry, and wrapped her up in a soft towel in a competent way I could never achieve.

"That'll hold her until Henry returns," Becky said, rocking the baby in her arms. She chuckled softly. "When I told him what was up, he flew out of here like a rabbit on the run."

I smiled. Henry was one big softie wrapped in a brusque, Maine manner. My smile evaporated when I thought of the mess I was in. "I'd better call Brad. I'm sure there are some legal issues here."

Becky nodded. "I think we should take the baby to Dr. Storey and have him check her out before any authorities are called. The mother didn't want the baby in the system. I don't much care for that idea myself."

I picked up the phone and punched in the number for Brad's cell. I couldn't help the tears that stung my eyes as I explained to him what had just happened. My emotions were on a merry-go-round of self-doubt and concern for the baby.

Brad listened to me and then spoke calmly. "The authorities will have to be notified, but my understanding of the law indicates Becky is right. You can place her with Dr. Storey, who would be considered a safe haven provider. He would then have to make the proper notification to the Office of Child and Family Services. He might even be willing to press upon the authorities the need for an immediate placement and ask for you to be made the temporary custodian of the child."

At his cold, professional words, my heart sank. The mother, whoever she was, didn't want the baby placed in the system, but I wasn't sure I wanted to take on the responsibility of this child myself, even for a short time.

"Keep me informed. I'm sure you and Becky are doing a good job with her. Let me see what I can do for you from this end," said Brad.

As I hung up with Brad, Henry returned from the store loaded down with diapers, all the fixings for bottle-feeding, clothes, blankets, lotions, and even a small, pink, stuffed lamb. When he saw the baby, his features softened. He approached Summer on tiptoes.

Becky pulled the towel away from Summer's face so Henry could see.

"Sure is a little mite," he said. "A pretty one at that." He turned to me. "You gonna keep her?"

My mouth turned dry. "I'm hoping to find the baby's mother. She must have loved her. The note said she'd been watching Brad and me for some time before choosing us to take her." The thought of being spied upon sent a shiver dancing across my shoulders.

"We'll do what we need to do," Becky said briskly. "We'll get her dressed and fed and then we're taking her to see Dr. Storey. From there, who knows? But I, for one, don't want to see the authorities take her away." There was a maternal warning in Becky's voice that I envied.

I left Becky and Henry in the kitchen and walked out onto the porch. Placing the basket on the white wooden railing, I lifted out the small mattress, searching for clues. But the plain, white, mattress cover told me nothing, and the empty basket was generic. My thoughts flew to the girl running down the beach. Was she the mother? If so, finding her would be like finding a needle in a haystack. There were a lot of young girls with long blond-streaked hair in New Hope alone. During the summer, even more.

Dr. Storey was a short, stocky man who, with his shaggy brown hair, dark button eyes, and wide smile, reminded me of a friendly teddy bear. Watching him gently examine Summer, I was glad we'd brought her to him first.

"She's a fine, healthy, baby girl," he said, handing the baby to me.

I took her in unsteady hands. "Have you seen her before? We're trying to find the mother."

He shook his head. "I'm not familiar with this patient." He studied me a moment. "Your husband called me. In light of the note the mother left you, he's thinking the baby should be placed with you until her situation is settled. How do you feel about that?"

I gulped, wondering if I should be honest and tell him the baby might be better off with someone else.

"That's a very good idea, Dr. Storey," Becky said before I could respond. "We'll see to it that she has the best of care. Won't we, Marissa?"

Still searching for words, I could only nod. With Becky's help, maybe I could do it. But that didn't mean I'd stop looking for Summer's mother. Something must be terribly wrong for a mother to give up a beautiful child like this or any child, especially when she cared enough to make sure her baby was placed in a nice home. Perhaps, finding her mother would be the best way to help this baby.

CHAPTER TWO

Within hours, Summer's addition to the household changed the entire atmosphere inside the house. Each time I walked into the kitchen, Becky was humming lullabies, holding the baby in the rocking chair we'd placed there. Lady became a four-legged guardian lying beside the basket in the sunroom or straightening with alarm in the kitchen every time Summer made a noise. Henry kept running in and out of either room with one excuse after another, stopping to look at the baby.

Brad called to tell me he was coming home early to see the little one for himself. At the excitement in his voice, my body filled with anxiety. I was being drawn into a scenario I didn't know how to handle and I didn't dare voice aloud.

I checked in with Becky to make sure Summer was fine, then walked out to the beach to gather my thoughts. On the sand, I kicked off my sandals and wiggled my toes in the sand. I turned and gazed upon Briar Cliff, the home I'd been given.

The large, three-story, brown-shingled house sat like a haughty New England matron alongside this stretch of sandy beach in southern Maine. The wrap-around porch on the beachside softened the vertical lines of the luxurious home. The sunroom, my favorite part of the house, filled one wing of it. With several floor-to-ceiling windows, the openness to the outdoors was satisfying. Growing up poor, I'd dreamed of living differently, but I would never have dared to dream of living in such luxury.

Beside the house was a tall maple tree—the original

Talking Tree. Following a tradition begun by my mother and Henry years ago, I sometimes sat beneath the tree's protective branches when I was troubled. Instead of the harsh ground beneath my Talking Tree in Barnham, the one my step-father Clive had chopped down, space beneath this tree held a white, wrought-iron bench that sat on a carpet of green grass.

Today, I'd use the sandy beach, not the Talking Tree, to sort out my feelings. I turned away from the house. Walking slowly, sifting through my thoughts, I strolled down the beach past a number of large homes similar to my own.

Everyone else was so excited to have a baby in the house. Why was I feeling so out of control? It wasn't like me. But then again, nothing was like it had been. Maybe that was the real issue. With a baby in the house, unexpected things like schedules not of my own making would take place. And I didn't feel competent, which bothered me. Every baby deserved more than I thought I could give.

A tall, spry, elderly woman stood up and waved at me from the porch of one of the houses. I smiled and waved back. Maude Miller was a character and a lovely old soul. She'd taken to me from the beginning. I'd never forget her kindness.

Maude's next-door neighbor, Eleanor Worthington, wasn't the same kind of person at all. That woman wasn't about to take to anyone else unless they were among what she considered the social elite. A snobby, old biddy my cousin, Allison, had called her. To avoid making contact with her, I hurried past the house.

Beyond the group of year-round estates lay a number of smaller summer cottages, more like what one would expect to find in a beach town. I slowed my pace. Perhaps, the baby's mother had come from one of these seasonal homes. Searching for a young girl with long, blond hair, I ambled along, studying the family groups lazing on the beach basking in the June sun or sitting on the porches talking. But no one matching the description I sought was among them.

Discouraged, I headed back home. As I drew close to the Worthingtons' house, Eleanor called to me and signaled me to stop. A substantial figure, Eleanor descended the porch steps and approached me like a ship parting waters with its prow, proud and sure of herself. Eleanor's posture, always erect, and her manner, always aloof, made it hard for me to feel comfortable in her presence.

"Marissa, I'm glad I spotted you! My daughter Courtney is coming for a visit from New York and is asking for your telephone number. I can't imagine why she'd contact you, but I said I would get it for her."

I ignored the barely hidden insult. I remembered meeting Courtney at the Worthingtons' annual garden party last summer. With finer features, Courtney Worthington was a smaller version of Eleanor physically, but any resemblance to her mother ended there. She seemed on the shy side, sweet, and friendly. I'd liked her immediately.

Eleanor handed me a pen and a paper. I wrote down my cell number and gave them back to her.

"Thank you," said Eleanor. "I'm busy with so many important projects for different organizations that it's difficult for me to find the time for something like getting your phone number for her."

At her condescending tone, I forced a smile. "I've got to be on my way."

Walking back to the house, I was curious to know why Courtney Worthington wanted to speak to me. We'd merely chatted for a brief moment at the party last July.

As I approached Briar Cliff, I could hear the wail of a baby coming from inside. I studied the house and wondered if this is how it would be if Brad and I finally had a family of our own.

I entered the house to sudden silence and found Becky in the kitchen feeding Summer a bottle. The baby moved her mouth eagerly, sucking with enthusiasm as she studied Becky.

Becky looked up at me and smiled. "She's such a good baby." The delight on her face made me happy. Becky had, at times, lamented the fact that she and Henry had no children and thus would have no grandchildren. I had a feeling this baby was going to fill that need for her for as long as possible.

"Do you want to hold her?" Becky asked me in a tone that begged me to say no.

I shook my head and sat in a chair at the kitchen table beside her. Gingerly, with one finger, I caressed the silky strands of hair on the baby's tender head. Like Henry said, she was a pretty little thing.

After a while, I stood and went into my office. If, as Brad wanted, we were to have custody of the baby for even a short while, we'd need a lot of baby equipment and heaven knew what else. I had to do some research on the internet to list what we'd need in order to take care of her.

Overwhelmed by all the unexpected changes to my life, I sat down behind my desk and drew a deep breath. Recalling the twisted history of babies in this house, I straightened in my chair suddenly determined to make things right. In a greedy scheme in the past, my uncle, Tim Hartwell, had been made to believe others were his parents. I vowed history would not be repeated. We'd do things differently, and we'd welcome Summer into our house. If her mother couldn't be found, Summer might be ours to cherish, but she'd be told her true story. She'd also understand her mother loved her enough to leave her with us.

The phone rang. I frowned at the unknown number and picked it up.

"Marissa? It's Courtney Worthington. How are you? Do

you remember me?"

"Hi, Courtney," I answered. "Of course, I remember meeting you. What can I help you with?"

"I know we've only met once, but I'm wondering if you might need some help. A friend of mine is looking for a summer job. I thought of you in that big house."

"Becky and Howard Cantwell take care of most of the things we can't..." I began, then stopped, as a thought came to me. "However," I amended, "there's been a new development here. How is she with children?"

"She's great with them. As a matter of fact, she's graduating with a degree in early childhood education. She hopes to find a job teaching. But first, she's taking a break." I could hear the smile in Courtney's voice.

"Why don't you tell me more about her," I said, immediately intrigued.

"Her name is Grace Paulson. She's my best friend," said Courtney. "She went to school here in the city with me at NYU. She's really smart and really, really nice. Everyone, including all her professors, admires her for her hard work and the way she can get things done. Besides that, she's a lot of fun. If she gets the job with you, I'll definitely spend the summer in Maine so we can do some things together."

I could feel my eyebrows rise. If I remembered correctly, Courtney and her mother didn't get along. "Well, have her send me a résumé and some references. I'll take a look at it. The situation here is uncertain, but it might work out."

"Thank you, Marissa!"

We chatted a few minutes more before hanging up.

Puzzled by the phone call, I returned to the kitchen. Becky handed Summer to me. "She's been burped real good. I told Henry I thought I should spend the night here. Is that okay with you?"

"Absolutely. I need you to show me what to do." The thought of being left alone with the baby made my stomach clench. There was so much to learn. In my arms, the baby kicked her feet inside her swaddle and made little gurgling noises. I held on tight, afraid I might drop her. I was anything but a pro at this. My cousins were naturals. But then, their mother Adrienne was a sweet motherly woman anyone would want to emulate.

Becky gave me an understanding smile. "Don't worry so. I'll be right here with you. But, Marissa, if she's gonna stay with you, you'll have to be able to handle Summer on your own."

I gazed down at Summer's sweet face, wondering how long it would take me to be comfortable with her.

The rest of the day went quickly as a never-ending routine took form. Summer would awake with a cry, I'd change her, feed her, cuddle her and then put her down for a nap so we could begin the process all over again. I wondered if this exhausting procedure was the same for all new mothers.

Becky showed me how to do everything—step-by-step—standing by in case I needed her.

As evening turned into night, I became exhausted from the effort of trying to do everything just right. After making sure Becky was comfortable in one of the guest rooms, I carried the baby in her basket to my bedroom. I pulled a wide, low table next to my bed and securely placed the basket with the baby on top of it so she'd be close by. Lady lay down next to it.

So tired I could hardly stand, I changed into silk pajamas and crawled into bed, settling back among the pillows. The tenseness that had knotted my body began to ease. I closed my eyes and let out a long breath just as the baby began to cry.

Groaning, I got to my feet. The howling, red-faced little girl flailed her arms and kicked her feet as if she hadn't recently been fed or changed. When I picked her up, Summer stopped her crying. Her gaze rested on me, and I had the unsettled feeling that I was being evaluated.

"I'm doing my best here, little one," I murmured to her. She'd just had a bottle so I checked her diaper. Dry. Thinking the problem might be gas, I patted her back.

One little burp.

"Okay, Miss Summer, back in bed for you," I whispered and gently lay her down. Summer kicked and fussed.

What now? I tried to hide my frustration as I picked her up again. Another woman might understand what was going on, but I didn't know if I was doing something wrong.

Holding the baby, I paced the room, humming softly to her. Summer looked up at me with what could almost be called a smile and let out a belch any teenage boy would be proud of.

"Good one," I murmured, and placed her back in the basket.

She let out a wail that brought a howling whine from Lady.

Becky appeared in the doorway to my bedroom. "What's going on?" She entered the room and came over to me.

Close to tears, I shook my head. "I don't know. She's been changed, fed and burped. Every time I think she's ready to go back down, she cries."

Becky frowned. "She sure slept a lot during the day. She might be one of those babies who is all mixed up and stays awake at night." She patted me on the back. "Go ahead and try to get some rest. I had a good break earlier. I'll be okay for a while. I'll take Summer into my room for a bit."

"You sure?" I couldn't wait to lie down.

At Becky's nod, I crawled into bed so stressed I didn't think I'd ever be able to fall asleep.

The morning sky was beginning to brighten when I woke. I heard a baby crying. Still caught in a dream, I frowned, wondering at the sound. Then it all came back. I sat up in bed and stared at the emptiness beside me. The baby, the basket, and the dog were gone.

I suddenly remembered Becky had taken Summer to her room, I climbed out of bed and hurried down the hallway into the guest room. Becky was sitting in the antique wooden rocking chair trying to soothe Summer.

"Good morning! Here, let me help you," I said.

I lifted the baby into my arms. As I brought her close, I felt something soak the front of my pajamas.

Becky started to get to her feet, but I waved her back. "I'll take her. I'm sorry I slept so long. Why don't you take a break?"

"Okay. Summer did pretty good through the night. I tried my best to get her to sleep."

"Thanks. I'm really grateful for the time you gave me to rest."

Becky crawled into bed, and I left her. I carried Summer back to my bedroom. After changing out of my uncomfortably wet pajamas, I changed Summer's diaper and put clean clothes on her.

In the kitchen, I'd just finished giving Summer a bottle of warm milk when Brad's Jeep rolled down the driveway toward me. I checked the clock on the microwave. 5:45 AM. Surprised to see him, I carried Summer over to the window and watched as Brad got out of the SUV. At his presence, the tension that had plagued me evaporated.

He waved to me and rushed inside, bringing cool morning air with him.

I smiled happily at him. "You're home early!"

"I couldn't sleep, so I decided not to wait to make the trip." He gave me a quick, sweet kiss on the lips and peered down at the baby in my arms. She stared up at him, her fussing momentarily forgotten.

"Wow, she's a beauty, huh?" he said softly. He traced the baby's cheek with a finger. "Just think, she might become ours." At the wonder in his voice, my insecurity reared its ugly head.

As if she realized how conflicted I felt, Summer began to cry. I spoke softly to her and she quieted.

"Here, why don't you take her? I need to get a burp rag." I gently placed the baby in Brad's arms.

Brad, surprisingly calm, lifted the baby to his shoulder and jiggled her. "I bet Becky loves having the baby here. When I told Doris why I couldn't have dinner with her this week, she went crazy. She can't wait to meet this little one."

Well able to imagine Aunt Doris' excitement, I felt my lips curve. She'd been waiting impatiently for news of our having children.

Summer began to fuss.

I quickly took a few more sips of coffee, grabbed the burpee and gathered Summer from Brad. After finding a seat at the kitchen table, I lay Summer on her stomach across my knees and rubbed her back in comforting circles like Becky showed me.

Brad pulled up a chair and sat. A tender expression crossed his face as he watched me. "You know, one of the reasons I married Amber was because she said she wanted a big family. Too bad she didn't really mean it."

I gave him a sympathetic nod. Brad had been married less than a year to Amber when she decided she didn't want to live in Barnham or anywhere else with him. She left in a hurry, taking everything she could from him. It had taken me a lot of time to convince Brad I wouldn't do the same thing to him. How could I? Brad was my rock, the one that kept me believing good things could happen to me.

"I've talked to the authorities," Brad said. "They've agreed to give us temporary custody. But by law, they must go through their due diligence. One of the reasons I came home early was to meet with the caseworker. They need to inspect our house for suitability, which means we need to set up a proper room for Summer."

I couldn't hold back the thought that rubbed my heart raw. "Brad, do you think she might be better off with someone more experienced? I don't know much about raising kids, and with my background..."

Brad cut me off with a wave of his hand. "Marissa, look at you! The baby is happy in your arms." He placed his gentle hand on my shoulder. "All we can do is to try our best to be good parents. There are no guarantees on how good we'll be, but we'll do the very best we can."

I bit the corner of my lip, an old nervous habit of mine. "What does your mother think about this?"

Brad looked away, then returned his gaze to me. "She's not sure we should do this. She's worried something might be wrong with the baby, that it's the real reason the mother gave her up."

Filled with a new sense of protectiveness, I stiffened. "I see." Though Ellen Crawford was kind and polite to me, I always felt as if I didn't quite measure up to her expectations because of what I was— a girl from a poorer section of town who'd lived a troubled life. Maybe Ellen would hold the same prejudice against Summer. At the thought, I tightened my arms around the baby. No one was going to judge this little one harshly because of her mother.

Summer's eyes began to close. "Oh, no you don't!" I whispered. I lifted the baby up over my shoulder. Summer stirred and let out a couple of loud burps.

"We're trying to keep her awake," I explained to Brad. "Yesterday, she slept most of the day and then was wide awake most of the night. I'm not sure when I finally got to sleep."

"I guess that's what we're in for, huh?" The smile on Brad's face was telling.

I frowned. "Brad, what if we don't get custody of her? What will happen to her? Or what if her mother comes back for her? Or her father? What do we do then? She has a right to know who her parents are and to be with them if at all possible."

He placed a finger in Summer's palm. She wrapped her tiny hand around it. "Let's not worry about it now. Something will work out. The note was pretty clear that Summer's mother wanted her with us."

I couldn't let it go. "Brad, maybe this should be about helping the mother keep the baby. Maybe this is what the note is really asking us to do." I took a deep breath. "She had to have been in the area for a while. The note said she'd been watching us for some time."

Brad's eyebrows lowered to form a vee. He studied me. "I know where you're coming from, Marissa, but sometimes it's best to let things unfold on their own. That way, fewer people can get hurt."

Confused, I stared into space. I wanted to please him and do everything I could to make him happy, but I didn't know if I could be a good mother to this child.

Brad leaned over and gave me a lingering kiss on the lips.

"Maybe, like Aunt Doris says, this is a miracle for us to enjoy, Marissa."

I nodded, but I wasn't sure what was unfolding before us—a miracle or a nightmare.

CHAPTER THREE

While Summer napped, Brad and I ate a hurried breakfast then went into my office to go over a list of things we needed.

"Whew! Who knew we'd need all this stuff," said Brad, studying the items I'd listed—clothes, décor and furniture for the baby's room, baby equipment, lotions and oils, and all the must-haves for body and health care.

"What's a snot sucker?" said Brad. "It sounds pretty scary."

I laughed. "It's a nasal aspirator. You use it on babies when they have a cold."

"Does Summer have a cold?" His voice held a note of concern I found endearing.

"No, but she might get one. It was one of the things recommended online."

Brad sat back in his chair and let out a whoosh of breath. "This baby business is something else. It's a good thing it usually takes nine months for a baby to arrive."

"I know but we'll do the best we can to get everything in just one day."

He grinned. "Okay. Who knew we'd get a baby this way?"

I smiled, but inside my nerves were throbbing with worry.

Becky was delighted to have us leave Summer in her care. Properly assured that all would be fine, Brad and I drove into Portland.

Our first stop was a well-known, big-box retail store. I followed Brad inside and came to a stop, overwhelmed by all

I saw. Cribs, strollers, baby seats, clothing and everything you could think of for a baby were lined up in several areas. Feeling like a fraud, I took a deep breath. By picking out a crib, changing table and the mountain of other things we'd need, I'd be going along with Brad's idea of keeping Summer forever even though I still felt obligated to search for clues as to the whereabouts of Summer's mother. Yet, if we found her, it wouldn't be a simple matter. I already felt the beginnings of a growing bond between Summer and me.

"Well, look who's here!" came a familiar voice.

I whirled around and smiled.

Adrienne Hartwell stood beside me. "This is so exciting! I didn't expect to see you here."

We embraced. Adrienne was Allison and Samantha's mother and a wonderful woman.

"It's not what you think. Not exactly," said Brad, joining us.

I told Adrienne the story of finding Summer on my porch. In the telling of it, I saw it for the lovely, unselfish phenomenon that it was. "So now we will take care of this little girl for as long as we can," I said. "We have to get final approvals of course."

Adrienne dabbed at her eyes. "Oh my! Such a wonderful story—both sad and happy. Is there anything I can do for the two of you?"

Brad wrapped an arm around my shoulder and drew me closer to his side. "Maybe you can give us some advice from time to time." He chuckled. "If you can get the baby away from Becky."

I smiled. "Becky loves having the baby around. She sings to her and finds all kinds of excuses to hold her. Even Lady is getting in on the act by staying right at Summer's side."

"Lovely." Adrienne clasped her hands. "Wait until I tell

the girls! They'll be thrilled for you. Allison's new little girl and yours may be great playmates someday." She gave me another hug and turned to Brad for a quick embrace before waving good-bye and picking her way through the maze of baby items.

At the idea of Summer having such wonderful cousins to play with, I filled with new excitement. If Summer's own family couldn't be found, then maybe the other Hartwell women and I would try to provide her with a wonderful, loving, extended family.

Brad and I finished shopping at the store and went on to a couple of specialty shops. By the time we were ready to head home, we were exhausted. Even so, as we entered the house, we rushed into the sunroom to check on Summer. We'd set up her basket there in a quiet corner so she could sleep peacefully, yet not be too far from Becky.

Lady, who'd been diligently guarding the baby, rose to her feet and wagged her tail at us. I gave her a pat on the head and stood watching Summer. Asleep, she moved her mouth as if she were nursing.

While she continued to sleep, I eagerly showed Becky the baby clothes we'd bought. Tiny flowers, butterflies, and ruffles adorned some of them. As I fingered the little jammies and onesies, I marveled at their small size. Becky and I ooohed and ahhhed over the dresses I'd bought. We also decided the soft blue bedding ensemble with moon and star details would look perfect with the pale yellow walls of Summer's room.

"What about the furniture?" Becky asked.

I smiled. "It's on its way. Brad made a deal with the salesman for immediate delivery."

Late that afternoon a delivery truck rolled into the driveway. Two men carried the white crib, bureau, and changing table, and several other large items inside.

Brad and Henry carried the furniture up the stairs, and

into Summer's room. While they assembled the crib, Becky and I tucked clothes into bureau drawers and organized items for skincare in the changing table. Lady sniffed the new items and strolled around the nursery as if to make sure all was in order.

When Summer woke up from her nap, I carried her upstairs and into her nursery. Brad, Becky, and Henry stood by as I showed her the crib, the bureau full of clothes and the changing table where organic lotions and creams were stored alongside diapers. She became more alert when I turned on the mobile, and soft music tinkled in the air as tiny stars rotated around a crescent moon.

Becky beamed at me. "This is as pretty a nursery as I've ever seen. Such a wonderful life this baby can have with you."

"We're not approved yet," I said, tucking Summer up against my breast. We'd had a call from the Office of Child and Family Services. An interview and tour were set up for the following day. I was already nervous about it. Despite other people's thinking of me as a mother, I was not yet comfortable with the idea that I was the best choice for Summer.

Later, I walked Becky and Henry out to their car. "I hate to see you go, Becky."

Becky hugged me. "You'll do just fine without me, Marissa. You know more than you think about taking care of babies."

So unsure, I watched them leave.

When I returned to the kitchen, Brad handed Summer to me. "Uh, she smells like she needs a diaper change."

"And?"

He gave me a playful grin. "And you do a better job of it than I do."

I bit back a snappish reply thinking, *He wants to hold the baby and to feed her but thinks I should be the one to change her diapers. Doesn't he realize how tired I am?*

I climbed the stairs to the nursery with the baby. As Summer stared up at me, a corner of her tiny lip lifted in a half smile. Though I knew it was probably gas, her smile made my irritation with Brad disappear.

Later, Brad and I ate dinner to the sound of tinkling music coming from the new baby seat we'd bought for Summer. Holding back a yawn, it seemed months, not just two days, since I'd found a baby in a basket on the front porch.

By the time I finally got Summer settled down for the night, I was too tired to do anything but collapse in bed.

Brad slid in beside me. Wearing an amorous smile, he cuddled close.

I loved the guy, but making love was so-o-o not happening. I gave him a sweet kiss on the lips and rolled over.

Tired from another night of little sleep, I sat with Brad and ate a quick breakfast. Brad yawned almost as much as I, though it was amazing to me how quickly he'd learned to sleep through the baby's crying.

As I waited for the caseworker to arrive for our custody interview, I felt as if I'd swallowed a hive of bees. I wondered how long it would take the woman to realize I was a fake. Tense, I checked Summer's clothing for the umpteenth time, fussing unnecessarily with a ruffle that wouldn't lay down. She looked adorable in a little pink outfit I hadn't been able to resist buying.

A small, blue car pulled into the driveway. I stared out through the kitchen window at the heavy-set, gray-haired woman who got out of the car and stood beside it. She spent some time studying her surroundings with interest.

Holding the baby, I went outside to greet her. Just as I

reached her, Summer threw up all over me and herself. Trying not to gag, I gave the caseworker a weak smile. "Are you Alice Tremblay? I'm Marissa Crawford. My husband Brad is just finishing a phone call. I'd shake your hand, but I'd better not."

The woman nodded sympathetically. "I see you have your hands full with the baby. Why don't I follow you inside?"

Brad appeared in the kitchen doorway as we approached. "Ms. Tremblay? Brad Crawford. Come in, come in." He stared at Marissa. "Uh, oh. What happened?"

"I guess I should've burped her more." Feeling as if I'd already failed a test, I brushed by Brad, eager to change the baby's clothes and my own.

When I returned to the first floor with Summer, Brad was finishing a tour of the downstairs' rooms.

"And the nursery?" Alice said, in a noncommittal tone.

"This way." Brad took her arm and led her up the stairs. I followed behind with the baby. Alice was puffing loudly by the time she reached the top landing.

Taking a deep breath, Alice said, "There are so many stairs to reach the baby. Have you thought of setting up something downstairs for daytime use?"

I gulped. Becky had suggested it, but I hadn't wanted baby equipment everywhere.

"That's something we can easily do," said Brad. "Right, Marissa?"

I nodded. "It will be much easier for everyone." Becky would be pleased with the changes, and I'd get used to baby stuff everywhere.

Alice stepped inside the nursery and gazed around. The faintest of smiles appeared on her face. She walked over to the changing table, picked up one of the organic lotions, and studied the label. Turning around, she faced us.

"I understand you can provide every material thing for

this child, but I need to know more about the two of you as people, as potential parents. I've brought forms with me that need to be filled out with your backgrounds and all. And then we need to talk."

Summer, sleeping in my arms, began to fuss. I checked my watch. "I need to fix a bottle for her." I also needed time to gather my thoughts. My background was problematic at best, but I couldn't lie about it.

Brad noticed my discomfort. "You can start with me," he said to Alice.

I gave him a grateful smile. "Perfect. I'll meet you down in the sunroom," I said and rushed away before Summer could begin her usual pre-bottle howls.

Downstairs, I placed Summer in her new baby seat and set to work to fix a bottle for her. As I was about to feed the baby, Becky and Henry arrived. I let out a sigh of relief. As soon as Becky got settled, I handed the baby and bottle over to her.

Becky grinned. "I couldn't wait to see her again!"

"Yup," said Henry with a wry smile. "She hurried me right along."

Their calm manner slowed my racing heart and gave me more confidence. My background was what it was. I would've changed it if I could. Alice would just have to understand that.

I entered the sunroom to find Brad busy filling out paperwork. Alice bobbed her head at me as I took a seat on the couch.

"I understand you have a large responsibility at Rivers Papers. How do you plan to carry on with that work and raise a baby?"

I rocked back against the soft couch cushions in surprise. I'd been so concerned about giving the details of my background that I hadn't considered my work at the paper mill a problem.

"Is this job at the mill something you can delegate to others?" Alice asked.

I shook my head. "Unfortunately, no. This is a commitment I made to my grandmother and to my cousin Samantha. Sam and I share some of the duties, but since she moved to California, I now handle most things on my own."

Alice's clucked her tongue. "Hmmm. I see."

"We have Becky here to help," Brad quickly added.

Alice frowned. "You told me she was the housekeeper."

"I have a nanny lined up." I crossed my fingers behind my back and willed Brad to wipe the look of surprise off his face. "Actually, I'm to interview her soon. She's a recent college student who graduated with a degree in early-childhood development."

"Good," said Alice. "What about you? Why would you want to take on someone else's child—a child whose own mother didn't want her?"

I let out a long breath, and all the thoughts I'd had about protecting this baby burst out of me in a stream of words. I poured my heart out with each syllable as I told her of my fears, my hope of being a good mother, and my decision to be the best I could be, even if I didn't know exactly what I was doing. "And so," I ended, "my commitment to this baby and every baby we might have is to be kind and gentle and loving— all the things I didn't have growing up."

Alice's eyes were wet as I finished. "Well, then, I think I have what I need. If you'll complete the paperwork, we'll see what can be done to keep Summer here for the time being."

"For the time being?" Alarm rose in me. "You won't put her into the foster care system, will you? Her mother didn't want that."

Alice stared at me with surprise. "She's already in the

system. We're working to get you approved as a foster parent. If the time comes to consider adoption, and there are no objections from anyone, that will be another matter. Ideally, we would be seeking termination of parental rights."

"But I thought..."

Brad cut me off. "It's understandable we'd have to follow the system's rules, but we don't want little Summer to be elsewhere."

"Yes, I know," said Alice. "Complete the forms with at least three references. We'll go from there. I suggest using family friends and neighbors for references. Questionnaires for them are included in the paperwork I gave you."

Alice gathered her papers together, put them into her briefcase, and stood. "For what it's worth, this whole situation is a puzzle to me. Obviously, the child's mother knew you. Do you have any idea who it could be?"

I exchanged glances with Brad and shook my head. "No. But I hope someday we'll find her. Summer deserves to at least know about her."

"Sometimes it's best to leave things alone," said Alice. "Through the years, I've learned that." She turned to go.

Confused by Alice's words, I walked her toward the door.

We stopped in the kitchen. Becky was holding Summer and rocking her in the old-fashioned rocking chair we'd moved there from one of the upstairs bedrooms.

Becky looked up at us and smiled. "Such a beautiful baby." Her voice held an unmistakable note of pride.

"And a lucky one," Alice responded, giving Becky a warm look. She turned to me. "Get that paperwork to me as soon as you can, along with information on the new nanny. And then we'll see about training courses for you."

I nodded. In order to prevent Summer from staying in the system, I'd do everything I could.

CHAPTER FOUR

"So what's this about a nanny?" Brad asked me when I joined him in the sunroom.

"In all the excitement, I forgot to mention that Courtney Worthington called me a couple days ago to ask if we needed any help."

His eyebrows shot up. "Courtney Worthington? Surely, she's not the one you're thinking of as a nanny. She doesn't strike me as the kind of person willing to work very hard."

"It's one of her best friends who needs a job—someone by the name of Grace Paulson. I've asked her to send me information. That's all. But if she's any good with Summer, she could be a godsend to us. Becky can't be expected to help out with Summer on a regular basis and keep on doing her regular duties. She's beginning to show her age. As a matter of fact, I've started to take over more and more of the household chores."

"A nanny makes sense, but before you hire her, I want you to make sure she's okay."

I smiled at Brad with affection. He was already sounding like a father. Why couldn't I feel better about being a mother?

To follow through on Alice's suggestions, I set up a changing area off the kitchen and ordered a portable crib we could place anywhere. It was almost comical to me that one tiny baby could require so much equipment and such a mountain of supplies. I wondered if this was part of the reason the mother felt unable to keep the baby. My thoughts flew to Rivers Papers. Was the mother someone who worked in the paper mill there? I decided to talk to Jonesy, one of the managers, to see if he had any information that might help me find Summer's mother. If she truly didn't want the baby, she could sign papers to give up her parental rights.

I was folding baby clothes when my cell phone rang. I checked the screen and smiled. Allison. I clicked onto the call. "Hi, Allie! How's that baby girl of yours?" Her little girl Lucy was nine months old.

"How about that baby girl of *yours*! My mother told me all about it!" Allison's voice trilled with excitement. "I love the name, Summer."

"She's a beautiful little girl," I said. "But, Allie, she's just considered a foster child until we can find the mother or adopt her."

"Find the mother? She wanted you to have the baby, didn't she?"

"That's what she said, but we don't know how desperate her situation was for her to make this decision. She might want to change her mind. The authorities want families reunited whenever possible, and Summer deserves that chance. And finding the mother is necessary in order to get her to sign her parental rights away if that is what she truly wants."

"I don't like the idea of trying to find the mother," said Allison. "There's a reason she wanted you to have her baby. She must've believed Summer would be a whole lot better living with you." The sound of a baby crying halted her words. "Hold on. Lucy's fussing."

I listened to Allison's soothing noises and then her voice saying more firmly, "No, Brian, stay away from your sister." Allison came back on the phone. "Can't talk long. Just wanted to let you know how excited I am for you and Brad. As soon as you can, head out to California. We've got to get all our little girls together—a gathering of cousins. I'm sure it won't take long before Sam's daughter, Renne, will be in charge. At two-and-a-half, she's just like her mother."

I laughed. Samantha Hartwell Roberts was a strong woman. I adored both my cousins. Without their encouragement, I might never have stood up to their autocratic father, who wanted me to turn the family seat on the Rivers Papers board over to his son, Hunter, the only male cousin.

Little Lucy's cries echoed in the background. "Gotta go," said Allison. "I'm sending you a few special dresses Lucy's already outgrown. I was saving them but I'd rather share them with you. Oh, and send pictures!"

"Thanks. Say hello to everyone out there." I hung up and stared at my phone, thinking again of the paper mill. Had someone seen me there? Someone who knew about Brad and me being without children? I punched in the number for Rivers Papers. At the receptionist's cheery hello, I asked to be connected to Jonesy.

"Hi, Mari," he said.

I smiled. He was the only one who ever called me Mari and I secretly loved it. After asking for his total confidence, I filled him in on the story about Summer and asked him to keep an ear and an eye out for anyone who might fit the description of the person I was seeking. We chatted some more about other matters, and I ended the call. If anyone could help me with this, it would be Jonesy, one of the kindest, most loyal people I'd ever met.

I waited until Summer woke up from her nap, then I dressed her in a white, cotton, knit dress decorated with scattered rosebuds. Shooing Lady away from us, I placed Summer in her infant seat and took several pictures of her. Before I could change my mind, I messaged them to Jonesy before sending them along to Allison, Samantha, and others waiting to see photos.

"What are you doing?" Brad asked, coming into the sunroom. When I told him about my call with Jonesy, he drew his eyebrows together. "Like Alice said, sometimes it's better to leave things alone. Be careful, Marissa. We don't know the story behind this mother."

"But that's exactly why I want to find out. What if we become attached to Summer and she's taken away from us? If we find her mother, it will answer so many questions we have. And it might mean we won't have to worry about her changing her mind." Against all my efforts to stay detached, I'd already bonded with Summer.

Brad's gaze penetrated me, reaching deep inside where I hid my feelings. His features softened as he studied me. When he drew me into his arms, I lay my head against his chest. He rubbed my back in comforting strokes. "Even if we end up losing her, we'd want her to have a special time with us, wouldn't we?"

Unbidden tears filled my eyes. I looked up at him. "I guess that's what foster parents do, right?"

He nodded a little sadly. "That's their job unless they're able to keep the children."

I buried my face into his chest once more and drew a deep breath. Had I made a horrible mistake by sending those pictures to Jonesy? If he found the mother, so many different things could happen.

After several nights of very little sleep, I got up out of bed and tiptoed downstairs, praying Summer would allow me a few minutes to myself. She'd been especially fussy lately. I thought it had something to do with the sticky heat wave that had gripped the area. A little rash had appeared on her skin.

Outside, dawn was streaking through the last of the lightening skies, spreading a rosy promise of another nice summer day in Maine. I made myself a cup of coffee and carried it out to the front porch. The floorboards beneath the rocking chair creaked as I settled into it. The cool morning breeze carried the scent of the water to me, making me long for enough time to be able to wander aimlessly along the shore. I drew a deep breath of the tangy air and pushed off with one foot, finding comfort in the swaying motion of the chair. As I glanced over to the spot where the baby's basket had been left, I tried to remember if I'd seen anyone unusual in the area over the past few weeks. But no one came to mind.

I wondered about other mothers. Did they resent having to be up at all hours of the night taking care of the baby while their partners slept peacefully? Were they unsure of themselves as a new parent when nothing seemed to keep the baby from crying? Did they sometimes want to cry from the constant drain on their emotions and bodies? I shifted in my seat and tried for a calming breath. Brad's Aunt Doris was due to arrive later that morning. I couldn't wait to see her. Doris was the closest thing to a mother I'd known growing up. Her house next door to mine had been a haven for me.

At the thought of Doris' presence in Maine, I felt tears sting my eyes. I was so exhausted. Becky was eager to help during the day, but I didn't want to put any additional stress on her. I intended to keep both Becky and Henry with me for as long as possible. I'd already promised to take care of them when they physically could no longer work for me. But right now their help was not enough.

"Marissa?"

I turned at the sound of Brad's voice coming through the screen door. He wasn't due to go to Barnham for a couple of days. "Marissa, the baby's crying!"

Frustration flashed through me. I leaped out of the chair and turned to face him. "Then go get her, change her diaper, and feed her a bottle!"

Brad held up his hands and backed away. "Whoa! Sorry ..."

I drew a deep breath. "I'm sorry too, but I'm so exhausted I can hardly see. You'll have to step up, Brad, and do your share when you're home."

"Sure, hon." He paused. "Guess I shouldn't have left it all up to you, huh?"

"Yeah." Chagrined by my snappish outburst, I sank back down into the chair. I needed to pull myself together. I couldn't take it out on Brad. He normally enjoyed doing things for the baby.

I continued rocking and listened for the sound of him taking Summer to the kitchen. As they passed by, I heard him making baby talk with her. Smiling at his sweet soft words, I closed my eyes. He was a good man, a good father. I'd take just a few minutes to rest, I told myself.

The next thing I knew, someone was tapping on my shoulder. I looked up to find Brad staring down at me.

"Are you going to be okay? I'm about to drive down to Boston to pick up Doris at the airport. It was cheaper for her to fly into Logan."

I dragged myself up from a deep sleep. Blinking against the sunlight, I murmured, "Where's Summer?"

"Asleep in the sunroom. I took care of her."

I grabbed hold of Brad's hand, drew him to me, and gave him a kiss. "Thanks. I needed that rest."

He grinned at me. "I love you, woman." He pulled me up and gave me the kind of kiss that made me feel like a very lucky woman, after all.

"Guess I needed that break," I murmured, inhaling his scent, loving the sturdiness of his body comforting mine.

"Yes, but I'd better go." He took hold of my hand and we walked into the house together.

I saw Brad off and crept silently into the sunroom. Lady, keeping guard, looked up at me and wagged her tail. Summer was asleep in the port-a-crib. As I studied the sweet little face, I noticed the beginning of a wispy curl at the back of her head and filled with tenderness.

"Baby Girl," I whispered, "what am I going to do about you?"

As if she'd heard the words, a frown formed on Summer's brow. She made a sucking noise and then her brow cleared. I patted her stomach until I was sure she was settled then tiptoed away.

I was sipping a cup of coffee in the kitchen when Becky called to say she wouldn't be able to make it in because her arthritis was kicking up. After assuring her it wouldn't be a problem, I hung up. I snuck a peek at the clock on the microwave. Maybe, I'd have time to pop into the shower before Summer awoke. Hopeful, I crept toward the stairway, imagining the soothing warm water on my skin releasing the tension of the last few days.

Summer's "feed-me" howls stopped me. I sighed and headed into the sunroom.

I'd just finished giving Summer a bath and dressing her when I heard the sound of a car in the driveway. Curious, I peered out the window. Samantha emerged from her mother's SUV. I smiled. Like Allison, my cousin Sam was the sister I'd never had. I twisted a lock of Summer's hair into a curl, held her close, and hurried downstairs to greet Samantha.

"Sam! Sam! I'm so glad to see you!" I cried, rushing through the doorway and outside.

Samantha grinned and gave me a careful hug to avoid hurting the baby. "When my mother told me what had happened to you, I decided to make a quick trip to Maine. I'd already promised Mom a trip soon, and I couldn't wait to see you and the baby." She held out her arms. "Ah, let me see."

I handed Summer to her and stood by anxiously while Samantha inspected her.

"She's beautiful," Samantha gushed. "And she's yours?"

I shook my head. "We don't know. We should be approved next week to officially become her foster parents. After that, if the mother can't be found, she'll be available for adoption. The Office of Child and Family Services has put out notices searching for the mother, but no one's responded."

Samantha hugged the baby to her. "I hope the mother isn't found. Summer is a little doll." She studied me a moment. "It's so nice to see you with a baby. I know you've been trying for one."

"Yes, but, Samantha, it might be a good idea to find her mother."

Samantha frowned. "You don't want to keep the baby?"

"We want to keep the baby, but maybe there's a way to help them both. Growing up as I did, I didn't think I should even have children, that I wouldn't be any good at it. But after having Summer here, I'm trying my best."

Samantha placed a hand on my shoulder. "I bet you're terrific at this."

I shrugged. "Brad might not think so. I yelled at him this morning for not doing his share."

Samantha laughed. "Welcome to the club. Derek has become a wonderful father but it took a little training. God, I love that man!"

I relaxed. I loved Brad too.

Samantha followed me inside the house. "Mom said

you've agreed to attend the Annual Summer Ladies Luncheon at the country club."

I couldn't help rolling my eyes. "I really don't want to go but I'd do most anything for your mother."

"And it's good for Rivers Papers too," prompted Samantha. "I'll go with you."

"Great," I smiled. "This is one event Ted Beers can't ruin for us."

Samantha laughed. "He's such an ass. Do you know he hasn't given up on publishing a book? He called Derek. He wants to do a photographic book on sports figures. Derek is so busy he turned him down, but you know Ted, he doesn't give up on any ideas."

"Oh yes. Now, he's trying to change the policy about running a nursery and day care for our young mothers who work at the mill. He feels it cuts into the company's profit. He says it's an expense we can avoid."

Samantha's lips tightened. "Sounds like him. Maybe I can go with you to the board meeting next week. The two of us can make sure the day care program stays."

"Hmmm. I bet we could." Ted Beers was the chairman of the board at one time. Samantha and I had tried to get him kicked off but he'd wormed his way back onto it and was chairman once more. He was one of the reasons, baby or not, that I could never turn my responsibilities over to anyone else but Samantha. We teamed up to keep Rivers Papers doing the right thing for everyone.

When I showed her Summer's room, Samantha squealed with delight. "This is adorable! I swear I'm ready to have another baby. At two, going on twenty-two, Renne is a little princess, directing everyone in the household to do her bidding. The twins are in preschool and are gone most of the day. I miss holding a little one like this." She gently swept a strand of hair away from Summer's face.

Watching her handle Summer with ease, I said, "You make it seem so easy. How do you handle all those children?"

Samantha gave me an incredulous look. "Easy? It's the hardest damn thing I've done in my life. But the rewards are there when a little voice says, 'I love you, Mommy.' Darren and Dawson, those clever twins, are getting real good at breaking me down that way." The corner of her eyes crinkled with laughter.

I joined in. Her boys were adorable, and Samantha knew it.

She stopped laughing and gave me a look of concern "Why? Are you okay? Can I do anything for you?"

"Can you give me five minutes to hop into the shower? Becky's sick today and I haven't had a chance."

Samantha chuckled. "Sure, go ahead. I'll put this little one down for a nap. Her eyes are closing."

I hurried into my room, grabbed some clothes, and raced into the bathroom. In minutes, I'd disrobed, scrubbed my body, and was drying myself in front of the mirror. Staring at my image, I could hardly believe the dark circles beneath my gray eyes and how drab my auburn hair looked without the benefit of the extra time I usually spent blowing it dry. It had been only a week since Summer was left at my doorstep, but, in some ways, it seemed like years.

Naked, I cupped my hands over my belly. I wondered how it was that some people made babies so easily and I didn't. Did it have something to do with the way Clive, my step-father, tried to touch me when I was growing up? I shook my head. No, that emotional damage had been healed by Brad. It had to be something else because otherwise, I was healthy.

I dismissed my worry, quickly dressed, and hurried downstairs. When I went into the sunroom to check on

Summer, I found her sleeping peacefully. Lady lay on the rug beside the crib. Seeing me, she wagged her tail.

Come, Lady," I said quietly. "She's all right."

Through one of the sunroom windows, I saw Samantha sitting out on the porch, rocking in one of the white wicker chairs that faced the water.

The dog gave a last look at the baby and lumbered beside me as I left the room and walked onto the porch. The screen door closed quietly behind me.

Samantha looked up at me and smiled. "Feel better?"

"Yes. A lot better. Thanks. It's amazing what a shower and a few minutes alone can do."

"Oh, yes. I know that feeling." Samantha's smile morphed into a frown. "With Becky growing older and not always able to be here, what are you going to do about help? A house this size is a lot of work and your participation at the paper mill is important."

I told her the story of Courtney Worthington's friend. "If the interview goes well, I'll hire Grace right away." I hoped she'd be really good at her job because I needed her or someone else to help me.

CHAPTER FIVE

Tears came to my eyes when I saw Doris Crawford step out of Brad's Jeep. At barely five feet, she had a surprisingly strong presence—a presence that had always given me a sense of safety. As I grew up, Doris was the one person I was able to turn to for comfort and common sense. I opened the kitchen door and ran to her with open arms. Lady followed at my heels, barking a greeting of her own.

Doris' face lit with pleasure as I threw my arms around her and squeezed as hard as I could.

"My!" she said happily, catching her breath as I released her.

I laughed. "It's so good to see you! And, Doris, wait until you see Summer. She's beautiful!"

A look of wonder filled Doris' face. "I can't believe it. You and Brad have a baby, after all."

"Come inside. She's sleeping upstairs but you can get a good look at her."

Brad held Doris' suitcase in one hand and took her elbow in the other. "Yes, let's go inside and get you settled."

Doris stood a moment and looked up at the house. "I forgot how beautiful this place is. And to think a baby will now live here."

"We hope so," said Brad. "We still don't know if the mother will come forward to claim her. Or it could be the father."

My heart stuttered to a shocked stop and then sprinted in nervous beats. I'd been so busy thinking of Summer's mother that I'd forgotten about her father showing up. That would make things really difficult. I stopped and took several breaths, telling myself to calm down.

Brad turned back to me. "Let's not worry about it."

I hurried to catch up to him, but my mind spun at the thought of an unknown father entering the picture.

Inside, I led Doris and Brad upstairs to Summer's room and opened the door quietly.

Summer lay sleeping in her crib.

Doris tiptoed across the room and gazed down at the baby. When she lifted her head, tears rolled down her cheeks in shiny streaks. "I can't help crying. She's so beautiful!"

Standing nearby, I took hold of Brad's hand. Every time I looked at Summer, I wondered if having her with us was a miracle or something that would break my heart. Only time would tell.

Doris gave me an encouraging smile. "It makes me so happy to see the three of you together as a family. Many were the days when you were younger that I didn't think that would ever happen for you, Marissa."

"I know," I said, remembering all that Doris had done for me. I realized then that a mother's love could come from anyone who chose to give it.

Over the next two days, I was thrilled to see the interest Doris took in Summer. Too soon it was time for her to leave.

Standing beside Becky, I stood in the driveway holding Summer waving good-bye as Brad and Doris drove away in his Jeep. Brad would return home at the end of the week.

"She really loves that baby, don'tcha know," said Becky, with a faint touch of annoyance.

I held back a laugh. It had been a contest of wills between

Becky and Doris as to who would hold the baby or feed her or play with her. Summer now wanted to be held all the time. It was something I'd have to deal with as gently as I could. Becky and I returned to the house and our morning routines.

A letter from Grace Paulson arrived in the morning mail. I took it into my office and eagerly opened it. I glanced through the body of it and reread the well-written opening, which detailed her qualifications. But it was the following paragraph that warmed my heart. In it, Grace told about her love of working with children. After reading through the three excellent recommendations she'd included with the letter, I was humming with excitement. I lifted the phone and called the number she'd given me. Grace answered with a cheery hello. I talked with her for a while and then, even more excited, I invited her to come to the house for an interview. She was staying at the Worthingtons'.

That afternoon, I opened the door and gaped at the tall, willowy, young woman standing there. With her smooth skin, light brown eyes and soft, curly, dark hair, she was among the most-stunning young women I'd ever seen—a Halle Berry look-alike. The smile on Grace's face lit her beautiful features.

"You're Grace?"

"Yes, but please call me Gracie. Everyone does."

I introduced myself and led Gracie into the kitchen to meet Becky.

"Nice to meet you, don'tcha know," said Becky, giving Gracie's polite hello a nod of approval.

After Gracie and Becky exchanged small talk, I took Gracie on a quick tour of the house. We peeked into the nursery at Summer, who was sleeping peacefully, before going downstairs to the sunroom to talk.

"I was delighted to read about your desire to work with children of all backgrounds," I began.

"I was adopted, so it's really important to me," Gracie said. "Our family is a mix of races and backgrounds. I have a brother from Viet Nam, a sister from Africa, and two white sisters from Russia. I'm from the island of Jamaica. My father is a Republican congressman who's done a lot to promote education for everyone. My education is one of his greatest gifts to me."

"And that's where you met Courtney? At college?"

"Yes."

"I understand from our earlier talk that you'll be staying with the Worthingtons at night and working here during the day. Is that correct?"

Gracie twisted a silver ring around her brown finger and looked up at me. "That may become a problem with her family, or at least with Courtney's mother. I don't think she realized I am black."

I frowned. "Even though we're neighbors, I don't know Courtney or her family very well. Frankly, I find her mother to be extremely difficult. I'm sure I will never measure up to her so-called standards."

Gracie smirked. "You can imagine how I measure up."

"Or not," I said, and we both laughed, comfortable with one another.

The sound of Summer's cries came through the remote, baby monitor on the table beside the couch. I rose. "Let's go see her."

We climbed the stairs to the nursery. At the sound of my soft hello, Summer's face brightened. I warmed with pride at her response to me. I lifted her out of the crib and gave her a kiss. "Look who's here," I murmured to her. "It's someone new. Gracie."

I handed the baby to Gracie and carefully observed her as she held Summer close. "I was fourteen when my youngest sister was born. It seems so long ago," Gracie said. "She was like my own real baby doll."

Under my watchful eyes, Gracie changed Summer's diaper. She was efficient but gentle. I smiled when Summer kicked her feet happily atop the changing table.

Downstairs, Gracie fed Summer a bottle and played with her for a few minutes. After accepting my offer of a job, she promised to return at eight the next morning.

I explained that Becky would be around all day, but I would not. I had a luncheon to attend. At the thought of the luncheon, a sigh escaped my lips.

Gracie and I exchanged knowing looks. "My mother doesn't like ladies' luncheons either."

I laughed, liking Gracie more and more.

Known for its unique golf course and its fine chef, The Waterview Country Club sat alongside the bay north of Portland. Memberships were heavily sought-after. Fortunately, George and Adrienne Hartwell sponsored Brad and me, which had put us at the top of the waiting list. We'd been members for almost two years. I hardly ever came to the club, but Brad used it quite often. Playing golf was a great way for him to meet people. When the law office he ran with his father in Barnham finally closed, he hoped to open a law practice in Portland.

I pulled up to the front of the clubhouse and waited inside the car for the valet to assist me and collect my keys. I gazed out the window to the golf course and beyond it to the water. It was such a pretty setting. The green of the course was offset by the darker green boughs of the evergreens mixed in with the hardwood trees lining the fairways. For golfers like Brad, the rolling terrain, and the onshore breezes added to the challenge of the game.

After the valet took my car, I went inside. I was standing in the foyer wondering where to go when Eleanor Worthington noticed me.

"Are you looking for something?" she asked me.

"Yes," I replied. "Where is the Ladies Luncheon being held?"

Eleanor gave my appearance a thoroughly disapproving exam. "You must be someone's guest. I haven't seen you here before."

At the condescending tone in Eleanor's voice, I bit back a sigh of exasperation. "Actually," I said with a forced calm, "Brad and I have been members for well over a year. I simply don't choose to attend most of the functions."

Eleanor lifted her eyebrows in surprise. "I didn't think we were accepting new members."

Relief streamed through me when Adrienne Hartwell appeared in the hallway. Spotting us, she rushed forward to greet me with a hug. "You're here at last. Sam and I are saving you a seat." She gave Eleanor a cursory nod and led me away. "Horrible woman, that Eleanor Worthington," Adrienne quietly said.

Adrienne's warm welcome lifted my spirits. Even after years of being away from Barnham, I sometimes felt as if I didn't belong in upscale places like this. I knew it was silly, but I couldn't help the old insecurities that made me feel that way.

I followed Adrienne into a small ballroom buzzing with conversation. Sam rose from her seat at one of the many round, cloth-covered tables and greeted me with a hug. "You look great. Not too much wear and tear on the new mom."

I laughed. "Not yet. I'm getting used to little sleep, and

Summer is getting better about not getting up so often. I swear that little girl is making up for lost time. She's eating like crazy, taking longer naps, and growing bigger every day."

"She knows she's in a good home," said Adrienne, giving me a warm smile. "Come. Let me introduce you to a few of my friends you have yet to meet." Taking my arm, she led me away from our table.

Thoughts of the baby disappeared as I made a sincere effort to memorize names and make conversation. But the moment I sat down to eat my lunch, my attention turned to the people back home at Briar Cliff.

Samantha gave me an understanding grin. "Go ahead and check on the baby. I know from experience you won't be comfortable until you do."

I smiled my gratitude, hurried into a quiet corner of the lobby, and punched in the phone number for home. After checking in with both Becky and Gracie and learning Summer was happily fed and sleeping well, I relaxed. I finished the call and slipped into the ladies room.

Eleanor Worthington was there with a woman I didn't know.

"Oh, Marissa. I was just telling Martha that Congressman Paulson's daughter is staying with us for a while," said Eleanor. "I understand she's working for you with that ... that foundling of yours. It's such an interesting story."

Foundling? Irritated by Eleanor's dismissive tone and choice of words to describe sweet Summer, I stepped back. *Foundling?*

Lines of distress appeared on the other woman's face. She held out her hand. "I'm Martha Goodrich. We haven't met but I admire you tremendously for taking in the baby. It's not always easy to do something like that."

"Summer is a wonderful, perfect, little girl." I couldn't

hide the defensive note in my voice. I turned to Eleanor. "I don't ever want her known as a foundling. She's a child whose mother must have loved her enough to see that she was safely placed with a good family. I'm sure there's much more to the story than either you or I know."

"Well," huffed Eleanor, "I think one should call it like it is."

"Enough, Eleanor," murmured Martha. "We need to get back to the table with the others." She gave me an apologetic look and hurried Eleanor out of the room.

Breathing deeply to control my resentment, I watched them go.

When I returned to the table, Samantha looked up at me and frowned. "What's wrong? Is it the baby?"

I shook my head. "I'll tell you later."

After lunch, Samantha took me aside. "Earlier, while you were gone from the table, I talked to Derek. He's agreed to stay with the kids a few extra days so I can attend the Rivers Papers board meeting with you. I'm really worried about Ted Beers' proposal to dismantle the company's child care facility."

"Me too." Having had the care of Summer for less than two weeks, I could better understand the need for working mothers to have such help. Besides, Samantha and I didn't want to allow the "bean-counters" to take over Rivers Papers, eliminating the benefits that made working there great for loyal families in Maine.

We made arrangements to travel to Riverton together in the next week. Then, anxious to get back home, I said good-bye to Samantha, thanked Adrienne, and left.

As I drove between the stone pillars at the end of the long driveway leading to Briar Cliff, I saw my house in a new light. With a baby inside, it now had the feel of a real home.

When I entered the house, Becky shot me a worried look.

"When Gracie got Summer up from her nap, she had a bit of a fever and her nose was running. I think it might be the start of one of those summer colds."

"Where is she now?" I asked, alarmed.

"She's with Gracie in the sunroom."

I hurried into the sunroom. Summer was lying on the play mat, her cheeks flushed. I knelt beside her and felt the soft spot behind her neck. It was warm. Too warm. Her forehead was warm too.

So afraid, I stood and clasped my hands together as my mind whirled with frightening scenarios. Summer might need to go to the Emergency Room at the local hospital. I was figuring how many minutes it would take to get her there when Becky came into the room.

Noticing my face, Becky shook her head. "Don't panic, Marissa. We'll get a humidifier set up in her room. And we'll keep her quiet. She'll be fine."

Adrenaline left my body. I sank down onto the couch. Summer's mother must not have realized how little I knew about these things.

After Becky and Gracie left for the day, I kept Summer at my side in her infant carrier, afraid to let her out of my sight. If she got worse, I'd take her to the emergency room no matter what the books said about summer colds.

I ate an early dinner and settled Summer in her crib. I went to the hall closet and pulled out a sleeping bag Brad and I had used for a camping trip. After spreading it atop the carpet in Summer's room, I tried to make myself comfortable. It was the best I could do. I knew I wouldn't sleep a wink worrying about her from my own bed. I turned out the light and lay still in the dimly lit room, aware of the snuffles coming from Summer's nose. Lady lay down beside me.

I'd just closed my eyes when Summer began to cry.

Rising, I lifted her out of the crib and carried her downstairs.

In the kitchen, I gave Summer a small dose of medicine and tried to feed her. After taking only a little bit of the formula, she pushed her bottle away and whined.

Throughout the night, between periods of fussing or eating, Summer slept. I did not.

Dawn was breaking when I rose to my feet stiffly. Summer was sleeping. I leaned over the crib and touched her forehead. It was a little moist and much cooler. Covering her with a light blanket, I left the room.

As I sipped coffee in the kitchen, I listened for sounds coming from the baby monitor in Summer's room and waited for Becky or Gracie to arrive, too tired to move.

CHAPTER SIX

A week later, I checked the clock in the kitchen. Samantha was going to pick me up to go to the paper mill for the board meeting. As usual, she was late. At the sound of a car pulling into the driveway, I waved a quick good-bye to Becky. "Tell Gracie I'll be back as soon as I can. And please remind her to put extra lotion on Summer after her bath. Her skin is so tender."

"Gotcha. Will do." Becky shooed me out the door. "You go ahead to your meeting. We'll be just fine."

I sighed and hurried out to Samantha's Volvo. In a matter of weeks, all my attention had become focused on one adorable little creature. Even Lady was feeling the effects and had taken to resting her head on my knees as I fed the baby.

"How're things going?" Samantha asked as I slid into the passenger's seat.

"Good. So far we're in a holding pattern. No word from either parent. The caseworker checked in with me yesterday, and things went well. We have another interview coming up next week. That might not be so encouraging."

Samantha frowned. "Why?"

"There are a number of people on a waiting list for a baby like Summer. Politics could get in the way." I fought uneasiness. Now that I knew the joy of holding a baby in my arms, I understood why others would fight for one.

Samantha reached over and squeezed my hand. "It doesn't seem right to ignore the mother's wishes and place her elsewhere."

"Unless the mother steps forward, what say would she have?" I shook my head. "Brad keeps telling me to take it one day at a time, but this waiting game is killing me. I hate not knowing what is going to happen to Summer."

"If you need more detailed references, you know Derek and I will do it."

"Thanks. I know. Allison and Blake told me the same thing." It helped to have my new family support me, but I knew it would take more than that to speed things up to a satisfying ending—or in this case, a beginning.

"We'd better talk about the company's day care center," said Samantha. "I've put together some figures as to cost and return on investment to present to the board. Ted only thinks of what it's costing the company, but when you figure in sick days not lost, we actually are doing okay."

I couldn't help smiling at the fierceness in Samantha's voice. Samantha and Ted were long-time rivals. Like oil and water, people said, and it was true. They'd dated briefly and ended up disliking each other intensely. I suspected Ted was frustrated by both Samantha's intelligence and her independence. I knew Samantha hated Ted's high-handedness. Until she met Derek Roberts, Samantha was not one to cross. Derek had brought out a whole other, softer side to her that I loved. Still, when it came to legal and work issues, the tough Sam was the one I wanted by my side.

The drive from New Hope to Riverton took a little more than two hours—time we spent catching up with one another and discussing the workings of the mill.

As we entered the small town, I took a fresh look at it. Familiar brick storefronts, their wooden trim painted in various colors, lined the main street. A brick church with a towering steeple captured one corner of the central city block and was opposed by an unimaginative, yellow, cinder-block building that housed the town offices. Steam rose from a stack down the street, indicating the mill, which sat at the edge of town.

Just before the approach to the bridge that spanned the Kennebec River, we turned left into the mill's parking lot.

Seen through the chain-link fence, the sleek white metal buildings sat in stark contrast to the faded, brick outbuildings on the property. As I stepped out of the car, I stood a moment to inhale the rich, piney smell that reminded me of Christmas holidays. I was well aware that the pleasant smell was really airborne resin that could coat the lungs if someone was over-exposed to it. That was just one of the environmental things Rivers Papers had to control carefully for the benefit of all.

A steady low, humming noise filled the air. I looked up at the roof of the building where huge fans were directing the heat and steam away from the mills. It filled me with awe to think my great-grandfather and his brother had begun with a simple mill years ago. Now, it was a major enterprise.

"Ready to go inside?" Samantha asked, giving me a comprehending smile. She'd confessed to me long ago that she too felt in awe at what our grandfathers had produced.

We carried our personal, yellow, hard hats inside and had our rubber-soled shoes inspected by the guard at the door. Smiling, he signaled for us to go on inside. In silent agreement, we headed for Jonesy's domain.

We covered our ears with the same OSHA-approved ear muffs workers wore on the job before stepping inside the large room that held the sights and sounds of a major paper operation. The long, air-conditioned room contained a huge, self-enclosed machine. The inside workings of the mammoth machine were represented on what was a three-dimensional display that dominated one wall like a huge television screen.

I knew the massive machine was fully enclosed to help

regulate heat, moisture, and noise. It had a 280-inch width and was capable of putting out 3,500 feet of paper a minute. When I'd first been shown the operation, I'd been astonished to learn the secret to running the machine was keeping an eye on the big electronic model on the wall, which told what was happening inside. I'd learned that each man stationed alongside the machine was responsible for a different part of it. A warning light at every critical point told the operators if there was a problem so they could check it out on their computers. It was as if the workers were working in a virtual reality. And that wasn't the only important machine at the mill. Hydro pulpers, grinders, winders and slitters, and super calendars—you name it, they had it. Rivers Papers was up-to-date. Samantha and I intended to keep it that way.

We passed through the room into the glass-enclosed, manager's office. The sounds from the main room immediately became muted. We took off our ear muffs.

A well-padded, pleasant-looking man rose from behind his desk and opened his arms.

Samantha rushed into them. "Hi, Jonesy! Long time, no see!" At his warm embrace, Samantha blushed with pleasure. She'd won his heart a long time ago when, as a little girl, she'd declared she wanted to run the company one day.

"You doin' okay?" he said, and I knew he was asking about Sam's sobriety. She'd been sober for several years now.

Samantha laughed. "With three little ones, I have no choice. I have to be okay."

"Good for you! It's been thirty-five years for me." He turned to me. "And you're a mother now, Miz Mari? That picture you sent me of the little one is fantastic." His blue eyes twinkled.

With his whitish-gray hair and trimmed, white beard, I thought of him as Santa Claus. More than that, he'd proved to be a loyal worker and a trustworthy friend.

"Though we'd like it to be permanent, it's a temporary situation for now," I explained. "Is there any news from here as to who, if anyone, might be involved in this situation?"

"Haven't heard a thing about it and can't think of a soul who might be the mother. I've talked to a couple of people privately, but they had no leads for me. They'll let me know if they hear anything, but I doubt anyone comes forward."

Unexpected relief rushed through me in a warm stream of happiness. Maybe, like Brad kept telling me, it was better if we didn't know who she was. I gave Jonesy a quick hug. "Thanks. I appreciate your looking into it. See you later."

I gave him a big smile, put on my ear muffs and followed Samantha out the door.

Board meetings took place in the conference room of one of the old brick outbuildings that overlooked the river. Samantha and I entered a room dominated by a large mahogany table, surrounded by brown leather swivel chairs. No one else had arrived yet.

The outside view through the windows drew my attention. The river below was more than a picturesque ribbon of blue winding its way through the town. It was the essence of Rivers Papers' strength. Without it, the mill never would have been developed.

I studied the inflatable flashboards that could raise or lower the water by a few feet and remembered what had been told to me. They were used for flood control in times of high or low water. Raising the "boards" allowed the generation plant to maintain head pressure, or the surge of the river, to turn the generators. When they could increase electrical output, it was a significant deal economically.

Samantha came up beside me. "I wonder if William and Edward Hartwell, as farsighted as they were for their time, could ever have imagined how extensive their small business would become." She turned to me. "It's up to us to continue its success in every way."

I placed a hand on her shoulder. "Don't worry, Sam. We're a good team."

"We'd better be. Ted Beers will do anything to get his own way."

The other members of the board, all eight men, arrived en masse. Samantha and I had yet to succeed in putting another woman on the board.

Everyone else had settled in their seats when Ted Beers strode into the room. A handsome, broad-shouldered man with hair graying at the temples, his confidence was striking. Taking a seat at the head of the table, he glanced at Samantha and me and frowned.

"To what do we owe this honor of having not one, but two, Hartwell women present?" He tried to cover the annoyance in his voice with a smile that neither Samantha nor I believed.

"As Marissa and I share the family seat on the board, I try to come to Maine as often as I can," said Samantha smoothly, though I noticed her flexing her fingers in her lap.

Ted turned to me. "I understand congratulations are in order. I heard you have a new baby. I suppose you'll be here less frequently."

My eyebrows rose with surprise. "My responsibility and participation in affairs of the mill won't be any less, just as the men here are not deterred from participation by happenings at home." I spoke calmly but I was boiling inside. I hated being put down that way.

Wendell Blake, a businessman from Boston whom I admired, broke the tense silence. "As major stockholders of the company, both of these women are to be welcomed." He smiled at Samantha. "Good to see you again. And welcome, Marissa. I'm always happy to hear what you have to say."

Other board members murmured their welcome. Disgruntled, Ted pulled out a leather folder from his briefcase.

I studied him. His trim body showed every sign of careful attention to detail, from his manicured nails to the perfect styling of his coffee-colored hair. His clothing was impeccable. Why I wondered, did such an attractive man have such a condescending, irritating way about him? It ruined him.

The matters on the agenda were handled in an efficient manner. Doing that was the only trait of Ted's that I admired. Soon it became time to discuss the day care center.

Ted cleared his throat. "As we all know, stockholders are always looking for ways to save money and maximize profitability. After reviewing the cost of running the day care center, I've concluded it's an unnecessary expense."

Samantha spoke up. "As you all know, we've talked about this before. I've done a study to analyze our situation." She passed papers to either side of her and continued. "The expenses of running the center are offset to a great degree by the lower number of days missed by staff taking time off to care for their young children. Some of our younger workers find outside day care so expensive it isn't worth their while to work at other businesses, even for better pay. By offering the benefit of day care here at Rivers Papers, we've been able to attract and keep good workers."

"One of the reasons the day care center was established was to reduce the cost of hiring and training new people," I added. "Our retention numbers are outstanding."

Ted shook his head. "Still, no matter what you say about it, it's an expense."

"Exactly," said Samantha. "One that enhances public

relations in addition to being an important employee benefit. It proves this company's willingness to do the right thing for families who've worked at Rivers Papers for years. In some cases, that includes more than one generation."

"Our job is to make the most for our stockholders," countered Ted.

"Yes, that's right, but our job is to do just that by running this business efficiently and wisely, maximizing return to the shareholders," said Samantha, her voice taut. "It has been well documented that recruiting, hiring, and training new employees is far more expensive than retaining long-term staff who are well motivated."

Wendell broke into the discussion. "The figures Samantha has come up with show the cost involved is such that no stockholder should be upset. Certain costs are considered the cost of doing business. This is one of them. In this low-density area of Maine where it's sometimes difficult to find good workers, I think it's a reasonable expense."

"It's just damn good PR and management of human resources," said another board member.

The look of disgust on Ted's face sent shivers down my back. As usual, he'd made it a personal issue between him and Samantha.

"I say we put it to a vote and approve continuing the day care center as it's presently run," I said. A vote was quickly taken and approved. The meeting ended soon after.

Ted left without speaking to either Samantha or me. I could tell it had taken him some effort to avoid doing so. He was a man who liked having the last word.

Samantha and I left the board room and walked over to the day care center, which was set up in another outbuilding. As we approached the building, laughter met us.

I smiled. "It's so great to hear the sounds of happy kids."

"I miss my little ones much more than I thought I would." Samantha grabbed my elbow. "C'mon, let's see what we can do to help the teachers. I didn't bring it up in the meeting, but I want to make sure they have all they need—things only we mothers would think of."

My heart swelled at the thought of being included as a mother.

Inside the building, the rooms were alive with activity. The children ranged in age from infants to kindergarten-age toddlers. I was impressed by the different way each of the four rooms was used—like age-appropriate classrooms in a school.

As we walked toward the back office, I stopped outside a small, dimly-lit room that was set up for the youngest. Five cribs lined the walls. Peeking in through the doorway, I noticed three infants sound asleep.

"I wonder how they get them to sleep at the same time?" I said softly.

"It can be tricky," Samantha said. "My twins were out of sync for a while. It about drove me crazy."

Susan Reynolds, the licensed director of the center, came up to us.

"Good to see you," she said softly. "What can I do for you?"

"We'd like to go over your equipment and supplies." Samantha grinned at her. "And to tell you that no matter what rumors you might have heard about closing the center, the board has approved keeping it."

Susan's face lit up. "Thank heavens! I don't know what some of our staff would do without our day care program." She waved us into her office.

I took a seat in front of Susan's desk and gazed around the office with new insight. I read through a number of items on a staff reminder board—simple, important, comforting reminders like washing hands after every diaper change. My eyes came to rest on another white board, this one entitled "Notes for Parents." One of the messages read: *Kaitlyn C has a rash. Go over protocol.* Another read: *Jack M needs to bring extra clothes in case of accidents.*

Susan smiled at me. "It's important for us to keep open, up-to-date communications with the parents. This board must be checked before a child is released for the day. With six staff members, including myself, we have to be sure that everyone knows what's going on."

"You and your staff are doing a great job," said Samantha. "My sister is thinking of setting up something like this on a small scale at the winery. I'll suggest to her that the next time she flies east, she pays you a visit."

"Now, what can we do for you," I said, taking out a paper and pen.

I listened with great interest as Susan went through a list of things the center could use. After approving the purchase of those items and more, as we'd done in the past, Samantha and I prepared to leave. I rose and shook hands with Susan. When I pulled away my hand, a folded piece of paper was in it. I felt my eyes widen and gazed at Susan. She merely smiled at me and looked away. I turned to Samantha but she'd missed the exchange.

It wasn't until later, when I was alone in the ladies' room, that I had a chance to read the note. I unfolded the paper and gaped at the words:

"I need to talk to you about something personal. Please call me at the phone number listed below."

A shiver skittered across my shoulders. Was this about Summer? Or her mother? My body turned cold.

CHAPTER SEVEN

On the drive home, Samantha chatted about Allison and the latest happenings at the vineyard Allie and her husband, Blake, owned in California. Her talking did little to distract me from my worries.

"You okay?" Samantha finally asked me.

I let out the breath I hadn't realized I was holding. "What should we do when we find out who the baby's mother is?"

Samantha turned to give me a questioning look. "Do you know who she is?"

I shook my head. "No, but I might have a way to find out. What then?" My stomach squeezed with worry.

"I say if you get to meet the mother, ask her why she wanted you to be the parents, not someone else," said Samantha. "Find out why she felt she couldn't keep the baby. Get her to answer all the other questions you've told me you have. Who knows what could happen? In today's world, lots of adoptive families have the birth mother in the picture. Maybe that's something you could do."

"What about the father?"

"That might be a different story, depending on how much he wants to be involved."

Feeling so confused, I clasped my cheeks and lowered my face. "I'm an emotional wreck. I don't know what I want to happen."

Samantha reached over and patted my shoulder. "One day at a time, Marissa."

Tears trailed down my cheeks. My life felt so out of

control and I wasn't handling it well.

As we pulled into Briar Cliff's driveway, I drew up in my seat. I had to be strong. New resolve filled me. By damn I'd do everything I could to make the situation the best it could be for Summer.

"Things will work out. You'll see," said Samantha, giving me a hug.

I hugged her back. "Thanks for all your support."

Inside the house, all was calm. Becky and Gracie were cleaning up from baking cookies for Brad, and when I tiptoed into Summer's room, I found her sleeping peacefully in her crib. The ever-loyal Lady rose from the carpet next to the crib and greeted me with happy licks.

Lady followed me into my bedroom. I changed into something more comfortable and was about to go downstairs when the phone rang. Brad.

"Hi, sweetheart! How are you?" I said, happy as always to hear his voice.

"Uh, okay. I've decided to come home early. As a matter of fact, I'm on my way. I'll be there in a couple of hours. There's something I want to talk to you about."

I swallowed nervously. His voice hadn't displayed any of his usual cheerfulness. "Is everything all right?"

"Sorta," he answered mysteriously.

My heart pounded. Something was wrong. "Do you want to talk about it?"

"Not yet," he said. "Gotta go."

At the click of the phone, I hung up, filled with concern. More mysteries. I took out the note Susan had given me, unfolded it, and punched in the phone number she'd listed. The phone rang and rang but there was no answer and no voice mail.

Frustrated, I disconnected the call and sank onto the bed.

Life had turned so unpredictable. I had no way of knowing what was happening next, and I was a planner who liked to have some idea of what to expect.

Downstairs, I chatted with Becky and Gracie about how their day had gone. Afterward, I went into my office to transfer the notes I'd made at the day care center into a report for the Rivers Papers board. I again tried calling the phone number Susan had given me, but once more, there was no answer and no active voice mail. *Had she given me the right number?*

I was doing desk work when I heard the sound of Brad's Jeep pulling into the driveway. Worried, I got up and raced outside to meet him.

He pulled himself out of the car. I knew by the way he stood—shoulders hunched, and without a smile, that something was seriously off.

Heart pounding with dismay, I ran into his arms and hugged him hard. "It's so good to have you home."

Silent, he wrapped his arms around me and drew me closer.

When we stepped apart, I studied him. "You have me concerned. Are you sure you're okay?"

His face gave little away. "We'll talk later after Gracie and Becky have left for the day."

My stomach knotted. I brushed a lock of caramel-colored hair away from his strong, troubled features. "I love you, man!"

At our signature gesture, his lips curved into his familiar smile. "Love you, woman."

Feeling better, I took his hand and led him inside. Lady greeted him at the door with little doggy yips of welcome, and Becky gave him a cheery hello. When he smiled at them, the tension that had gripped me eased.

Gracie joined us in the kitchen, holding Summer. "She's

all changed and ready for her next bottle."

Brad held out his arms. "Here, let me do the honors."

Gracie handed the baby over to him then checked her watch. "Okay if I leave now, Marissa? Courtney and I are going into Portland for a concert. There's a great group performing downtown."

"Sure. It's time for you to leave anyway. Have fun."

Becky went to the pantry and picked up her purse. "It's time for me to be off too. Your supper is in the oven."

I gave them each a hug. "Thanks for everything."

After they left, I felt myself relax. It was wonderful to have such help, but I'd come to treasure the moments Brad and I had alone with Summer. I sat at the kitchen table and watched Brad feed Summer in the rocking chair. He'd turned out to be a wonderful father, eager to hold the baby and to feed her. I smiled affectionately at him. He was even getting better about changing diapers. "My, you make a great Daddy."

He looked up at me, his brown eyes shiny with unshed tears.

I felt my heart drop to my shoes. "What's wrong?"

"I went to my doctor in Barnham last week. Today I had a long talk with him. I'm in great shape except for one thing." He took a deep breath. "My sperm count is low. He's pretty sure that's why you haven't gotten pregnant."

The pain etched on his face made me feel queasy. Swallowing hard, I started to reach for him. Summer kicked and cried and pushed the empty milk bottle away. I handed Brad a burp rag and, stomach churning, watched helplessly as he lifted Summer over his shoulder.

"It's a good thing we have a shot at keeping Summer. She might be the only baby we have." A sad puff of air escaped Brad's lips. "Who knew I'd be so desperate for a kid, huh?"

I tried to think of something to say, but my emotions were

so mixed up with shock it took me a few moments to get the words out. "You're always telling me to take it one day at a time, Brad. Things will work out."

"I hope so," he murmured, and rubbed Summer's back.

"Surely there's something you can do." I'd once noticed an article about it in a magazine but hadn't bothered to read it.

"I have a list of things that can help the situation— routine things like watching my diet, taking antioxidants, and changing my underwear." He gave me a smile that wasn't real. "No more 'tighty-whities' for me. I'll show the list to you later..." His voice trailed off. "God! I feel like a damn eunuch."

At the resigned note in his voice, my heart pounded with dismay. "Don't do that to yourself. You are a strong, virile, healthy man whom I love very much."

He nodded his head, but his look told me that the insecurities he'd felt after his first wife dumped him were clouding his judgment.

I thought of Susan's note. I'd planned to tell Brad about it but now I knew I wouldn't. I'd handle it on my own. I couldn't upset him any more than he was.

As soon as Summer had taken her last bottle of the evening and was settled down for the night, I drew Brad up out of the couch where he'd been glumly watching television.

"C'mon. Let's go to bed."

He gave me a grimace but followed me up the stairs to our bedroom. Inside the room, he unbuckled his pants and headed for our walk-in closet to change out of his clothes.

"Oh no, you don't!" I said, playfully and tugged him to me. "I've been waiting all evening for this moment. I love you, Brad. I want to make love to you."

His face lit with satisfaction. He lowered his lips to mine. When his tongue entered my mouth, shivers of delight rolled through me. There'd been a time when he'd had to show me how tender, how sweet, how giving love could be. It was my turn now.

I pulled him down on the bed and cupped his face in my hands. "I love the way you make love to me. I want you now. All of you—body, heart and soul." I unbuttoned his shirt and stroked his strong, muscular chest before trailing my fingers down his body to his belt. He lay back on the bed as I unbuckled his belt and undid his zipper. His gaze didn't leave me as I reached inside his pants to the bulk of manhood already responding. At my touch, he let out a moan of pleasure. A sense of satisfaction swept through me. I loved this man who'd taught me so much.

We hastily undressed.

Aware of his need to feel secure about himself, I slid on top of him, determined to prove to him how manly he really was. We made love, easily climbing to satisfaction together and then lay spooned against each other, happy and sated.

"I love you, Marissa," Brad murmured in my ear, cuddling me to his chest. "Will you stay with me?"

My eyes widened with surprise. I turned to him. "Of course! We're a team, remember? Don't worry, we'll work things out. Together. Understand?"

He closed his eyes and nodded.

People always thought only women wanted babies, but men wanted children too. And Brad was a good man. An only child, he'd always loved the idea of having a large family. He'd already shown what kind of father he could be. Somehow we had to make things work.

CHAPTER EIGHT

The next morning, Brad and I went over the list of recommendations the doctor had given him and decided to do a little shopping. "We'll have lunch afterward," I suggested, eager for him to stop dwelling on the issue. I could think of nothing else. If we couldn't have children of our own and Summer was taken away from us, what would we do?

We left Summer with Gracie and took off for the outlet malls on a mission that meant more than buying things. It was to be a healing time for Brad.

After a successful shopping trip, we strolled along the streets of New Hope. I breathed in the salty tang of air. I'd fallen in love with the beautiful, little, seaside town the first time I'd seen it. Wooden buildings lined the narrow streets that wound along the inlet shoreline and followed the edge of the harbor. The weathered sidings of the buildings had withstood Maine summers and winters for so long they'd faded to silvery gray. During summer months, the structures came alive with the noisy activity of tourists entering and leaving them, carrying away packages like pirates raiding a town of its treasure.

"Good to be home," Brad murmured, taking hold of my hand. We sidestepped a couple so intent on reading a map of the town that they had no idea where they were going.

I smiled at Brad. He was acting more like his old self. The harbor with its fishing boats and bobbing pleasure boats always seemed to bring out the best in both of us. I lifted my head to watch seagulls spread their wings and swoop in the air above us like wind-loving kites.

"Shall we go to The Lobster Trap for lunch?" It was still one of my favorite places for seafood.

"Sure," said Brad. "A lobster roll and a cold beer sound good."

Situated right on the harbor, The Lobster Trap's large wooden deck extended over the water at the harbor's edge. The July day was perfect for dining al fresco—the temperature in the low seventies and enough cloud cover to keep us from getting too hot. A cooling onshore sea breeze was steady. Chiding myself for not coming to town more often, I took a seat at a table next to the wooden railing.

"It can't get better than this," Brad commented. He checked over the menu and sat back.

A young girl approached our table.

"Hi, I'm Cherie! I'll be your waitress today. What can I get for you?" Cherie smiled at me and turned to Brad.

I placed my order and Brad followed, also ordering a cold, draft beer.

"I'll be right back with your water and your beers," beamed the friendly waitress, briefly settling her gaze on me.

I stared at her. With fine features, dark, shoulder-length hair, and blue eyes, the girl was striking in appearance. But that wasn't what had caught my attention. There was something familiar about her. I tried to think of when I might have seen her. My thoughts quickly turned to Summer. Was this her mother? They both had blue eyes. Goose pimples that had nothing to do with the cool sea breeze puckered my skin.

Cherie brought our drinks to the table. I placed a cold, tentative hand on Cherie's arm. "Have I seen you before?"

Cherie's eyes registered surprise. "I worked for a caterer here in New Hope last summer. You might've seen me at one of the local parties."

I sat back in my chair. "That's right. That's where I've seen you—at the Worthingtons' garden party. You're not working for The Pampered Guest anymore?"

Cherie shook her head. "No, the hours at the catering company were awful."

"So you're here just for the summer?" I knew I was being a bit intrusive, but I couldn't help myself.

"I ... I don't know," Cherie responded. "I'm not sure about school." She turned and walked away.

Brad frowned at me. "What was that all about? You were almost rude to her."

Shame heated my cheeks. I shrugged, unwilling to tell him how determined I was becoming to find Summer's mother. I didn't ask any more questions of her, but I knew I'd remember the name, Cherie.

The days flew by in quick succession. Monday morning came all too soon. I stood outside the house holding Summer, seeing Brad off for another work week in New York. I couldn't wait for the time when we'd no longer have to live our lives this way. This week would be especially hard, because, when Brad returned to Maine, his mother would be with him. It would be a couple of tense days. No matter how hard I tried, I felt as if I never measured up to Ellen Crawford's standards.

Brad stuck his head out of the window of the Jeep. "See you Friday. Love you, woman."

I smiled at our old pattern. "Love you, man!"

He pulled out of the driveway. When I returned to the kitchen, Summer was wide awake. I placed her in her baby seat and started up the musical mobile. I poured myself a second cup of coffee and checked the clock. Gracie would be here soon. Then I'd have a chance to take a shower and wash my hair. I carried Summer in her baby seat into my office and began to go over the monthly figures for Rivers Papers. Ever since I'd discovered Ted Beers trying to cheat the company in sneaky little ways, I'd made it a mission of mine to check all figures for the company carefully.

The ringing of my cell phone caught my attention. I checked it. Unknown number.

"Hello?"

"Marissa? It's Gracie. Something's come up. I can't come in today. I'm sorry, but I don't know what else to do."

"Are you okay? You sound upset."

"I can't talk right now," Gracie said and hung up.

I stared at the phone with dismay. Something was terribly wrong for Gracie to end the call that way. She was one of the most polite people I knew.

Becky and Henry arrived a little later. I breathed a sigh of relief. After they got settled, I'd have Becky watch Summer while I went upstairs to shower.

Becky smiled when I asked her. "Of course. I'd love to sit with Summer. Where's Gracie?"

"Something's come up. She's not coming in today." I drew my eyebrows together, still concerned about the call. "Has she mentioned any problems to you, Becky?"

Becky shook her head. "No, she hasn't. She sure is a nice girl. Good worker too."

Shrugging off my worry, I headed upstairs, eager to get cleaned up. Who knew having time to shampoo your hair would turn into such a luxury?

While I was in the privacy of my bedroom, I called the number Susan had given me in Riverton. Again, no answer, no voice mail. I called the mill and asked for Susan. One of her teachers answered the phone.

I introduced myself and asked to speak to Susan.

"I'm sorry," came the reply. "Susan's gone for the next week or so. It's her vacation time. What can I do for you?"

After assuring her I needed no other help, I hung up, dismayed. If the note Susan gave me had something to do with Summer, it could spell trouble. I made a mental note to call her within the week. When I returned to the kitchen, I found Becky holding Summer in the chair and singing softly to her. My heart warmed at the sight of them, rocking back and forth in rhythm to the sweet little song.

"I'll fix her bottle," I told Becky. "Then I'll give you a break and feed her."

The furrows on Becky's forehead deepened.

I stopped. "Is everything okay?"

Becky took a deep breath. "You aren't trying to get rid of me are you?"

Surprise caused my eyes to widen. "No! Why would you think that?"

"You've been doing more and more of the housekeeping. And now you have Gracie here. What do you need me for?" Becky's cheeks flushed with emotion. Her eyes became suspiciously moist.

"Oh, Becky!" I hurried over to her and put an arm around her. "Why would I want to get rid of you? You and Henry are family to me."

Tears glistened in Becky's eyes. "I know I can't do all the work I used to do ..." Her voice trailed off.

"Stop," I said gently. "I don't expect you to." I sat down in a chair at the kitchen table and faced her, trying to make her understand. "After all the years of working here, you and Henry deserve a nice retirement. We know how hard, how unappreciated you were, working for my grandmother. Brad and I have decided your salary will be provided whether you and Henry are able to continue working for us or not. As a matter of fact, Brad has talked to Henry about coming in only twice a week. Maybe we should have you do the same."

Becky's face drained of color. "Are you firing me?"

I shook my head. "Of course not. I'm merely suggesting cutting back on your hours."

Becky squared her shoulders. "Sounds like firing to me," she muttered.

I took hold of one of her hands. "Think it over, Becky. Try cutting back on your hours to see if you like it. Wouldn't you like to do some traveling? See other places?"

Becky shook her head stubbornly. "This is where I belong, don'tcha know."

"You belong with us here as part of the family, not as the housekeeper you used to be." I hoped she'd hear the affection in my voice and know it would make sense. I'd never want to hurt either Becky or Henry, but it was obvious the work had become too much to ask of them. They deserved what we were offering.

Throughout the day, Becky was quiet as she went about her work. I silently noted the extra care she took in performing her usual duties in the house and working in the kitchen. When Becky had worked for my grandmother, too much had been expected of her. But today's easy lifestyle didn't demand such help, even in a house as big as Briar Cliff. Besides, I was used to working hard. The thought of sitting around all day while others did my work was totally abhorrent to me.

Before Becky left for the day, I gave her an extra big hug. "We love you, Becky. Please don't be upset at my suggestion. It was meant to please you."

Becky gave me an impish grin. "Well, I have noticed it's hard on Henry to be here so often. I'll talk to him about it."

I smiled to myself. Becky wasn't ready to give in, but she was listening.

###

After dinner, I sat in the sunroom watching Summer play atop the activity blanket I'd laid out on the carpet. Lying on her back, she kicked and reached for the toys hanging above her. I was amazed by how bright and alert she was. We had no exact birth date, but everyone agreed she was now three to four months old. At the sound of the doorbell, I frowned. I wasn't expecting anyone, and it was beginning to get dark. I rose, picked up Summer, and moved cautiously toward the kitchen door. Lady followed us.

"Who is it?" I called through the door.

"It's me, Gracie," came the reply.

I swung the door open and stepped back to allow Gracie inside. "Hi! It's good to see you! Is everything all right?"

"Can we talk?" she said.

At her troubled expression and the way she was wringing her hands, I knew something was terribly wrong. "Sure. Want a cup of coffee? Or maybe a soda?"

"Coffee would be nice." Gracie went into the kitchen and sat down. Seeing her, Summer waved her arms and kicked her feet with excitement. Gracie's face brightened. She held out her arms for the baby.

I handed Summer to her and set about making two cups of coffee. I had a feeling we'd both need it. I noticed now that Gracie's eyes were swollen from crying. After I served the coffee, I settled into a seat at the table. "Do you want to tell me what's going on?" I asked gently. The hot coffee slid down my throat but didn't make me feel any warmer.

"I can't stay at the Worthingtons' anymore." Fresh tears coated Gracie's tawny-colored eyes.

"Because?" I prompted.

"Because Mr. Worthington is a lying, cheating bastard,

and his wife is even worse." Gracie's sharp words came out fast, like bullets from a handgun. Her nostrils flared. "I moved into a motel this afternoon. But I can't afford to stay there for long."

My heart thumped with alarm. "Let's start at the beginning. What exactly happened?"

Gracie's lips thinned. "As I was getting ready for bed last night, I heard a knock at my door. Thinking it was Courtney, I went to open it in only my underwear. Her father pushed me back into the room and closed the door. He's not a small man, and it took me a moment to catch my balance. Even then, I couldn't keep him from shoving me back onto the bed. I fought him and called for Courtney. She came into the room. So did her mother."

Gracie let out a trembling sigh. "You can imagine what happened next. Her mother went crazy, calling me a whore and every other name you can think of. Courtney tried to calm her but it went on and on."

"Of course, she blamed you," I said, knowing very well how mean Eleanor could be.

Gracie let out a bitter sound. "And so did he ... the lying scum! He told her I'd invited him to come into the room and went after him!" She took another breath. "Courtney began crying and accused her father of cheating on her mother many times. That's when things got really bad. He hit Courtney, and she took off. I packed up my things and went to the motel downtown. I haven't seen Courtney all day and she won't take my calls."

"Is she all right?" I asked as calmly as I could, though my stomach boiled with acid. I hated physical violence. It was no stranger to me.

"Physically, she's probably fine," said Gracie. "But she was in bad shape, otherwise. She hates both her parents." She took a sip of coffee, giving herself time to calm down.

I observed her pain and felt anger build inside me. "I've never cared for them myself," I admitted. "Harrison has a reputation as someone who fools around, and Eleanor is difficult at best."

Gracie's eyes narrowed. "There's no way I can stay there, even to protect Courtney. I don't take that kind of bullshit from anyone."

"Why don't you move out of the motel and come here? The extra time here might naturally add to your workload, but that could be in exchange for room and board." The more I thought about it, the more it made sense.

"Do you mean it?" Gracie's face lit with relief. "I'd love to be able to keep my job with you. I don't know if I want to go on for my masters, so I was thinking of taking some time off. This would be perfect."

"Okay, we'll do it. Do you need a ride to the motel? How did you get here?" I didn't recall hearing the sound of a car.

"I rode Courtney's bike," said Gracie.

Full of resolve, I got to my feet. "Let's put the baby in the car. I'll drive you to the motel to pick up your things. We can talk to management. I'm sure they'll understand. They probably need the extra room at this time of year anyway."

In town, we explained the situation to the desk clerk and quickly loaded Gracie's things into my Land Rover. Though I looked, I saw no signs of Courtney anywhere.

Back at the house, I placed Gracie in the room next to Summer's and left her alone to get settled. I wasn't sure what Eleanor might have to say about my giving Gracie a new home, but I really didn't care. Coming from my background, the verbal lies and physical abuse in the Worthington home made my stomach roil.

CHAPTER NINE

I awoke and glanced foggily at my bedside clock. 8:15 AM. I sat up in a panic. Summer usually got up by six o'clock. I hurried out of bed and ran down the hall to the nursery. The door was open and the crib was empty.

Heart pounding, I stood a moment in shock.

"Are you looking for this little one?" Gracie walked down the hallway toward me carrying Summer.

I clasped a hand to my chest. It was foolish, but for a moment I'd felt as if Summer had been kidnapped. "What time did she get up?"

"Around seven." Gracie handed me the baby. "She's been changed and fed."

Hugging Summer to me, I inhaled the scent of the organic oils in the lotion we used on her skin. I kissed the head nestled against me. Feeling the soft, smooth skin against my lips, my body filled with joy. Summer made little sounds of contentment.

"Thanks so much for getting up with her. That was a pleasant surprise," I told Gracie. "I didn't expect that."

Gracie shrugged. "It seems only fair since you're giving me a place to live." A frown marred her face. "I still haven't been able to reach Courtney. I've no idea where she went. I can't imagine she'll want to stay at her parents' house."

"What about their son? Does he live there? I don't recall seeing him lately."

Gracie's laugh was dismissing. "Young Harry is a horny little guy who's away at prep school most of the year. He spends a lot of his time here in the summers crewing in sailboat races." She shook her head. "He even hit on me once, until I set him straight. I feel sorry for him. His mother spoils him, and his father thinks he's a lazy good-for-nothing."

I squeezed Summer affectionately. I'd never want her to be treated like Harry Worthington.

By the time I'd bathed, dressed, and finished breakfast, it was ten o'clock. Wondering if Becky had accepted my idea of cutting back on hours, I kept checking the kitchen clock. Neither she nor Henry had arrived.

I turned to Gracie. "Looks like we're on our own today." I explained the plan I was trying to work out with Becky.

"I'll do the dishes," said Gracie, rising from her seat at the table. The sound of Henry's truck turning into the driveway made her pause.

I waved Gracie back down to her chair and went to the kitchen door to greet them.

Wearing a big smile, Becky burst through the doorway. Henry followed behind her, unusually spry.

"Well, we've done it!" announced Becky. "It's all his idea, don'tcha know." She elbowed Henry playfully in the side. "Who knew it was a dream of his?"

"What are you talking about?" I stepped aside so Gracie could join us.

"We're going on a cruise for a few months. Can you beat that?" The look of disbelief on Becky's face brought a smile to my own.

"Is that right, Henry?" I said, so surprised I could hardly speak.

"Yup, been a dream of mine." He put an arm around Becky. They gazed at each other like teen-aged lovers.

Gracie clapped her hands together. "Wow! That's so exciting! When do you leave?"

Becky's expression sobered. "That's just it. We got a special deal because we signed up late. So we're gonna leave next week. And we'll be gone for three or four months!"

"That okay, Marissa?" said Henry. "With you and Brad urging us to take it easy, we thought it'd be all right. The money your grandmother left us will pay for it and then some."

"All right? It's wonderful news!" I hugged them both. "I'm so happy for you!"

Becky tilted her head toward Gracie. "This girl's a real good find. She'll do fine with me gone."

"And I know of someone to handle the yard work," added Henry. "'Course, he aren't good as me but he'll do."

The baby's cries came through the monitor on the kitchen counter, interrupting us.

"I'll get her," said Gracie. "And then, Becky, will you show me all your routines?"

A look of pride crossed Becky's face. "'Course, I will. I want you to do a good job for me while I'm gone."

"And please show me," I quickly added, realizing I'd relied too heavily on Becky to carry on duties from my grandmother's days. It was time for me to be in control of my own house.

Whenever possible, Gracie and I stayed alongside Becky taking notes on how she cared for the house, where she shopped for the best meat and fish, going over her favorite recipes, and the many other small details that made running this big house go so smoothly.

When we were finished, I took Becky aside. "I'm sure there are a thousand things for you to do before you leave on your trip, including doctor appointments. Why don't you take the rest of the week off and come say good-bye over the weekend? Brad will want to see you, and I'll want another chance to say good-bye."

Becky grinned. "I was afraid to ask for any time off, but you're right. Henry and I need time to get ready for this trip." She giggled. "Can't believe it."

I chuckled with her. There was a new spring to Becky's step—a well-deserved one.

Gracie and I were in the kitchen with the baby when Courtney surprised us by appearing at the kitchen door. She gave me a quick hello and rushed over to give Gracie a hug.

"I'm so sorry about everything," Courtney murmured.

"Where were you? I was so worried about you," Gracie said. "Have you talked to your parents?"

Courtney's face crumbled. "I went next door to Maude Miller's house and ended up spending the night there. This morning, I decided to move out of my parents' house. I packed up while my mother was at one of her meetings. And then, this evening after my father got home from work, I told them I was moving out." She gazed at Gracie. "My father's still furious with me and my mother never wants to see me again."

"I'm sorry," said Gracie.

"My parents don't understand how awful they can be. They never will," said Courtney.

"So what are you going to do?" I asked, wondering what it all meant.

Courtney took a deep breath. "May I stay here with Gracie? I'm willing to do anything you want and I'm a fast learner."

"I see," I said slowly, uncertain how to respond. "Let me talk to my husband and then we'll let you know. As it is, your timing couldn't be better. Becky and Henry are leaving on a cruise. We could probably use the help." Hiring more people wouldn't interfere with my plan to take care of Becky and Henry.

"I've already promised to stay and help Marissa for as long as it takes," said Gracie.

"I know I can't go home again," said Courtney. "Not now, maybe, not ever." Her eyes filled with tears, and I realized all of Courtney's tough talk hid a broken heart.

While Gracie and Courtney took Summer outside for a walk along the beach, I went into my office and called Brad.

"What do you think we should do?" I asked him after explaining the situation to him. "With Becky and Henry gone, it might be helpful to have Courtney here with us."

"Yes, but the Worthingtons might think we are aiding and abetting, so to speak," responded Brad like a lawyer. "I certainly don't want to get into a ruckus with neighbors. Especially neighbors like them."

Before I could protest, he added, "However, we are discussing adults here, so I'm less inclined to worry about such a reaction. I suggest we offer each of the girls a guest room and adjust any pay accordingly. When I get home this weekend, I'll sit down with them and draw up a written agreement between us."

"Your mother is accompanying you. How is she going to feel about this?"

"Whether my mother is staying with us or not, Marissa, we all have to agree on a number of living arrangements."

I felt my whole body relax. I'd been making it seem so complicated. "Thanks, Brad. You've made me feel better." I couldn't help smiling at the thought. "How are you going to feel with the house full of women?"

He laughed. "Guess I'd better get used to it, huh? How's

the little one?"

Pride filled me as I told him about Summer's fascination with her hands and how she'd begun to reach for things. We talked for a while longer before ending the call. I left the office and found the girls with Summer in the sunroom.

They looked up at me with worried expressions.

I took a seat on one of the couches. "Brad and I are willing to work out arrangements with you both for room and board. You'll each be given a guest room. When Brad comes home this weekend, we'll work out pay and living arrangements so we all have privacy."

"Oh, thank God," murmured Courtney, letting out a long breath.

"Thank you so much, Marissa," added Gracie in her quiet, dignified way. "I hate to think that because of me, Courtney would end up with no home."

"I'm sorry about what happened, Courtney," I said. "I know you're upset. However, I think it's important to keep things low-key. Your parents are probably not going to be happy with the idea that you're staying here."

"They're gonna be pissed," Courtney admitted.

My mouth grew dry. Like Brad said, I didn't want any quarrels with the neighbor—and Eleanor Worthington was an impressive adversary.

When Courtney went out to her car to get her things, Gracie spoke quietly to me. "I promise not to be in your way and make it uncomfortable for you."

"Thanks," I said. "Brad's mother is going to be with him when he comes home this weekend. *She* makes *me* uncomfortable!" Gracie and I exchanged amused smiles.

After Courtney settled in her room, she came downstairs and joined me in the kitchen. "Marissa, I meant what I said. I'm willing to work anywhere. All I need is some direction."

I gazed at the earnest expression on Courtney's face. Though she wasn't tall like her mother, she had her broad shoulders and a sturdy, solid body. Her dark hair was cut short in a stylish pixie cut that accented her large blue eyes.

"Don't worry, Courtney!" I said teasingly. "We're going to put you to work. I promise. We'll work a lot of that out this weekend."

"Thanks," said Courtney quietly. "I don't want to make trouble for you and Mr. Crawford. That wouldn't be right."

"I appreciate that. Brad and I are trying to do everything we can to adopt Summer. We need to have things running smoothly here at home."

Though Courtney nodded her agreement, I knew there'd probably be repercussions ahead. She was an unhappy young lady from a troubled family.

CHAPTER TEN

I woke to a cold summer rain. I stretched in bed and lay there waiting for Summer's cries to come through the baby monitor. The morning with Summer was one of the times I enjoyed most with her. The baby's smile, the newness of it all, had become precious to me.

Through the open window, I could hear the water of the bay meet the shoreline with a thump before sweeping back in a rhythmic pattern that almost lulled me back to sleep. I hugged Brad's pillow to me. I missed him like crazy. He was the one I knew I could count on to be there for me.

I climbed out of bed and took care of my morning routine but my mind stayed on Courtney. It had struck a nerve of mine to learn Courtney sought help from a next-door neighbor like I had done growing up. Did every family have such pain?

At the sound of Summer's stirring, I entered the nursery. The warm yellow of the walls and the blue and yellow designs in the décor added a touch of brightness to the otherwise gray day. Best of all was the smile that crossed Summer's face when she looked up and saw me.

I lifted her up and hugged her to my chest, more accustomed to this new role I'd been so afraid to try. Summer squealed and clapped a hand on my cheek. I took hold of Summer's fingers and kissed her soft skin.

Downstairs, freshly changed, Summer sat in her baby seat kicking restlessly while I quickly put together her morning bottle. As I rocked the baby in the chair Becky loved so much, the sound of its movement back and forth against the wooden floor was soothing. I wondered what the day would bring. Perhaps I'd have the time to catch up on the online accounting course I was taking. Others had told me to relax, to give up on the idea of completing a college degree, but after working so hard to pay for a few courses on my own, I couldn't give up. My financial circumstances might have changed, but my determination to be the best, most knowledgeable person hadn't.

Gracie appeared dressed and ready for the day. "Am I late?"

I shook my head. "Ordinarily, you wouldn't be here for another twenty minutes."

Gracie smiled. "I know, but living here changes that."

"When Courtney comes down, the three of us can sit down and talk about it."

I left Summer with Gracie and went into my office. I'd begun to write a list of duties around the house when the phone rang. The display read: Office of Child and Family Services. I picked up the phone. "H-h-hello?"

"Marissa? Alice Tremblay. We have an emergency here and I'm wondering if I can ask for your help."

"Is this about Summer?" My stomach flooded with acid.

"Actually, no. It's about a little newborn boy. His mother is a recovering addict who stopped using prescription drugs during the pregnancy. But because she's afraid of going back to them, she's agreed to go into a twelve-week rehab and training program for clean-living parents. Her baby needs a place to stay for at least the first six weeks. All of our registered foster families are unavailable. Since you've completed all the paperwork and meet our requirements for foster parenting, my supervisor has agreed to allow him to go to you if you're willing."

"Can I think about it?" I said, overwhelmed by the idea.

"And, of course, I have to talk to Brad."

"Certainly. With your beautiful setting and all the help you have, I thought of you immediately. You understand it may be for only six weeks. We don't know at this point."

"Anything else?" My head had begun to throb at the idea of taking on another child. I was still unsure about my role with Summer.

"Babies coming from backgrounds like this need a lot of special attention. Though he isn't going through withdrawal, there can be problems depending on how much the mother actually used during the pregnancy. We'd assign someone, probably one of our nurses, to come and talk to you about it if you wanted. Think about it and call me back as soon as possible."

Numb, I hung up. *Another baby? A difficult one at that? Did I want that? Could I do it?* My mind spun with uncertainty. I held my head in my hands, wondering what would be best.

In the quiet of my office, my thoughts wandered. Brad and I didn't know if we'd ever be able to have children of our own. He'd kiddingly said at one point we needed to fill the house with children. Was this fate leading us to that very decision? Was that to be my role—a foster parent? Would we always be saying good-bye to children and letting others have them? I didn't know if I could handle that.

I picked up the phone and called Brad.

He listened quietly as I told him the situation.

"What do you think?" I asked. My nerves tightened into knots of uncertainty. "Should we do it?"

"You mean should *you* do it? Most of the responsibility for this little boy will be yours, Marissa. Is this what you want?"

"Alice said with all the help we have, she immediately

thought of us."

"Maybe we should ask Gracie and Courtney how they feel about bringing another baby into the house," he said. "They'll need to help."

"Of course, but it's you I'm concerned about. You'd be the father if only for a short time. Is this what you want?" I didn't tell him I was worried about acting as a mother to a second child when I wasn't entirely comfortable mothering one.

The silence that followed seemed unending. Then Brad said, "It may be the only way I can be a father." The pain in his voice was wrenching. I knew then that I'd do anything to make Brad feel better about himself.

"Okay, Dad, you're about to have another baby," I said. "We'll do it. It's only for six weeks."

"All right, if that's what you want, we'll do the best we can for the little guy." Brad paused. "I love you, Marissa."

"I love you too, Brad." And I did. More than he'd ever know.

I did a little research on the internet and was surprised to learn one baby is born addicted every hour. I read on:

" The rise of addicted babies continues to be an ever-growing problem. Much like the 'crack baby' epidemic of the 1980s, the last decade or so has seen an alarming increase in the number of prescription-drug-addicted babies. These babies may cry excessively and have stiff limbs, tremors, diarrhea, and other problems that make their first days of life excruciating. In addition, prescription-drug-addicted babies are prone to problems like stunted growth, birth defects, and seizures."

I sat back in my chair and let out a long breath. Alice had said the baby wasn't going through withdrawal, but after reading some of these facts, I had no doubt this little baby would be more difficult to handle than Summer. And with Becky away, I'd need the cooperation of Gracie and Courtney. I rose from my chair and went to talk to them.

Both girls listened quietly to what I told them and quickly agreed to help around the clock if necessary. I gave them each a hug. *Funny how life works out*, I thought. Having Becky temporarily gone and Courtney here in her place was a lucky thing. I couldn't have, wouldn't have asked Becky to take on more.

Alice was ecstatic when I called to inform her we'd take the baby. "He's a doll," she gushed. "Big brown eyes, dark curly hair and a sweetness about him not many babies have at this young age."

"What's his name? And how old is he?" It felt a little like getting a puppy—learning who you'd raise, if only for a very short time.

"His name is Silas."

I smiled. I liked it. Summer and Silas.

"He's seven days old. He's been kept in the hospital for testing and to make sure he gets off to a good start. As I told you, he's not going through withdrawal, but he's having a bit of a tough time. I'll bring him to you this afternoon."

After talking with Alice and asking more questions about Silas' condition, I hung up the phone feeling more confident. If any problems arose that we couldn't handle, someone on staff would see that Silas got proper medical attention.

I left Gracie and Courtney with Summer and drove into Portland to the baby store I was beginning to know quite well. A short time later, I drove home with a port-a-crib, sheets, clothes, toys, diapers, extra bottles, pacifiers, a baby monitor and a soft toy giraffe that made soothing sounds.

At home, the girls helped me set up Silas' portable crib and arrange clothes and supplies in another guest room. And then the three of us waited anxiously for Silas to arrive.

When Alice's blue Ford pulled into the driveway, I rushed outside to greet her. Too excited to wait for her to get out of the car, I peeked through the window at the blue bundle curled up in the car seat. Alice smiled at me and climbed out of the car. "Go ahead. Pick him up."

I opened the door and reached in for the baby. He opened his eyes and stared at me. His mouth opened wide. He let out a high-pitched howl that sent a shiver down my back. I lifted him into my arms. Crooning to him, I stroked his velvety chocolate cheek. He turned his head toward my finger. "Ah, he's hungry," I said, proud I knew the signal.

Gracie, holding Summer, stepped up beside me, followed by Courtney and Lady.

"Look who we have here," I said, holding up Silas so everyone could see. Silas continued howling.

"He's so cute," said Courtney. Then she made a face and backed away. "Eeeuw. Marissa, look what he did. You're going to have to change your clothes."

I looked down at my jeans. Silas has soiled them through the lightweight blue blanket wrapped around him.

"That side effect should clear up soon as his system begins to calm down," said Alice soothingly. Alice handed me an envelope. "Here are some notes for taking care of him, including instructions for his formula."

"Let's get him changed," I said, trying not to retch. "Courtney, will you look at the instructions and put together his bottle?"

Courtney ran inside. The others followed me inside. I carried Silas to the changing station we'd set up in the back pantry. Singing softly to try and calm him, I cleaned him up, changed his diaper and dressed him in new, clean clothes.

Alice looked on with approval. "You've come a long way, Marissa. It's a pleasure to see you working with him. He responds to the softness of your voice. Some babies from situations like this startle easily with loud noises."

I'd do whatever it took to make him happy. My heart had melted at the sight of this tiny, handsome little boy.

Gracie held out her arms. "Why don't I feed him so you can go change?"

I smiled my thanks and handed Silas to her. "I'll be right back."

When I returned to the kitchen, Silas had fallen asleep in Gracie's arms. Summer was in her baby seat nearby seemingly fascinated by all the activity. Lady was sitting on the floor between her two charges.

"Any questions before I go?" Alice asked me. "You already have the sheet of instructions I gave you. You can always call the office or my direct line. I'll see you in a week or so."

Suddenly nervous, I glanced at Courtney and Gracie. "Any questions?"

At the shakes of their heads, I said, "I guess not. I'll walk you out."

Later that afternoon, holding Summer, I stood beside Silas' crib in the sunroom. Wrapped tightly in a swaddle, Silas lay still, but his mouth moved in his sleep. A frown crossed his forehead and vanished. Summer reached for the baby.

"We have to let him sleep," I told her softly and moved away. It seemed strange to have two babies in the house. I wondered if this was how Samantha felt having twins.

I put Summer down for a nap. I left her sleeping peacefully and hurried into my office. Lifting the phone, I called Brad.

"How is he?" Brad said.

"His name is Silas and he's beautiful! Compared to Summer, he seems so tiny. His skin is velvet soft and what little hair he has is curly. And his eyes are amazing—so big and beautiful. I sent you a picture of him. He was sleeping so you won't be able to see his eyes, but you can get a good look at his face."

"Hold on!" said Brad. "I'm checking my cell. Yeah, I got the photo. He's one cute little guy." He paused. "Just so you know, my mother thinks this is another mistake of ours—taking in a child like this."

I couldn't worry about his mother now. I was too worried about trying to be a mother to two babies. "She's going to be surprised when she sees all the changes in the house. If you thought we had a lot of baby gear before this, wait until you see it now!"

"About that, I've decided to head home early. We'll be there tomorrow night in time for dinner."

"Okay," I said, wondering how we'd get the house ready for our company while I learned how to handle the new situation.

"Listen, I've gotta go," said Brad. "I have a lot to do before I can leave. See you soon. Love you!"

"Love you, too."

When I walked into the kitchen, Gracie looked up from doing dishes. "Everything all right? You look upset."

"My mother-in-law is coming for a visit. Tomorrow. We've got a lot to do. Where's Courtney?"

"She went to get the rest of her things." Gracie rolled her

eyes. "It won't go well. Her mother is a...well, you know."

I nodded. Heaven knew what Eleanor Worthington would say when she learned Courtney was staying with me. It wouldn't be anything nice. I glanced at the two baby monitors on the kitchen counter and shrugged off my concern. These babies were more important than anything Eleanor might say.

I picked up a paper and pen and went to the refrigerator to make a grocery list when Silas' cries came through the monitor.

"I'll get him," I quickly said. I was anxious for the baby to get to know me. "Can you get his bottle ready?"

"Sure." Gracie got to her feet.

I hurried into the sunroom and stopped. Lady was pacing back and forth in front of the crib like an anxious mother.

"Don't worry so, girl." Giving her a pat on the head, I raised my voice above Silas' howling. "I'm here. He'll be fine."

I peered into the crib. Silas' body had gone rigid inside his swaddle. I lifted him up into my arms and brought him to my shoulder. Crooning sweet words to him, I patted his back. But his crying continued—a shrill, high-pitched sound that pierced my ears and my heart. Bouncing him gently in my arms, I walked back and forth in front of the window. His crying continued nonstop.

I went into the kitchen to find the bottle Gracie had said she'd fix, but no one was there. At the sound of Summer's cries through her baby monitor, I understood. I set Silas down in his baby seat. While he continued screaming, I finished preparing his bottle. I picked him up again and settled in the rocking chair. Murmuring softly to him, I held the bottle to his lips. He sucked eagerly, then turned his face away and started screaming again. I tried everything I could think of to get him to take the bottle, but he continued to turn away.

Gracie returned to the kitchen with Summer. Making

little hiccupping sounds, Summer's cheeks were blotchy from crying so hard.

"I think Silas's screaming scared her," said Gracie. She gave Summer a hug before placing her in her baby seat. "I'll get her bottle."

"Silas hasn't stopped crying. I don't know what else to do." Feeling helpless, I got to my feet and began pacing the room with him. It suddenly went quiet.

I peered over my shoulder at his sweet face. He'd fallen asleep. "Poor little guy. He's exhausted."

From her baby seat on the floor, Summer began to cry for her bottle.

The sound startled Silas. He woke with alarm and started crying again. I could feel him pull his legs up to his body as he let out a scream. Gas, I thought. I lowered myself into a seat at the kitchen table, laid him in my lap and gently patted his stomach, rubbing it in soothing circles. He calmed and then filled his diaper right through the swaddle onto me.

Gracie gave me a helpless look from the rocking chair, where she was feeding Summer. "Uh, oh. What can I do for you?"

I let out a shaky sigh. "I'll change him and myself." Smelling the mess, feeling the wetness against my skin, I couldn't help the sting of tears. Was this what I had to look forward to for the next six weeks?

Courtney walked into the room rolling a huge suitcase behind her. "What's going on?" she asked above Silas' cries. She looked with dismay from me to Gracie and back to me.

Relieved to see her, I said, "After I get him cleaned up, I need you to take him for a few minutes. Maybe you can get him to take his bottle."

I cleaned up Silas, changed his diaper, and put a new onesie on him. Taking an extra few moments, I stroked his arms and legs. I'd heard it was a way to calm a baby. Soft nonsensical baby talk streamed from my mouth. He stilled and I trailed my fingers down his cheeks. He turned to them, trying to nurse.

Wrapping him in a blanket, I called for Courtney.

Courtney took him and held him carefully. I watched her carefully to make sure she was holding him properly then led her to a kitchen chair. "Here's his bottle and a burp rag. I'll be down in a minute."

As soon as Silas took the bottle, I raced up the stairs two at a time, peeled out of my clothes and washed up. In only my panties and bra, I sank down on the edge of the soaking tub and drew in deep breaths. I can do this, I told myself, wondering if I really could.

Feeling better wearing fresh clothes, I returned to the kitchen to find both babies half-asleep as they worked on their bottles. I stared at those little creatures, so different, so beautiful, amazed that at least for the time being they were in my care. Never in all my dreams would I have imagined such a scene. I still didn't know what it all meant.

CHAPTER ELEVEN

After a grueling night of being awake with babies, I struggled to find the energy I needed to get things on an even keel and the house ready for Brad's mother. Summer had developed another runny nose and was cranky. Her temperature was barely above normal, but I knew she felt miserable. With Courtney and Gracie looking on, I carefully cleared her nose. We got out the humidifier and set it up. Though I was calmer about this cold, I called Dr. Storey's office to make sure I was doing everything right. After being reassured I was being a good mother, I relaxed a bit.

I made a list of the things that needed to be done around the house, then called Gracie and Courtney into the kitchen.

"Is this about Operation Mother-in-Law? Gracie asked, a teasing sparkle in her eyes.

At her humor, I laughed. "Wait until it happens to you."

Courtney's lips twisted. She let out a sound of disgust. "I probably won't have a mother-in-law and, heaven knows, my mother is never going to visit me."

I studied her. She seemed so young for someone who'd recently graduated college. But then, I'd had to grow up fast, whereas she'd always lived in the lap of luxury, though I now knew that lap wasn't too comfy.

"What can we do to help?" Gracie asked.

I handed her the list. "I'll take care of the things at the bottom, but I need you to do the rest. If you have any questions, ask me. Between doing baby stuff, I'm going to work here in the kitchen."

Courtney reviewed the list of duties I'd given them and frowned. "Why are you fussing so much?"

"I know I'm going a little overboard, but I want things to be perfect for Ellen's visit." *Okay, maybe I was going a lot overboard. But Ellen already thought taking in babies was wrong and I wanted her to see how right it was.*

That afternoon, I'd finished making a Maine huckleberry pie and was sitting in the rocking chair with Silas when Brad drove into the driveway. I gasped and jumped up. According to my watch, he was at least three hours early. I glanced at the flour on the counter top and down to where it had spilled on the floor. I'd intended to mop it up later. Empty baby bottles were stacked in the sink. I'd wanted to wash them in the dishwasher but hadn't gotten around to it. Summer was sleeping and the girls were working outside, sweeping and scrubbing down the porch.

I thought of the nice, clean pair of slacks and crisp blouse laid out on my bed upstairs and brushed off my cutoff jeans and stood, adjusting Silas over my shoulder. He was calmer, but his stomach was acting up. The T-shirt I was wearing was spotted from a messy burp. This was my life now— bottles and burps and baby talk.

I took a deep breath and walked outside to greet Brad and his mother.

Brad helped Ellen out of his Jeep before turning to me with a big grin. "Hi! Thought we'd surprise you."

I smiled gamely. "You certainly did, as you'll soon find out."

He hurried over to me. "Let's see what you've got here." He lifted aside the edge of the green blanket wrapped around Silas. "Ahhh. Nice. He sure is little."

Silas tried to focus on the man behind the voice.

"Hi, little man," said Brad softly. He turned to me. "Like

you said, he's got big, beautiful eyes."

Ellen came over to us. "You're becoming quite the mother." She smiled at me.

"Thanks. I'm trying."

"May I hold him?" Ellen asked.

I hesitated. Silas hadn't had an accident in a while but his spitting up had become worse.

"Well?" Ellen held out her arms.

After pausing a moment, I placed him in her hands. As soon as she had him over her shoulder, Silas spit up all over her. The look on her face was a silent scream I understood all too well.

I took him from her. "I'm sorry, Ellen. His system is still struggling a bit."

Her smile was a moment in coming. "Well, if I'm to be a grandmother, if only for a short time, I expect this will happen from time to time."

Tears came to my eyes. This was as nice a peace-offering as I'd ever received from her.

"I'll take your suitcase inside so you can get changed," Brad said, looking aghast at the stains that ran down the back of Ellen's shirt.

"Yes. I'd like that," said Ellen, and I wanted to hug her for her calmness.

As we went inside, I took a fresh look around the kitchen. It wasn't in perfect condition but it was a place where a family obviously lived. The tension that had built inside me over the visit now seemed foolish.

After everyone was changed and freshened, we gathered on the porch. The late July day was picture-postcard perfect. Blue skies embraced a yellow sun that smiled down at us in lemony rays. Water calmly lapped the shore in steady musical whispers. Sailboats in the water beyond the shore skimmed the bay's surface, their sails like white wings reaching for the heavens.

Courtney and Gracie, who was carrying Summer, joined us to announce that Silas had finally fallen asleep. Seeing me, Summer held out her arms to be taken.

Smiling, I took her and whispered sweet baby talk to her as she nestled against me. Brad looked on with a look of satisfaction that touched me. A fleeting look of pain changed his features and withdrew. I knew he was wondering about more children and wondered if someday we'd be able to do as he wanted and fill the house with them.

As I rocked Summer in my chair, I relaxed in the seaside scene. The peace that had wrapped around me was unexpectedly shattered when a young man jogging along the beach headed our way shouting. His arms flailed in agitation as he stormed in our direction. He stopped at the bottom of the porch stairs and glared up at us. His eyebrows formed a V of anger as his gaze settled on Courtney.

She rose and clasped a hand over her chest. "What are you doing here?"

"What are *you* doing here, Courtney?" His sharp words pierced the air around us. "You'd better get home. Dad's freaking and Mom's crying." He jabbed a finger in Gracie's direction. "And it's all *your* fault!"

Courtney started forward and stopped. "Get out of here, Harry. You don't know what you're talking about!"

"I'm talking about your leaving home!"

Shock silenced the scene and then Summer began to cry.

Holding the baby to me, I stared helplessly at the boy who'd caused this commotion. Tall and thin, Courtney's brother had his father's large handsome features. Dark brown hair covered his head in soft waves. Wisps of it hung over his brow above wide-set blue eyes. His lips were small and curved, almost too pretty for a boy.

Brad went down the porch steps. Taking Harry's arm forcefully, he drew him away from us. They stood on the lawn, facing each other. Brad had drawn himself up in a protective pose. I knew him well enough to recognize from his stance how angry he was. I hoped Harry Worthington would understand that words spoken quietly had a force of their own.

Uttering a sob, Courtney rushed inside. Gracie followed her. The screen door closed behind them with a swishing noise that echoed in the stunned silence on the porch.

Ellen turned to me. "So she left home?"

"The family has a lot of issues," I said, wondering at the nerve of the gangly prep-school kid who'd tried to hit on Gracie. Did the Worthington men think they had the right to do such things?

Slump-shouldered, Harry made his way down the beach toward his home. Brad returned to the porch wearing a look of disdain.

"Stupid kid thought he could convince his sister to come home. Guess he doesn't know the whole story. I told him he'd better talk to his parents."

"Do you see why I said it was okay for Courtney to stay here?" I hoped he sensed the same turbulence in that household that I did.

"Yeah. I can't believe that kid threatened me if she stays here. He said his parents will see that we don't have any friends left in this town."

My insides clenched at the thought.

"Maybe you should ask her to leave," Ellen interjected. "You're trying to be part of this community. They could ruin it for you." She looked directly at me.

I cringed. It was a throwback to old times in Barnham,

where if he, the basketball star, had dated me, a loser, it would've harmed his popularity.

Brad let out a disgusted snort.

I spoke as calmly as I could to Ellen. "I couldn't live with myself if we made her leave and something bad happened to her. No, we'll do the right thing and let her stay. Right, Brad?"

"Absolutely," he said crisply.

"Well, then ..." Ellen's words trailed off as the screen door opened.

Courtney came out onto the porch. "I'm sorry my brother was being such a jerk. Do ... do you want me to leave?" She clasped her hands in front of her.

I knew the feeling of not being wanted around and reached out a hand to her. "Come here."

As she took my hand, I gave hers a squeeze. "We said you could stay here, and we'll stand by you. As long as you do good work for us and live peacefully here, you are welcome to stay."

Fresh tears came to her red-rimmed eyes. "Thank you, Marissa!" She turned to Brad. "And thank you, Mr. Crawford. You can see why I can't go home."

Brad's lips thinned. "I can well imagine it."

Gracie appeared with Silas, who was kicking and crying. "I've got him changed. I'll fix a bottle for him if someone will hold him."

Brad held out his arms. "How about giving me a try?"

He took the baby and sat down in a rocker. The movement of the chair stopped Silas' crying momentarily, then he started up again. Brad got to his feet and started pacing with him.

"Wow, is he always this way?" he asked me.

"A lot of the time."

"Summer's much easier, huh?"

He'd no sooner said the words when Summer rubbed her

nose and started to cry. I stood. "Guess I'd better take care of her nose."

"I'll do it," said Courtney. "I know how. You showed us this morning." She held out her arms.

"Do it gently," I reminded her and placed Summer in her arms.

Gracie appeared with a bottle for Silas.

"May I do it?" Ellen said. "It's been so long since I've done anything like this, but I'd like to try."

I hid my surprise. Ellen looked dazed by all that had happened, but she was gamely holding out her arms for Silas.

Brad handed the baby to her.

I watched as Ellen easily held the baby to her chest and offered the bottle to Silas. He quieted when she spoke softly to him. She looked up at me and we exchanged warm smiles.

"Guess I'll go inside to check on Summer." I rose to my feet to give Ellen and Brad some time alone.

When I returned to the porch with Summer, Silas had fallen asleep in Ellen's arms. My admiration for her grew.

I handed Summer to Brad and took Silas from Ellen. "We'll put him in his crib. I don't know how long he'll sleep, but he's comfortable there."

"Such a sweet little boy," said Ellen. "Too bad the mother was an addict."

"She's smart enough to get some help for the long-term hopes she has of raising him. I've done a little research. I had no idea so many babies were born to addicted mothers. And I'm not talking about addiction to only street stuff but to prescription drugs—drugs you and I might take for pain or whatever. It's a dangerous situation."

"Yes, I know. One of my friends back home had a terrible time getting off painkillers after having knee surgery."

Silas woke up and let out a scream, drawing his legs up in

a position of pain.

Carrying Silas, I left the porch and went upstairs to the room we'd designated as his. It was a peaceful room with pale green walls. We'd moved the rocking chair from Summer's room into his. Sitting down, I hummed an old lullaby and began rocking him and rubbing his back in comforting circles. He calmed and looked up at me with the dark eyes I found so irresistible. The brown skin on his brow smoothed as the pain subsided. Studying him, I wondered what the future would hold for him. I clutched him a little tighter as if I could protect him from the ups and downs of life. Fatigue washed over me, but even so, I knew it would be hard to let him go.

CHAPTER TWELVE

Gracie and Courtney agreed to take care of the babies so Brad, Ellen, and I could have a pleasant dinner together without interruption. Coming from a home where meals were sketchy at best, I enjoyed putting together a nice meal with attractive place settings. We ate simply—fresh grilled swordfish, sliced tomatoes from Henry's garden, and fresh green beans. Ellen watched her diet carefully so I was gratified when she eagerly dug into her slice of huckleberry pie without comment. Brad, as usual, had his pie with vanilla ice cream.

The calm around me, the fullness in my stomach, and pure exhaustion caused me to nod my head as the conversation continued. The room dimmed and I sat back in my chair.

"Marissa? Darling?"

Startled, I roused to find Brad standing at my side, gently shaking my shoulder.

I pulled myself up straight. "Oh, I'm sorry ..."

Brad took hold of my arm. "I'm taking you upstairs. You need your rest."

It wasn't even eight o'clock, but then I couldn't remember when I'd last had three straight hours of sleep.

"I'm sorry," I mumbled to Ellen and left the room with Brad.

Upstairs, Brad turned back the covers on our bed.

"The babies ..."

"The girls will take care of them," he said. "They're here to help."

He watched as I quickly brushed my teeth and changed clothes. I sank into bed and closed my eyes, unable to do more than thank him. Trying to prove to everyone I was a good mother had worn me out.

Morning sunlight streamed through the windows, washing my face with warmth, urging me to open my eyes. I rolled over on my side. Brad's length lay beside me. I spooned up against him and inhaled the scent that was his alone.

He turned and faced me with a grin. "How are you, my Sleeping Beauty?"

I laughed. I was no Sleeping Beauty and I knew it. My usual daily grooming routines had been discarded as I'd tried to learn my new role of Mommy.

Brad cupped my face with his strong hands and kissed my lips. At the taste of him, desire traveled through me. Thought I was still tired, the sexual chemistry between us was there. He smiled as if aware of the jolt he so easily caused inside me. "You're beautiful, you know, even falling asleep at the table."

I wrinkled my nose. "I hope your mother wasn't offended."

He brushed a lock of hair away from my face. "I think she's really beginning to understand what kind of person you are and why I love you so much."

My eyes stung at the tenderness in his voice. I would always be grateful to him for his patience with me, teaching me to trust him.

I gave Brad a lingering kiss and reluctantly pulled away. "I have to check on things. After taking on the duties of the babies, the girls must be exhausted."

"At some point last night, I told them they could have the morning off. I hope you don't mind."

"Not at all. That'll give you and your mom more time alone with the little ones." I checked the bedside clock. 8 AM. "Give me a chance to take a shower and get dressed, then I'll relieve them."

I hurried through my routines, anxious to see how everyone was doing.

Ready for the day, I entered the kitchen to find Ellen holding Summer.

"Good morning," she chirped happily. "Did you have a nice sleep?"

I nodded, feeling a little sheepish at my lack of attention to her. "'Guess I really needed it."

She smiled. "I can see why."

"Where's Silas?"

"Sleeping. Gracie said to tell you he should be good until nine o'clock. When I offered to stay with Summer, she immediately agreed. Both of the girls went back to bed."

"That's fine. What can I get you? Would you like some coffee or juice?"

"I'd love another cup of coffee," Ellen said, rising and placing Summer in her infant seat.

I turned to get the coffee and stopped. I couldn't wait another minute. I picked up Summer and hugged her to me. The clean-smelling lotion we used on her filled my nostrils. She placed her tiny hands on my cheeks. Lifting her fingers, I kissed them.

As I resettled Summer into her seat, Ellen said, "You're a good mother, Marissa."

I straightened. "Do you really think so?" Ellen's sister-in-law was Doris, the woman I often thought should've been my mother. And though Ellen might not know all the details, she was well aware of what kind of mother I had.

Ellen took my hand. "I know I haven't always been easy

on you, and I'm sorry. Mothers can be overprotective of their children. After Amber left Brad hurting so much, I didn't want it to happen to him again. I see now I shouldn't have worried about it. You're everything Brad has told me you were."

Overcome by emotion, I threw my arms around her. We stood for several seconds holding onto each other. Odd, how it had taken two babies to make her see me for who I really am. Or, I quietly admitted to myself, perhaps those same babies had allowed me to show more of my feelings.

I dabbed at my eyes with my T-shirt and went about fixing us coffee. Brad joined us. We sat at the table in companionable silence while Summer kicked in her seat and stared up at the mobile twirling above her head.

A gentle knock at the kitchen door brought me to my feet. At the sight of Becky and Henry, I eagerly opened the door to them.

"Good morning! Come in."

I smiled at Becky's new hairdo. Cut short and newly colored a soft brown, the style made her look years younger. Henry, I noticed, was sporting a bright-colored golf shirt and what looked like new pants. They looked adorable together.

I gave each of them a hug and introduced them to Ellen.

Brad whistled at Becky playfully. "You're looking good."

"Time for a change, don'tcha know," she said, blushing like a school girl.

Brad elbowed Henry playfully. "A three-to-four-month cruise? You old rascal."

Henry's features softened. A smile crossed his face. "Yup. 'Been a dream of mine."

"That's what Marissa told me. I'm very happy for you. And when you're ready to come back, we'll be here for you."

Henry smiled and nodded. "We'll be back. Yup."

Becky went over to Summer and picked her up. "This is

such a precious child," she said to Ellen. "I'm hoping these two get to keep her. She's already wormed her way into everyone's heart."

"You haven't met Silas yet," I said. "He's staying with us for six weeks or so. Wait until you see him. He's a tiny boy with a lot of gumption."

"Oh my!" said Becky. "Another baby? How will you or Gracie handle two?"

Silas' loud, high cries came through the baby monitor, startling us.

"Come with me," I said to Becky. "I'll explain everything."

As we returned to the kitchen, Becky was holding Silas. "Such a darling," she said, showing Silas to Henry. "Maybe we should postpone our trip. Marissa might need me here."

At the look of dismay on Henry's face, she laughed. "Just kidding. But I'm serious, Marissa, I want to see pictures on a regular basis."

"Me too," said Ellen.

I felt a mother's pride in her children and smiled.

Amid warm hugs and many wishes for a wonderful trip, Becky and Henry left. I set about cleaning up the kitchen while Brad played with Summer, and Ellen rocked Silas.

My hands were in some soapy water when the doorbell rang. I wiped my hands on a towel and went to the kitchen door to answer it.

Maude Miller stood there. Of good height and slender, worry added creases to her old Maine-weathered face. Her blue eyes shown with intelligence and the kindness I'd always admired.

"Hello, Maude. Come in," I said, wondering what had brought her to our door.

She stepped into the kitchen and glanced around. "I hope I'm not interrupting anything." She held out her hands in a helpless gesture. "I'm here because of Courtney Worthington."

I tensed. Was she about to un-friend us?

Maude studied me. "I understand she's staying here."

"Yes," I answered. "Why?"

"Well, as you might imagine, Eleanor is fit to be tied over it. She's telling everyone you're enticing Courtney away from them with all kinds of promises."

Indignation filled me. "But ..."

Maude held up a hand to stop me. "Courtney came to me and told me what was going on. She stayed with me one night but didn't want any trouble to come to me by staying longer. And now I want to make sure you're okay having her here."

I glanced at Brad, who had come over to stand beside me.

"We're well aware of the trouble in Courtney's home. We've offered her a place to stay in return for her becoming the second nanny here. Both girls are legal adults who are working here in exchange for room and board. Each has her own room and plenty of food." His voice had assumed the crispness and finality that he used in the courtroom.

Maude gave us a look of satisfaction. "Good. I just wanted to make sure she was all right and you both were fine with it. Eleanor may try to make your lives miserable, but I'll stand beside you."

Relieved, I let out the breath I'd been holding. I didn't want any troubles standing between us and the Worthingtons. They were powerful, nasty people.

CHAPTER THIRTEEN

Just before noon, Gracie came down to the kitchen. Silas was back down for a nap. Summer had just finished eating and was sitting in her seat on the porch with Brad and Ellen.

"Good morning," I said, washing up Summer's bottle.

Gracie checked the clock and laughed. "Good afternoon, you mean. That sleep sure felt good. Thanks."

Courtney joined us, stretching and yawning. I was about to talk about fixing lunch when the sunshine, streaming through the windows, tempted me with another idea.

"Why don't the two of you watch Silas while he naps? Brad and I will take Ellen and Summer to lunch. Then, when we come back, Brad wants to talk to you about our arrangements. After that, you can have the rest of the day off."

"Sounds good," said Gracie. "I need to do a little shopping of my own."

"Yeah, me too," said Courtney. "Now that I'm going to stay here, I need to pick up all kinds of things."

I left them rummaging in the refrigerator and went to the porch. Ellen was playing with Summer, holding toys out for her to try and grab. Brad was reclining in one of the rockers, his feet on the railing, a smile settled like sunshine on his face.

"How about us taking Ellen to The Lobster Trap for lunch?" I said to him before turning to Ellen. "Does that sound good?"

She smiled. "It sounds delicious."

Summer kicked her feet happily in her seat. "The two girls are going to grab lunch here and stay with Silas while he naps.

I think he's a little young to be out in the sun and breeze. But I thought we'd take Summer with us. I want to try the new baby carrier we got for her. That way, we can walk down the beach to town."

"That would be nice," said Ellen. "It's such a beautiful day."

Brad jumped to his feet. "Sounds like a plan."

Adjusting the baby carrier was more of a production than we'd first thought, but soon the four of us were moving along the sand edging the water. Summer looked adorable in her floppy sun hat and sunglasses. At the look of pride on Brad's face as he marched along with her tucked in front of him, I realized I wasn't the only one who'd be crushed if we were forced to give her up.

Ellen and I walked side by side in better concert than we'd ever been. Carrying sandals, we splashed in and out of the shallow water where it met the sand. It being a Friday, the town was burgeoning with tourists when we reached it. We made our way through the throngs of people milling about and stood in line at the restaurant, waiting a few extra minutes to secure a table in the shade.

After being seated by the hostess, I took Summer out of the carrier and held her in my lap. She kicked her bare feet happily and seemed intent on studying her surroundings.

"What a darling baby!"

I looked up to see the girl who'd waited on Brad and me before. "Thank you. Your name's Cherie, right?"

"Yes." She squatted next to my chair. Wiggling a tempting finger in front of Summer, she studied the baby, then folded back the lip of Summer's bonnet for a better look. A moment later she rose. "Now, what can I get you?"

After our orders were taken and Cherie had walked away, Brad gave me a quizzical look. "What was she doing? Just looking at Summer?"

I nodded, but I was a little uneasy by the attention she'd given the baby. My mind went into overdrive. Was she the mother? Or did she know the mother?

When Cherie brought us drinks, I studied her closely. Apart from having blue eyes, I saw no resemblance to Summer. Brad noticed my actions and frowned. I sat back in my chair and told myself to relax. I'd been rude to Cherie before. I wouldn't do it again. I became preoccupied as I attempted to eat my salad while holding a wiggling baby. At one point, Ellen took over so I could finish my meal.

When dessert came, we put Summer in the baby carrier. The fresh air and the lapping of the water below the deck helped to lull her to sleep.

Later, as we rose to leave, Cherie hurried over to me. "Say, I was wondering if you need a babysitter. Between shifts here at the restaurant, I have time to babysit for others."

Surprised, I smiled at her. "Thanks, but I've got enough help."

"Oh." A look of disappointment crossed her face. "Okay, then. Come back." She gave a lingering look at Summer and walked away, leaving me with plenty to think about.

That afternoon, Brad and I met with the girls in my office. We quickly agreed on the arrangements that were already in place. Brad, in lawyer mode, went over the details and asked the girls to sign the agreement designating their pay, their hours and the right to have room and board in exchange for their expected duties.

After signing the agreement, each girl shook hands with Brad and left the room. We'd given them the rest of the day off.

"I think the meeting went well, didn't you?" I said, as I prepared a bottle for Silas, who was doing his screaming act in Ellen's arms on the porch.

"I guess. There's no way you could handle the babies alone. Not with Silas' needs and Summer becoming much more active."

"I know other mothers do it, but I'm glad to have the help, believe me."

Brad came up behind me and drew me back against his strong chest. He nuzzled my neck, sending shivers down my back.

"I love you," I murmured, and felt an instant reaction from him. He might have doubts about his virility, but I didn't. I turned around and faced him. Drawing his face to mine, I kissed him.

"Oh! I'm sorry! I didn't mean to interrupt," said Ellen, coming into the kitchen with Silas.

Startled, I dropped my arms.

Brad pulled me to him and turned to his mother with a smile. "Gotta make our time together count."

She laughed. "Don't mind me. I'm getting a burp rag for Silas. Summer's awake. I thought you'd want to know."

"Thanks," I said, feeling a little guilty. In Brad's arms, I hadn't even heard Summer's whimpers coming through the baby monitor.

Brad tilted my chin. "She's okay."

I was now beginning to understand a fine line between the roles of mother and wife. I'd read about that in magazines and decided talk to Allison and Samantha about it.

That night, after everyone was asleep, I lay awake pondering the day's events. The way Ellen and I had come together through motherhood pleased me so much. My thoughts flew to Cherie, the girl at the restaurant. Her behavior seemed odd to me. Brad might not like it, but I intended to find out more about her.

Brad rolled over and saw me lying on my back, staring at the ceiling. "Is everything all right?"

I smiled and reached for him.

His body responded. Aware of his need and mine, I reveled in his touch. Our lovemaking became free and easy, and oh so fulfilling as we took what we'd learned about each other and made it work to our mutual satisfaction once more.

"You're such a beautiful mother," he murmured.

I smiled. I knew others thought me beautiful, but I couldn't think of myself that way. Not when I looked so much like my mother. I had her heart-shaped face, her gray eyes, her auburn hair. But there was a softness to my face she'd never had. I clung to that idea because I never wanted to be like her.

The weekend visit ended with my standing outside once more waving Brad off to another week in Barnham. Ellen left with him, promising to return soon. We'd talked about the holidays and she'd agreed that perhaps it was time that she and Brad's father, Jim, came to us to celebrate instead of Brad's and my making the trip to them. It was another new step in building a stronger relationship between us.

It still didn't make it any easier to say good-bye to Brad. He seemed more reluctant than ever to leave us, though he'd admitted to me, with babies crying at any hour of the night, he'd be sleeping a lot better at his parents' house.

I walked back inside the house and stood a moment in the kitchen staring at the chaos. It was a good thing Becky wasn't there to see the mess. The girls' work was not up to her standards. But I didn't care. They were great with the babies.

After pouring myself a second cup of coffee, I went to work cleaning up the breakfast dishes. I'd just finished sweeping the floor when the trill of the phone caught my attention. I saw caller ID and caught my breath. Office of Child and Family Services.

"Hello?"

"Hi," said Alice. "I just wanted to give you a heads-up. My supervisor is going to be dropping by your house sometime today. An issue has come up. Sorry, I can't say anything more. I'm not even supposed to be telling you this."

"What's this about?"

"Gotta go," said Alice softly and hung up.

The ends of my nerves snapped to attention. Something must be horribly wrong.

The morning dragged by. With a big mess and little time, I frantically oversaw the cleaning of the house. Every time Silas spit up, I changed his clothes. I put a little ribbon in Summer's hair and put on her prettiest dress. The waiting was interminable.

Finally, a dark green sedan pulled into the driveway. Silas was crying and Summer had spit up on her dress and pulled the bow out of her hair. Not a good time for a visit from someone from the Office.

I went outside to greet the woman who emerged from the car. Heavy-set and with a sharpness to her features I found intimidating, she stood and looked around. Taller than I'd expected, her gray hair was pulled back into a severe bun. Dark eyes studied me as I approached.

"Hello? May I help you?" I asked, pretending I hadn't known she was going to drop by. I'd put on a flowy skirt and a sleeveless summer top which she eyed with a hint of disapproval. My heart sank.

"I'm Lisa Thomas from the Office of Children and Family Services."

"Welcome." I extended my hand, hoping she wouldn't notice how cold my fingers had become with nervousness.

She gave my hand a perfunctory shake. "May I come inside?"

"Of course. How can we help you?"

"A matter has come up that we need to discuss." She headed for the kitchen door. I quickly matched her steps, wondering at her serious expression and brisk manner.

I led her through the kitchen and into the sunroom, thinking the pleasantness of the room might soften her forbidding stance.

As we took seats facing each other, Courtney entered the room. I'd told the girls to expect the visit. They'd been given instructions to offer us something to drink.

Courtney smiled at me and turned to Lisa. "May I get you some refreshment? Coffee? Iced tea? A soda?"

Lisa frowned at her. "May I ask who you are?"

"Courtney Worthington. Why?"

Lisa merely nodded. "A cup of coffee would be nice. Just a little sugar."

Courtney turned to me. "And you?"

"Just water." I noticed Courtney's hands were shaking. "Perhaps Gracie could help you."

"She's busy with Silas," Courtney said and hurried out of the room.

Lisa leaned forward and stared at me. "I understand you have two young girls here helping you. Is that right?"

At the way she said young girls, I had my first inkling as to what this visit might be about. "Gracie is a recent college graduate and Courtney will be a senior. They work for us in return for room and board and wages."

"I've received a phone call from someone who claims there's a lot of wrongdoing taking place here. Things of a sexual nature."

I felt my jaw drop and then tighten so hard my teeth hurt. It was all making sense to me now.

"Was this caller Eleanor Worthington, by chance?" I asked.

Lisa shook her head. "At this point, I'm not able to tell you who it was."

Furious, I waved away her words. "You don't need to affirm or deny. I know it was her. She's a mean-spirited woman."

"The fact remains she's brought up a matter which would be of concern to us," Lisa said calmly, confirming my suspicion. "This person has claimed that an innocent girl is staying here. It was hinted that this girl has been encouraged to be part of an abnormal relationship."

A gasp of dismay interrupted Lisa. We both turned to the sound. Courtney stood in the doorway of the sunroom. Her face had gone white. "She did it! My mother promised to hurt you if I didn't agree to go back home and apologize to my father." With a sob, she turned around and left the room without delivering the drinks to us.

I rose to my feet.

"I'll come with you," said Lisa, leaving me no choice.

We found Courtney in the kitchen sitting at the kitchen table crying.

Gracie entered the kitchen, carrying Silas. "What's wrong?"

"It's my mother," said Courtney between sobs. "She promised to get back at Marissa if I embarrassed her in front of her friends by refusing to live at home."

Lisa turned to me. "How did the girls come to live here?"

"Gracie applied for the job. We agreed she'd work here during the day and stay with Courtney at her house. Then an incident took place at Courtney's house, and Gracie decided she couldn't stay there. We agreed to have her stay here. And then Courtney had problems at home and, after temporarily losing our housekeeper, we agreed she could work here for room, board, and wages. They each have their own room and their own pay. And they do a wonderful job with the babies and the house. Brad and I are well aware of Eleanor Worthington's dislike, if that's what all this is about."

Lisa remained noncommittal. "Perhaps you'll show me the rest of the house? And I need to see the babies."

"This is Silas," said Gracie, showing Lisa the sleeping baby.

"Isn't he beautiful?" I whispered, thankful he wasn't in one of his screaming modes. I motioned toward the stairs. "Summer is upstairs. She should be sleeping for another half hour or so."

Lisa followed me up the stairs to Summer's room. I opened the door and we quietly tiptoed inside. Summer was asleep on her back, clutching the pink lamb Henry had bought her. Lisa glanced around the room, went over to the changing table, and checked out the lotions and the little outfit I'd laid out. Silent, she turned and headed for the door. I followed and quietly closed the door behind us.

Facing Lisa in the hallway, I worked to keep my irritation out of my voice. "Anything else?"

Lisa shook her head. "I've seen all I have to."

We returned to the kitchen, where the girls sat talking quietly.

They stood.

Courtney cleared her throat. "My mother is an unhappy woman. A lot goes on in that house that isn't good."

"I can attest to that," said Gracie quietly.

Lisa studied them both. "Thank you for your honesty. Good luck to the two of you."

I walked Lisa out to her car, realizing she'd never been given the coffee she'd requested. I started to ask if she wanted something to drink and decided not to. Her presence made me uneasy. I couldn't help wondering what this episode might mean for Summer's adoption.

CHAPTER FOURTEEN

A s soon as I returned to the kitchen, Courtney ran to me. Her look of misery tore at my heart.

"Oh, Marissa! I'm so sorry for all that's happened. While you were finishing up with Lisa, I talked it over with Gracie. We think I should stay somewhere else. Then, maybe my mother won't be such a pain in the ass."

I shook my head. "You don't have to leave on account of us. Brad and I discussed it before we offered you a job. We certainly don't like any unpleasantness with our neighbors, but it's become a matter of principle to allow you to stay here. You've proven to be a big help. Do you want to keep the job?"

"Oh, yes! I want the job and I want to stay here, but I don't want my mother to keep pulling her dirty tricks on you!" Courtney's eyes filled with tears.

"Let's just take each day as it comes," I said, well aware of how emotional Courtney could be at times.

"I agree," said Gracie. "After knowing Courtney for some time, I think her parents do mean things like this so Courtney will be upset enough to give in to their wishes."

I studied Gracie. For someone so young, she sure had a lot of people sense.

Hearing Silas' cries, I left the girls and went upstairs to give them more time to talk things over.

I cracked open the door and peered into Silas' room. On his back, he was kicking and waving his arms. I walked over to the crib and leaned over the railing. "Hello, little boy," I said softly.

At the sound of my voice, he grew silent and stared up at me. Crooning sweet words to him, I lifted him up out of the crib. He was quiet in my arms for a few minutes before letting out a cry which I now recognized as his "I'm hungry" cry. I smiled. After just a matter of days, he seemed to be on a more regular routine. As I carried him to the changing table, it felt as if he might even have gained weight.

I changed him, taking the time to caress his thin limbs as some books had recommended. As I carried him down the stairs, I wondered at all the feelings of love he brought out in me. I drew Silas closer. His mother loved him too. I hoped she'd be able to get through rehab and claim him like she wanted, even if it meant I'd lose him. He was such a precious baby.

When we entered the kitchen, Courtney asked if she could feed Silas. I understood she wanted to feel useful and handed him over to her. Summer was still asleep.

I decided to take a walk on the beach. There was someone I wanted to talk to.

Standing outside my house, I drew in a breath of tangy sea air. The sunny day was beginning to cloud over, casting a gray color to the waves rolling in and mirroring my worried thoughts. If Courtney continued to stay with us, it might permanently destroy any relationship between her and her parents. I didn't want to be a partner to that. But Eleanor's behavior was outrageous. Shouldn't we stand up to her bullying?

My mind still spinning, I walked down the sandy shore. When I reached Maude Miller's house, I left the beach and walked up to her front door. I was about to ring the bell when I heard shouting next door.

Harry Worthington emerged from the house, onto the porch, yelling and swearing.

Eleanor opened the screen door and shouted, "I'll throw you out of here if you don't shape up and do what I say."

I cringed at the anger in her voice and stood quietly, hoping she wouldn't see me. No such luck.

Eleanor rushed onto the porch and shook a finger at me. "Courtney leaving home is all *your* fault, Marissa Crawford!"

I shrank. This wasn't the perfectly coiffed, perfectly in-control person I knew. This disheveled, distraught woman was acting crazy. It made me wonder if she was on some kind of medication or if she needed some. I didn't know her well enough to assume one or the other.

I punched the doorbell and waited anxiously for Maude to appear. Eleanor was still shouting at me when Maude answered the door. Her eyes widened at the sounds coming from the Worthingtons' house.

"Better come in," she said, grimly. "It sounds like Eleanor is on one of her rants."

Relieved I wouldn't have to face the woman's wrath, I stepped inside. "Does this happen often, these rants of hers?"

"Only if she hasn't taken her medications," said Maude. "Without it, her highs are too high and her lows too low."

Suddenly I understood Courtney's inability to reason with her mother. If Eleanor had some sort of mental issues, like I now suspected, fights between them might not be that rare.

"What can I do for you?" Maude asked, motioning me into her sitting room.

I sat on a sofa and faced her. "After the three of us talked this morning, Gracie and Courtney decided Courtney should stay somewhere else. I told her she didn't have to do that, but I don't know either Eleanor or Courtney well enough to know if it would be foolish for her to stay with us. I thought you might help me with that decision. After observing Eleanor today, I think it might be best to tell Courtney not to go anywhere else. What do you think?" I knew Maude would be straightforward with me. She was known for it.

Maude drew a deep breath. "Courtney's staying with me wasn't the first time she'd done so. Things used to get really tense at home and she'd slip over here. Eleanor finally accepted that it was going to happen from time to time."

Looking at this older woman who bore the scars and wrinkles of time, tears came to my eyes. Maude was for Courtney what Doris had been for me—a safe haven.

"I love that child, you know," Maude said in her brisk, Maine manner that did nothing to hide her real emotions.

"Yes, I know," I said. My protector Doris loved me too. I thought of Harry and wondered if he, too, had someone he could turn to. I didn't think it would be either one of his parents.

"If it becomes necessary, Courtney can stay here with me for as long as she wants," Maude said.

"Thanks. I'll tell her. She's an adult and can make her own decisions, but I feel better knowing she has a choice between two supportive homes. I'm not encouraging her to leave home, just providing a safe place for her while she works things out."

"Of course. Neither am I," said Maude. "I've known for a very long time that Eleanor has some issues that need to be addressed, but Eleanor refuses to acknowledge it."

"I guess coming from her background, Eleanor doesn't want to admit to something that might harm her social status."

Maude actually snorted. "Her background? Eleanor Worthington is from a very poor situation. How she landed Harrison, I'll never know. Some say it's because she got pregnant with Courtney."

I blinked in surprise. Eleanor's snobby treatment of me

now seemed ridiculous.

"Strange, isn't it, how some people act," Maude said, rising from her chair. "Come join me in the kitchen. I've made some cookies for a church meeting. Maybe you'll take a few home with you for the girls. Peanut butter cookies are Courtney's favorite."

Liking her more than ever, I followed Maude into the delicious-smelling kitchen. She might have a spare frame, but it protected a very big heart.

Later, with a package of cookies for the girls, I bid Maude good-bye. As I walked back home along the beach, I thought of the hidden stories behind most of us. Now that I knew a little bit more about Eleanor, I was surprised to find myself feeling sorry for her. I knew very well what it was like to pretend to be something you weren't. For years, I'd maintained a front of being self-sufficient, when all I'd wanted was to be loved and to feel safe.

The cool water splashed on my bare feet as I playfully danced in and out of the water's edge and decided I needed to talk to someone else.

At four o'clock, the downtown dinner rush hadn't yet begun. I pulled into the parking lot of The Lobster Trap and got out of the car wondering how best to approach Cherie. Brad might be annoyed with me, but I had to make sure I'd covered every possibility in finding Summer's mother.

When I walked into the restaurant, the hostess came right over to me. "May I help you?"

"I'd like to speak to Cherie, please."

The hostess shook her head, disturbing her blond ringlets. "She's off until next Sunday. Can I help you with anything? Is she in trouble or something?"

I warded off that thought with my hand. "No, no, nothing like that. I'll come back and talk to her later."

Defeated, I got in the car. Alice and others had told me to let things go, but I couldn't. Next week I'd talk to Cherie. After that, who knew?

I drove through the gates of Briar Cliff and parked the car in the garage. As I walked toward the house, it seemed so peaceful. In the distance, I heard the lap of the water. Birds sang from the top branches of the trees. A playful breeze moved the boughs of the pine trees that edged the property, whispering a song on the wind.

Courtney met me at the door, her eyes red, her cheeks puffy. Holding Summer, Gracie looked distressed.

A sinking feeling filled me. "What's the matter?"

"My mother came here looking for you. I made a deal with her. She'll leave you alone if I go back home. She doesn't want her friends to know I've left home because of what happened to Gracie." Fresh tears filled her eyes. "I can't let anything bad happen to you or Gracie or the babies. I waited to leave until you came home."

Fighting a range of emotions from disappointment to anger, I gave her a hug. "I'm sorry. I wish I could do something to help you." I held her away from me. "Are you sure this is what you want to do?"

She let out a sigh. "It's best this way. Believe me, I know."

"You understand you always have a safe place to stay with me or with Maude."

"Thank you. I'm hoping to make my mother understand that she needs help. Gracie thinks she and I need to see a counselor together. I'm beginning to think she's right."

Gracie handed Summer to me. Then she and Courtney went upstairs. They returned a short time later, each carrying a suitcase.

"Gracie said she'd see I got anything I might've left behind," Courtney said, trying not to cry.

I gave her a hug and watched as Gracie helped Courtney load her luggage into her car. From the somber expression on Gracie's face, I knew she was upset.

As she returned to the house, tears filled Gracie's eyes.

"It's not your fault," I said, wrapping an arm around her.

"Yeah, but that's the excuse Courtney's mother will use. It's so unfair!"

"I know," I said quietly. "But maybe now Courtney will push to get help for her mother. She's a sick woman."

"I hope it works." The look Gracie gave me showed her doubt.

Summer's cries caught our attention. I picked her up just as Silas let out a wail.

The babies' schedules took over the remaining days of the work week. By Friday morning, I eagerly awaited Brad's arrival. I hoped his presence would allow me a little more time to myself. I needed it.

I was busy in the kitchen, doing the last of the dishes when the phone rang. I checked caller ID. Office of Child and Family Services.

I grabbed up the phone.

"Congratulations," said Alice. "You've been officially approved as foster parents."

My spirits, which had soared at the word congratulations, plummeted. It was good news, but not the news I'd been waiting for. "No word on Summer's mother?"

"No, but I have news about Silas' mother. Odelle is doing so well in the rehabilitation program that she's being allowed to make a special visit to see Silas. Are you willing to meet her with Silas somewhere?"

"Why doesn't she come here?" The thought of packing him and his gear up was daunting. "It would be easier for me, and this way she can see him in his temporary environment."

"That's very generous of you." Alice's voice held a note of approval that pleased me. "Let's say two o'clock this afternoon. I'll bring her out there. Is that all right with you?"

"Yes, that will be fine." That would give Gracie and me time to put some order to the mess I still saw around me.

Alice and I chatted about both babies, and then I hung up, eager to meet the mother of the little boy I already loved.

Gracie and I kept glancing anxiously at the kitchen door. While she paced nervously, I sat in the rocking chair with Silas. We'd put him in a new little outfit. The subtle blue and yellow plaid of his shorts and his yellow T-shirt looked adorable against his dark skin.

"I wonder what she'll look like, be like," said Gracie, taking a seat at the kitchen table near me. She reached over and lifted Silas's hand in hers. "She's probably young and tough."

"Yes. And I picture her as tall and strong. After all, she suffered through withdrawal for her baby." I gazed down at Silas and back at Gracie. "I hope I like her."

"Me too," said Gracie. "I'd hate to see Silas go to someone who might not take care of him properly."

That very thought had been eating away at me since the phone call from Alice. As a foster parent, I would give my all to help this child, but I had little say if the law allowed birth parents or their families to take him away.

Gracie elbowed me. "Here they come." She stood and went over to the baby monitor and listened. "Good. Summer's still sleeping."

Rising to my feet, I watched Alice's car travel toward us. A shiver crossed my shoulders. Inside was the woman who would shape Silas' life. I hugged him to me, aware of how much he and Summer had changed me. Alice parked the car and got out. I held my breath as the passenger's door opened.

Odelle Thompson was so different from the image I'd formed in my mind that I gasped. Gracie looked at me and we chuckled softly in understanding.

Carrying Silas, I left the house and walked forward to greet Odelle. A little over five feet, she appeared to be as wide as she was tall, or maybe her yellow, flowing top over her black pants made her appear that way. As I drew closer, I became mesmerized by her dark eyes. Bright and shiny, they oozed an intriguing vitality. A wide smile lit her face. She appeared to bounce along the ground on light feet as she ran to greet me.

"Can I see him? Can I see him?" she squealed.

I held out Silas to her.

Tears ran down her cheeks as she held him to her ample breast. Watching her, tears formed in my own eyes. The love she showed him was so obvious.

Silas stared up at Odelle. I saw now the resemblance between them in both the eyes and in the shape of their mouths.

Odelle looked at me. "Thank you so much for taking care of him for me, Mrs. Crawford." Her mouth trembled. "I was so afraid of going back on pills. And now I'm stronger." She patted her hips and gave me an impish grin. "Not thinner, but stronger."

I smiled. Odelle was nothing like I'd imagined, but oh, so much better. "You're Silas' mother. That makes you wonderful. And please call me Marissa."

Fresh tears filled her eyes. "Thank you. He's the best thing that's ever happened to me."

"Shall we move inside?" Alice said gently.

"Sorry, I've forgotten my manners. Come in." I turned to Odelle. "I want you to meet Gracie. She's my nanny and helper. Like me, she loves Silas too."

When we entered the kitchen, Gracie was nowhere to be seen. "Gracie must be with Summer. She'll be down soon." I indicated the rocking chair. "Won't you have a seat? What can I get you to drink? Coffee, tea, water, soda, anything? And how about you, Alice? What can I get you?"

"I'll have a diet coke," said Alice.

"Me too," said Odelle. She hesitated. "Uh, I'd better make that water. I'm trying to lose weight. That's what got me in trouble, to begin with. Diet pills and everything else."

"That's the reason Odelle agreed to participate in our program, so she wouldn't be tempted to go back to it if she had post-partum depression."

"Yeah, and trying to lose baby weight," added Odelle. "But I'm doing fine. I just want to be able to be with my baby. They tell me three more weeks and I can enter the family program. Then he can stay with me."

I blinked in surprise. *I'd only have three more weeks with Silas?* I turned to Alice.

She gave me a sympathetic smile. "That's how the program works."

Odelle and I exchanged glances.

"I appreciate all you've done for him. Really, I do," she said.

Too emotional to speak, I could only nod my head. This is what I'd agreed to—taking him for a short period of time. I tried for calm as I got the drinks for everyone. But when I sat down, I couldn't stop feeling depressed by the thought of Silas leaving.

Gracie entered the room, carrying Summer. "Hello, everyone!" She smiled at Odelle. "This is Summer."

Odelle smiled. "What a beautiful baby!" She turned to me. "She's yours?"

"We don't know," I said.

"We're working on it," Alice said smoothly.

Odelle looked from her to me with understanding.

Summer let out a happy cry and reached for Silas. Seeing her, he kicked his feet with excitement.

"Wow! They recognize each other!" Odelle said, changing Silas's position so he could better see Summer.

Gracie took a seat closest to the rocking chair so the babies could watch each other.

I hurried to get Summer's bottle ready. Soon she'd start fussing.

Silas started to cry. "He might need his diaper changed," I said to Odelle as I handed a bottle to Gracie. "He was fed a little while ago."

Odelle rose. "Where can I change him?"

"Come with me. I'll show you his room."

Odelle followed me out of the kitchen and up the stairs. Behind me, I heard her trying to soothe Silas.

I opened the door to Silas' room and stood back. We'd set up a second white crib there, along with a matching changing table, rocking chair and small bureau. Not opting to do anything permanent, I'd placed removable Winnie the Pooh decals and sayings on the green walls. A big stuffed Winnie the Pooh sat in the rocking chair.

"This is beautiful," exclaimed Odelle. "I love Winnie and Eeyore and all the rest!"

I smiled. "I've already started a collection of children's books in case we..." I couldn't go on. The thought of losing Silas so soon and now the thought of losing Summer was suddenly too much.

Odelle placed her free arm around me. "I'm sorry, hon. It's gotta be hard, not knowing."

I swallowed a sob. "Yes, so hard."

"Why don't you show me what lotions you use on him and we'll get him changed," Odelle said soothingly.

I gathered myself together and forced a smile. "Sure."

I showed Odelle the stacked diapers in the changer and handed her the jar of organic diaper ointment I used on him. After his wet diaper had been exchanged for a dry one, I showed her how I massaged his limbs. He stared up at the two of us with those amazing eyes of his—Odelle's eyes. A corner of his lip lifted.

"Oh, he's smiling at us," said Odelle.

"Yes," I whispered. I didn't care that it was probably caused by a gas bubble. To me, it would always be a genuine smile.

Odelle lifted Silas and hugged him to her. "I'm so, so glad to see him. Thanks, Marissa."

"It's you, Odelle, not me who made it possible. It sounds like you're doing a terrific job of staying clean and learning how to be independent."

"I'm trying. I wish his Daddy could see him." She let out a bitter sound. "He took off when I was at my worst. I don't even know where he is. But I'll always be thankful he gave me this little boy."

"So what'll you do when you leave the family program?"

She shrugged. "I'm not sure. I was going to become a nurse's aide but then a lot of things happened."

I placed a hand on her shoulder. "I'm sure Alice will help you."

"I'd like to think so. I want the best for this little man." She rubbed Silas' back. He settled against her shoulder and closed his eyes, calm and happy.

We returned to the kitchen, where I found Gracie and Alice deep in conversation as Gracie fed Summer. Gracie looked up at me with surprise.

I gave her a questioning look.

"I was asking Alice about the need for family services counselors. Originally, I was going for my master's degree in that area. Then I wasn't sure I wanted to go ahead with it. But after being here with you, I've decided I want to go back to school after all. My advisor feels it won't be a problem to sign up this late. I'd been accepted earlier and backed out."

"Oh but ..."

"Don't worry. I'll be here for a few weeks longer. Alice said she'd help you find someone to take my place. And Becky will be back."

I lowered myself into a chair at the kitchen table, wondering how many more changes to my life the day would bring.

CHAPTER FIFTEEN

After an early supper, Brad and I sat on the porch. With Gracie off for the evening, we had some time alone with the babies. Brad held Summer in his lap, making little lamb noises for her. I rocked Silas in a chair beside them. For once, the babies' feeding schedules were in sync.

I drew in a deep breath and exhaled, worried about Brad. He'd arrived home unusually quiet, and I needed to know what was wrong.

"Want to tell me what's going on?" I asked him.

He looked startled. "Guess I've been pretty quiet, huh?"

"Uh, huh. You have me worried. Is everything all right?"

He shook his head. "My father and I had a big disagreement this morning because he wanted us to take on a complicated case and I told him I wouldn't do it." He leaned forward with an earnest expression. "I explained I didn't want to be tied up in a case that might delay my departure. I told him I wanted to be out of the firm as soon as possible." He shook his head. "You can imagine where that led."

"Yes, I can," I said quietly. Jim Crawford had been unhappy with the idea of his son moving to Maine, disrupting their partnership. But Brad had insisted upon it, agreeing finally to maintain a partnership on a part-time level. Over time he'd been sucked into doing more and more work in New York.

"I'm sick of it, Marissa. I want to be home with you and Summer. This commuting back and forth is killing me."

"I'd love it if you could be here permanently." I didn't dare say more about it. I wanted Jim to understand it was Brad's decision alone.

"As much as I love my father, I'm tired of working with him. I want to have my own small practice, take care of things my way, and decide alone what cases I'll take on."

"I understand," I said, again holding my tongue.

"So I told him I wouldn't be working on any new cases. I'd wrap up the ones we have and that's it."

"And?"

"And he's pissed. But I think he'll come around. Mom talked to him about our life here, and he knows it's best that we're together—especially if we're trying to adopt Summer. And then there are the other babies we might help." He studied me. "That's what you want, right? Taking in other babies?"

I looked down at Silas falling asleep in my arms. He was off to a good start because of what we'd done to help him. I recalled the tears of gratitude on Odelle's face and slowly nodded. It was a role I'd never dreamed of doing until a few weeks ago.

"Yeah, I think that's what I want."

His gaze never left mine. "I want to make you happy, Marissa."

"Oh, Brad! I *am* happy with you. Don't ever doubt that." I reached over and squeezed his arm. "I love you, man!"

He grinned. "Love you, woman."

Silas woke up screaming. I rose. "We'll talk later."

"Or something," said Brad playfully, giving me a sexy look.

I laughed and left him making more soft animal noises for Summer, who was gleefully babbling in reply.

Later, with the babies asleep again and Gracie still out for a late evening, I went upstairs to our bedroom. Brad had been sending me silent but clear signals all evening and I was more than ready to join him in a romp. Sometimes, covered with spit-up or feeling crummy without a shower, I yearned to feel womanly. He had a special way of making me feel beautiful.

I slipped out of my clothes and headed for the bathroom. A lingering hot shower would feel just right.

I turned on the water in the large, double-headed shower. We'd had it installed when we updated the bathrooms shortly after our wedding. Standing in the streams of warm water hitting me front and back, I let out a sigh of contentment. With Odelle's visit and Gracie's intention to leave for school, it had been a day full of surprises.

I was rinsing off my hair when I felt his presence.

"Nice."

My body reacted with an ache of desire at the sound of his deep sexy voice coming from behind me.

I smiled as Brad drew me up against him. His body reacted as our skin met. I turned to face him, loving the feel of him. Water rained down on us, but I barely noticed as Brad's lips came down on mine. His tongue entered my mouth with an urgency that sent tingles of pleasure through me. It had been a while since we'd made love and I'd missed it. Brad had obviously missed it too.

He put his arms around me and began moving against me. The tension and worries of the week evaporated as I responded freely to his movements. He lifted me up, and I wrapped my legs around him, showing him in a way words could not, how much our love meant to me.

"Love you," he murmured. I lost all sense of self as we let our passions take us on a well-known, satisfying journey.

When we stepped out of the shower, Brad hugged a fluffy towel around me. His eyes twinkled with humor as he smiled down at me. "Guess you missed me, huh?"

I laughed. "Oh yeah. I always do."

He cupped my face in his hands. Studying me, his expression turned serious. "You're always with me in spirit, you know?"

I smiled. I knew very well what he meant. For all the corny talk about soul mates, I was sure I'd found mine.

Later, as we lay in bed, I turned to him. Trailing my hands down his body, I enjoyed the feel of him lying beside me. He was always so responsive in our lovemaking. It was still hard for me to believe his situation. I cuddled up to him. Resting my head on his chest, I heard his strong heartbeats. He was following all the doctor's suggestions. That's all we could do for the moment.

Before sleep overtook me, my thoughts turned to Summer. I still hadn't given up on finding her mother. When Brad left on Monday morning, I intended to follow up with Susan's unanswered phone calls in Maine and to talk to Cherie at The Lobster Trap.

Brad's departure Monday morning was especially hard because I knew he really didn't want to leave. Gracie stayed inside with the little ones while I walked him out to his car. Inside the privacy of the garage, he took me in his arms. "I'll come back as soon as I can—maybe on Thursday if I can take care of a few things early."

"I'll miss you," I murmured, reaching up to touch his lips with mine.

Our lingering kiss was sweet, full of a special tenderness that followed a night of lovemaking. Reluctantly, we parted. I stepped back to allow him room to get into his Jeep.

He waved and backed out of the garage. I followed the car into the open area and watched as he pulled away. With

Summer and Silas in our lives, I minded his absences more and more.

I returned to the house and was soon caught up in the morning routines. Later, with both babies down for their morning naps, I went into my office and closed the door.

Picking up the note from Susan Reynolds, I eagerly punched in the number she'd given me. I was counting on her to be back on the job at the child care facility at the paper mill. The phone rang and rang. I was about to hang up when I heard a click.

"Hello?" Susan sounded out of breath.

"Susan, it's Marissa Crawford. You asked me to give you a call. I've tried several times..."

"Oh I'm so sorry," she said, interrupting me. "I lost my phone. Then we were away on a family trip."

"No problem. I'm just curious. What did you want to talk to me about?"

"Hold on," she said. "Let me close the door to my office."

I heard her feet tapping across the floor, the closing of a door, and finally the sound of her situating herself at her desk. As I waited for her to speak, I had the weird sensation I knew what she was about to say. With my free hand, I clutched a pen, ready to write.

Susan cleared her throat. "Thinking I'd be a good resource, Jonesy came to me about a private matter of yours. I thought of and eliminated any possibilities of someone here being the mother of your baby. I didn't think any more about it until the day before you came here to the mill for the board meeting."

"And?" I asked impatiently.

"My daughter Lily, who's at Riverton High, told me about someone in her class she suspects of recently having a baby."

"Recently? Does Lily know when?"

"The girl dropped out of school in February, during winter break. But when my Lily happened to see her in Portland in early May, she looked like her normal self. When I recalled the picture Jonesy showed me, I thought this particular girl might possibly be the mother—similar features and all. And living in the area, she'd know about you. You've made the papers here many times with some of the philanthropic work done by you for the town."

My body had grown so cold I could hardly move my frozen jaw. "What's her name? And where does she live?"

"Her name is Celeste Durand. No one knows where she's living now. Some say she went to stay at a relative's house. Apparently, her father kicked her out of the house. He's since left town. He wasn't exactly a stellar citizen here. There are stories of drunkenness and a lack of ethics. He'd apparently been out of work for some time."

"You say your daughter saw her in Portland?"

"Yes," said Susan. "She tried to talk to her, but Celeste took off when Lily called to her."

"Do you have a picture of her? Is there one in the school yearbook?"

"I'll check," said Susan. "If I find one, I'll email it down to you. I hope I've been of some help, Marissa. I have no idea if this young girl is the mother of your baby, but I know you well enough to understand you'd want to follow any lead."

"Thanks. I appreciate your help more than you know." After we hung up, I sat in a daze. I didn't know whether the little bits and pieces of information presented to me would be a help, but I'd consider every possibility. In the meantime, I had another lead to follow up.

After a late lunch, I headed to town. I suspected most of the lunch crowd would be gone from the restaurant, and my suspicions proved right when I pulled into the restaurant's almost-empty parking lot. I got out of the car and stood a moment, trying to come up with a non-threatening way to speak to Cherie. I decided to be as forthright as I could.

The inside of the restaurant was quiet. Just a few customers remained inside the dining room. A cold onshore breeze had come up, and the outside deck was empty. I looked around for Cherie.

The hostess approached me. "May I help you?"

I smiled. "Is Cherie in today?"

"She just left by the back door. You should be able to catch her outside. She's got her bike with her."

"Thanks," I said, turning and heading for the door. Outside, I saw Cherie walking her bike down the side of the street, and took off.

"Cherie! Cherie! Wait!" I called, sprinting toward her.

She stopped and turned, facing me with a puzzled expression.

I caught up with her. "Something's come up. I might have need of a babysitter, after all. I won't know for a couple of weeks. Since you were interested in the baby, I thought I'd better find out a little more about you. Can we go somewhere to talk?"

Her eyes widened. "Sure."

We went to the local Java Joint and sat outside. After placing and picking up our order, I settled in a chair at the table, opposite Cherie.

I reviewed my mental list of questions. "You seemed so interested in my baby, Summer. Have you done a lot of babysitting?"

She shifted in her chair. "Well, I have a younger sister who I've taken care of. Our own mother died when we were very small."

"I see. So you like babies in general, or was there

something special about mine?

Cherie looked away from me. When she returned her gaze to mine there was a sadness in her eyes that deepened their blue color. "She ... she's beautiful. That's all."

"Are you here just for the summer?"

She shrugged. "I'm not sure. I've got a few family issues to work out. I might stay on through the winter. I had to drop out of beauty school in Portland, but I'm hoping to save enough money to go back and finish."

My mind went on full alert. She'd lived in Portland. If she was taking care of her sister, and that sister was Celeste, it would make sense that Lily had seen her there.

"So there's a sister..."

Cherie frowned at me and got to her feet. "Yeah. Listen, I've gotta go. I'm late in getting home."

I pulled out a business card from my purse and handed it to her. "I didn't get a chance to explain my situation to you. My present babysitter is going back to school in a few weeks. I'm hoping to know by then if I will need your services. The baby ..." Unexpected tears filled my eyes. I stopped talking, unwilling to go on.

She gave me a worried look. "Is the baby all right?"

"She's fine, but there's a legal complication that has to be resolved. We're trying to adopt her but we need to find the mother." I knew I was being overly open, but I had a feeling about this girl I couldn't deny.

"Oh, I'm sorry. That's a shame." She pushed back her chair and rose. "Thanks for the card. I hope things work out for you. I'd love to take care of her."

I rose too. "Thanks. I hope to hear from you."

She studied me a moment, then went to retrieve her bike. Knotting my hands, I watched her ride away. *Were my instincts about her right?*

I walked back to the restaurant and stepped inside.

The hostess waved and walked over to me. "Did you get ahold of Cherie?"

I smiled. "Yes, but I failed to write down her last name. Can you give it to me? I might be able to use her for babysitting services when she's not here at the restaurant."

"Oh, okay. Sure. It's Finnell."

Disappointment coursed through me. Celeste's last name was Durant.

CHAPTER SIXTEEN

When I got home, I checked on the babies. Summer was down for a nap. Gracie was feeding Silas. Pleased that Gracie had things under control, I went into my office to see if anything had come in from Susan. Nothing.

Later, as I was folding laundry, my cell rang. Thinking it might be Susan, I hurried to it. Grabbing the phone, I tapped the answer button before realizing the screen indicated it as a call from the Office of Child and Family Services. I drew in a breath and prayed for good news.

"Marissa? It's Alice Tremblay. Good news, I think. Odelle has been given permission to move on to the next phase—the part of the program where mothers are reunited with their children. So Silas will be leaving you by week's end. Just wanted to give you notice."

Unprepared for such news, I sank into the rocking chair in the kitchen.

"Marissa?"

"I heard you," I answered in a wobbly voice. "When will she pick him up?"

"I'm trying to arrange it for Friday morning. Is that a good time for you?"

"I'll have him ready." My heart ached at the thought.

"It may be too soon to ask, but are you willing to take another baby? We're going before a judge tomorrow. It's a case of child neglect."

"I ... I don't know. I'm not sure I'm cut out for this." My emotions were in overdrive. Continuing to be a foster parent might tear me apart.

"I'll let that thought settle. We'll talk about it after Silas leaves," Alice said gently.

"Yes, that would be better. I'll see you Friday." I hung up and let out a long shaky breath.

Gracie walked into the kitchen, took one look at me, and sat down in a chair beside mine. She took my hand in hers. "Are you all right?"

I shook my head. Tears rolled down my cheeks. I wasn't all right. Not at all. Not when I was about to lose a little boy I'd fallen in love with.

"It's Silas," I managed to say. "He's leaving us on Friday."

Gracie placed a hand on her chest. "Already? Odelle is taking him?"

I sighed. "I'm happy for her, I really am. But I wasn't ready for him to leave us. You know what I mean?"

"Oh, yeah, I do," said Gracie. "We're used to him, and he's used to us. And we're just getting him settled into a routine here. How's that going to work out for him?"

Remembering Odelle's tears and the way Silas had slept peacefully in her arms, I wiped my eyes. "He'll be with his mother. She'll take good care of him, I know."

At the sadness in my voice, Gracie placed a hand on my shoulder. "You've done a good job with him, Marissa."

I straightened in my chair. I *had* done a good job with him. He'd calmed down, now enjoyed being hugged, and was becoming a much healthier, happier boy. I couldn't imagine what he'd be like if his mother hadn't gotten off drugs during the pregnancy. I was pretty sure he wouldn't be doing as well as this. At the thought of his leaving, I decided the best I could do for myself was to keep busy. And I wasn't about to tell anyone else about another possible foster baby. Not until I'd made some honest decisions for myself and I'd talked to Brad about it. He too would be upset at Silas leaving.

Rising from the chair, I made my way to the stairway and climbed up to Summer's room. She was due to get up from her nap. When she awoke, I wanted to be the one to hold her in my arms.

As I liked to do, I stood on my porch in the early morning light gazing out at the movement of the water, thinking about my life. Did I owe others a chance at a better beginning, a better life? I knew the answer, of course. I just had to steel myself for the challenges of opening my house and heart to those little ones who would come and go. I walked over to the porch railing and lowered myself onto it, deep in thought. When I'd first struggled with the idea of taking over this house where such deception had taken place, Henry had reminded me it was the people inside, not the house, that had been so bad. I'd thought then that I had a chance to do something special with it, to make it a loving home.

I descended the stairs to the lawn and walked over to the Talking Tree. Wrapping my arms around it, I felt the rough bark against my cheek. This old tree had heard many sad tales from my mother and her brother. I decided this was another thing I'd change about Briar Cliff. The Talking Tree would be a place where children came to play. Envisioning that, I knew I'd made my decision.

Pretty certain Brad would be pleased with my choice, I smiled and watched the water play a kissing game with the shoreline. I'd call him right away. We'd discussed it last night and hadn't made any decisions. We'd left it that we'd both think it over.

"Marissa?" Gracie called to me from the porch. "Call for you!"

Without the worry of indecision weighing me down, I felt as if I could fly as I hurried over to her.

She smiled and handed me the phone. "It's Brad."

"Hi, darling," I said into the phone as Gracie left me.

I sat in one of the rocking chairs. "I've been thinking about you."

"Me, too." I could hear the smile in his voice. "I've been thinking about Silas leaving. I want a chance to say good-bye to him so I'm heading for home today instead of tomorrow."

"That's great," I said, "because I've thought about Alice's proposal about taking in other children and I've finally decided."

"Yeah, me too."

"And?"

"You go first," said Brad.

"Okay, here goes. I think it must be our destiny to do it, what with my having inherited this house and my grandmother's money. I believe it all happened for a reason. And as you said, our house should be filled with children—other people's children. And maybe, someday, ours. What do you think?"

Silence met me.

"Brad?"

"I hoped you were going to say something like that. I'd decided I wouldn't ask you to do it, that it had to be up to you." The gruffness in his voice told me how he felt. I wished I could magically reach through the distance separating us to hug him.

"Well, then," I said. "I'll let Alice know. And when you get home this evening, I'll have another reason to call you Daddy."

He chuckled. "I guess that's how it's going to be. Love you, woman!"

"Love you, man."

As I disconnected the call, I was smiling. I'd been given a house and an inheritance, but nothing could equal what I'd found in Brad.

I went inside and heard Summer awakening, I climbed the stairs to her room, wondering what category Summer would fall into—other people's children or mine. I prayed for a happy answer soon.

After the bedlam of morning feedings and bath time, both babies were put down for naps. Excited now by my decision to continue as a foster parent, I went into the office and called Alice.

When I told her what Brad and I had agreed to, she let out an audible sigh of relief.

"You can't know how pleased I am. The state of Maine and every state in this country has a huge need for foster parents. As you know, it's not a choice made lightly. Our best homes are those where decisions like this have been carefully thought out."

"I almost said no," I said honestly. "It's going to be hard to see Silas go."

"Well, now that you mention it, I have something else for you to consider. With Gracie leaving you in a couple of weeks, you're going to need someone else to help you. Would you..."

My mind raced ahead of her. "Odelle? Are you talking about Odelle?" I said, interrupting her. The idea filled me with joy. I'd seen Odelle in action with Silas. And she'd seemed so nice, so open, so much fun. I'd felt like we'd connected.

Alice chuckled. "Yes. As part of her training, Odelle has opted to take child care courses. She wants to become a certified, child caregiver. She's started on some online courses. In six months, she could have her provisional certificate if all goes well and she stays straight."

"But she could work here while she's doing the courses?"

"That's what I'm thinking. Silas is used to you and your house, so he could be with her during the day while she's working for you. Then, at night, she can take him home and work on her courses at home. I haven't spoken to her about this. That's something you need to do if you're interested."

I sat back in my chair. This would be perfect. I'd have the help I needed and I'd still get to see Silas.

"Think about it, Marissa. In the meantime, let me tell you about the little girl I'm hoping to be able to send to you."

As if in a dream, I listened to her describe the next child to enter my life.

"The courts have taken Kaylie Moffet and her two step-brothers from their mother's home. There's no father in the picture for either Kaylie or her step-brothers. The mother has been charged with neglect and child abandonment. She left Kaylie and her step-brothers, four and six, alone in the house for hours on end several times while she went gambling in Bangor. She's admitted to being a prostitute to feed her addiction to gambling and drugs."

"That's so sad," I said, wondering how far some people would go for their addictions.

"It's also very sad that the mother has little or no remorse," said Alice. "In fact, she says she doesn't want the children. The two boys are together in another home that is unable to take Kaylie. So we need to find a special home for Kaylie before any adoption can take place. Because she's been neglected for most of her nine months, she's underfed and needs extra care in learning how to bond with people. I'm not going to fool you, Marissa, it will take time and patience for this little girl to feel safe and to be happy."

My heart went out to the little one. "I want to try, Alice."

"Good. I'd like to bring her to you as soon as possible."

I took a mental inventory of all our equipment. "I can put

her upstairs in one of the guest rooms until we can prepare a more permanent arrangement for her. If Silas is going to be around, we'll leave his room for him. Kaylie can use the port-a-crib until we get a full-size one for her."

My excitement grew at the thought of another girl. "Brad is coming home today. Tomorrow we'll be able to get a room set up for her and other equipment. And clothes, of course." The house that had seemed so oversized at one point now was perfect for its use. At the rate things were going, soon all seven bedrooms would be filled.

"The state will reimburse you for some of the expenses," Alice said. "We'll get that settled over the next few days. In the meantime, are you willing to take her as soon as possible?"

"When might that be?"

The clearing of Alice's throat gave me some warning. "Uh, I was thinking this afternoon. Is that all right? With Silas leaving tomorrow, I figured you and Gracie could handle three for one night."

I chuckled. Good thing I was prepared for it. "Sure. Bring her along."

"Good. She's a dear little thing. Understandably, she's quite shy."

"I'll warn Gracie," I said. My mind whirled with all the things I'd need to do to get ready for baby three.

As we had once before, Gracie and I sat in the kitchen waiting for Alice to arrive with a baby for us to take care of. Summer kicked happily in her seat as she reached for the mobile animals above her head. Silas was down for a second nap.

"Wonder what she looks like," said Gracie. "No little girl can be cuter than Summer."

I gave her a sideways glance. "We cannot play favorites."

Gracie laughed. "I know, but you have to admit Summer is a cutie."

I grinned. As she grew, Summer's blond hair had started to curl ever-so-slightly. A ready smile crossed her face at the slightest opportunity.

At the sound of a car, I stood to watch Alice's blue Ford roll down the driveway toward us. Gracie and I smiled at each other, and I went outside to greet our new little girl.

Alice got out of the car, walked over to me, and gave me a hug. "Thank you, Marissa. You don't know what this means for Kaylie."

"I hope I can do a good job with her. Can I see Kaylie now?" I felt like a new mother asking to see her baby for the first time. And in many ways, I was just that.

We stepped over to the car together. I peered through the window. A tiny girl sat in a car seat, slumped to one side, sound asleep. I slowly opened the car door and peeked in.

"Hello, sweet girl," I said softly.

Her eyes opened, and I peered into the dark depths of them. She sat silently staring at me in what was almost an eerie way. Her silence, her lack of any reaction, her studying of me was so unlike Summer I was taken aback.

I held out my arms. "Wanna come?"

Again, she didn't react.

"Go ahead and bring her out," Alice suggested.

I unbuckled the seat belts and lifted her into my arms. It felt as if she weighed nothing. Her limbs, I noted, were thin.

"Hello, Kaylie," I murmured, wiping a strand of dark hair away from her face.

She eyed me carefully.

Gracie came outside, carrying Summer.

Kaylie's gaze followed their movement. She made no

noise, but simply watched them.

"Hi, Kaylie," said Gracie, approaching us. "This is Summer."

Summer laughed and reached for Kaylie, who shrank from Summer's outstretched hands and turned her head away. Alice and I exchanged knowing glances.

"Staying here with other children closer to her age will be good for her," said Alice. "But, as you can see, she'll need some special time alone with you."

Kaylie was a pretty little girl, with tiny features. But her eyes lacked luster, and her lips remained unsmiling. I decided I'd give my all to see changes in her. I drew her closer and rubbed her back. She remained in my arms, her thin legs dangling.

Alice noted my dismay as I tried to rearrange her limp body in my arms.

"One of the ways you can tell a child has been deprived of bonding is to see if they cling to you. She isn't doing that now because no one has held her much or taken the steps to show her what it is to bond with someone else. I've brought you some information on it, as well as a special formula for her bottles. The fortified milk will help her grow well, along with the solid foods she normally would be eating. I believe she'll come around, staying here at the house with you," said Alice. "I hope so."

"We're going to show them, aren't we?" I said to Kaylie, jiggling her carefully in my arms.

She only stared at me.

When we went inside, Lady rushed to meet us. I held on tight to Kaylie, sure she would cry, but she merely stared at Lady. When Lady licked her dangling hand, the merest flicker of a smile appeared on Kaylie's lips and quickly disappeared.

I'd seen enough to have hope.

CHAPTER SEVENTEEN

The sound of Brad's footsteps in the upstairs hallway caught my attention.

"We're in here," I called to him from Summer's room, where I was changing Kaylie's diaper.

He walked into the room and grinned at me.

"Welcome home. Come see Kaylie," I said, speaking softly.

Her gaze left me as Brad walked over to us. I braced for tears from her, but she remained calm at the sight of a stranger. She was a stoic little girl.

"Wow! She's small for her age, huh?" He wrapped his arm around me and gave me a kiss. "Guess it's going to be me and all you girls."

I smiled. "Maybe not. I'll tell you later. Right now, I need to try to get Kaylie to take a bottle. Alice left us some helpful information. It explains that someone like Kaylie isn't used to being fed on a timely schedule. To begin with, we'll give her milk with extra nutrients, along with some finger foods. We want her to learn to trust us and to know we'll take care of her."

"Sounds good. Where's Silas, my little man?"

"He should be getting up from his nap soon. Why don't you go check on him?"

Brad watched as I finished putting fresh clothes on Kaylie and lifted her up. Gently, he trailed a finger down her cheek. "Hi, Kaylie."

Her eyes widened, but again she didn't cry.

Rubbing her back, I said, "That's Brad. Daddy Brad."

"Does she ever smile?" Brad asked, looking concerned.

I shook my head. "I haven't seen a real smile yet. That's something we can work on together."

"Okay, I'll go get Silas." Brad left us.

Talking softly to her, I carried Kaylie downstairs. As we passed by the screen door to the porch, Kaylie turned her face to the sound of Summer's babbling and Gracie's laughter.

In the kitchen, I placed Kaylie in the baby swing we'd set up for her. At nine months, she was not much larger than Summer, who we figured was now around five months old. I turned on the swing and stood by to make sure she was all right. A light of interest flickered in her eyes as she began to move back and forth.

"See, Kaylie, you can watch me fix some food for you," I said, as Lady lay down on the floor near the swing.

Soon, I hoped, she'd know preparing food was part of the process. It was hard for me to imagine letting a child go hungry; but then, I'd never fought addiction like her mother. It was also hard to imagine a mother not wanting her children. I wasn't sure what having Kaylie here meant for Brad and me in the future. As much as I was a planner, I decided to go with the flow. Heaven knew, things had become so unpredictable, I couldn't begin to guess what would happen next.

I finished preparing Kaylie's bottle and turned to her. Her eyes focused on the bottle in my hand.

"Ah, so you're hungry."

I lifted her out of the swing and settled with her in the rocking chair. She took to the bottle immediately, grasping it with her two hands. I rocked back and forth, crooning softly to her. After she finished the bottle, I sat her up in my lap and rubbed her back. A small lady-like sound emerged from her as if her body was reluctant to let go of even a burp.

Brad walked into the kitchen with Silas. "He and I have had a man-to-man talk. It seems he wants his supper. Gracie said she'd get it for him if I'd play with Summer." He gave Silas a hug. "Sure am going to miss this little guy."

"That's what I wanted to tell you. It may work out that Odelle can take Gracie's place when she leaves for school."

Brad's eyebrows lifted with surprise. "Oh? Would she live here?"

I shook my head. "I don't think so. She has her own place."

"Good. I'm anxious to have more alone time with you, without someone else being here all the time." He gave me his sexy grin and wiggled his eyebrows playfully. "Know what I mean?"

I laughed. I knew very well what he meant. We'd hardly finished our romp last weekend when Gracie surprised us by coming home early.

Holding Summer, Gracie came into the kitchen. "I'll take Silas now."

Brad exchanged babies with her and followed me out onto the porch. Thinking the warm fresh air would be good for Kaylie, I settled into one of the rocking chairs on the porch.

Brad and Summer sat in a rocker next to us. Lady lay down in front of the chairs.

Kaylie watched with interest as Brad clasped Summer's hands in his and played a game of Pat-a-Cake.

"We can do that too, Kaylie," I said, taking her small hands in mine. We went through the motions of clapping, patting, and rolling the cake, before marking it with a B.

"For baby and me," I ended.

Watching us, Summer laughed and reached for us.

Kaylie held up a hand as if to reach for Summer. Seeing the two of them together, I grinned. Alice was right. It would do Kaylie good to be with someone close to her age.

Later, when it was time to put the babies down for the night, Brad and I decided to set up the portable crib for Kaylie in our dressing room. If she cried, I wanted her to know I'd be there to help her. It would be another way to help her realize she'd be cared for. After we got the crib up and Kaylie settled for the night, I crawled into bed beside Brad. "What a day!" I let out a long sigh.

"Come here." Putting an arm around me, he drew me to him.

"You okay?" He gave me a kiss on the forehead and lifted my face to his. "This is what you want, right? Babies and children coming here and leaving?"

"Well, I hope there's more staying here than leaving," I admitted. "I want to do what we can to help other kids, but I want some, like Summer, to be ours, really ours, forever. You know?"

He wiped a strand of hair away from my face. "Yeah. I've always thought we'd have a large family." His tawny eyes filled with a teasing sparkle. "Of course, I haven't given up on making a few kids of our own. That's something we'd better work on. The more we try, the better the odds."

Laughing, I pulled his face to mine. If the amount of love I felt for him had anything to do with it, we'd have a million children.

Brad's lips met mine. My body felt as if it were melting with pleasure. I wasn't sure if the magical attraction between us was rare; I only knew it was something I'd never tire of.

Eager to welcome Brad home in the best way possible, I lifted my nightgown over my head and ... heard Kaylie's cry.

Quickly slipping my nightgown back on, I sighed and climbed out of bed. First things first, I reminded myself.

"I'll be back as soon as I can," I said to Brad.

He grinned. "I'm not going anywhere."

I tiptoed into the dressing room. Kaylie had pulled herself to her feet and was hanging onto the crib's rails, looking scared. Her mouth had formed an O. The sounds coming out of it lacked the lusty cries of either Summer or Silas. Instead, they were more like the mewling of a child who'd discovered too often that no one would answer. My heart went out to her.

"Hey, baby," I murmured, picking her up.

I checked her diaper. Dry. It wasn't time for a feeding, but I didn't hesitate to carry her downstairs to the kitchen. The sound of Lady padding after us was comforting.

After placing Kaylie in the swing, I mixed up a bottle for her. As the swing moved back and forth to the sound of tinkling music, she watched me solemnly.

I finished preparing the bottle and placed it on the kitchen table beside the rocker. Kaylie's eyes remained focused on the bottle as I picked her up and carried her to the rocker. After getting settled in the chair, I offered her the bottle. She took hold of it and began to greedily drink as if she hadn't been recently fed.

"Ah, so that's how it is," I said. "We'll work on slowing you down as time goes by."

Before she'd even finished the bottle, Kaylie's eyes closed.

I carried her upstairs to her crib and made sure she was comfortable and asleep. Then, full of anticipation, I returned to Brad and our bed.

He was there, just like he'd promised—only he was sound asleep, snoring peacefully.

So much for showing him a proper welcome home.

Silas awoke from his morning nap with a wail that echoed in my heart. His mother was due any minute to pick him up. I changed his diaper and dressed him in the blue and yellow plaid outfit that looked so cute on him.

"There, Mr. Handsome Boy, you're ready." I picked up the tote filled with the boy clothes we now had no use for and carried it and him down the stairs to the kitchen. Gracie was sitting near the swing, watching Kaylie go back and forth.

Gracie looked up at me and smiled. "She likes it!"

When she got up to fix Silas' bottle, I took her seat next to the swing.

"Having fun?" I asked Kaylie. Her arms were waving in the air at each motion of the swing. Her gaze focused on me and then on Silas.

Brad came into the kitchen carrying Summer. "It's a beautiful day out there. The fog has lifted, and it's going to be warm."

We all turned at the sound of Alice's car in the driveway. I clutched Silas to me and went to greet Alice and Odelle.

Odelle emerged from the car and ran to me. "Can I take him now?" There was a hint of tears in her eyes as she turned her attention to Silas.

He studied her. Then a smile crossed his face—a real smile this time. A smile that made me feel like both laughing and crying. He'd changed so much in the weeks that we'd had him. He was becoming more and more responsive.

"It's perfect timing," I said, handing him over to his mother. "He's about to have a bottle. And, Odelle, I want you to meet my husband. He came home from his business trip early to say good-bye to Silas."

A beaming smile lit the young mother's face, making her beautiful. "That's nice."

Odelle headed toward the house as Alice walked up beside me. "How's it going with Kaylie?"

"I think she'll be fine. She really loves the swing we have

for her. It's been interesting to see her reaction to it."

"And otherwise?"

I let out a sigh. "I realize it will take time to make connections to us, but I'm optimistic. Last night she seemed to reach for Summer's hand. I think you're right. Having the two girls together will be very helpful to Kaylie."

Alice gave me a satisfied smile. "Thank you again, Marissa."

"It's Brad's decision too," I reminded her.

"I'll be sure to thank him. Now, let's go see that brood of yours."

I chuckled at her description. It hadn't been that long ago I hadn't wanted children. Now, I apparently had a brood of them.

Inside the kitchen, chaos reigned. Impatient for his bottle, Silas began to wail while Odelle was getting situated in the rocking chair. Summer was pointing at the swing, wanting to use it. Kaylie was crying and looking scared from all the confusion.

I went over to her and lifted her out of the swing. She'd apparently been left alone so often she wasn't used to all the noise and activity.

Whispering baby talk to her, I patted her back. Her stiff body softened against my side, though she remained detached from me. *Patience*, I told myself and rubbed her back.

With Summer in the swing, Silas taking his bottle, and Kaylie quiet now, the kitchen became peaceful enough for me to introduce Brad to Odelle.

I watched carefully as they exchanged greetings. I'd been so impressed with Odelle at our first meeting, I wondered if I'd still feel the same. But the sparkle in Odelle's eyes, the quick smile, the humor as she spoke about herself—it was all still in place.

"Yessir," she was saying. "I've learned not to worry too much about the size of me and concentrate on the size of my heart."

Brad smiled. "You've got a great boy, Odelle. I'm going to miss him." He reached out a hand to caress Silas' head. "He and I have had a lot of guy talks. Right, Silas?"

Silas' gaze lit on Brad and a corner of his lip lifted.

"Oh, that's nice," said Odelle. "Real nice. I have no idea where Silas' daddy is and I probably never will. That's okay by me, but Silas might not think so later on."

"Marissa tells me you've done a great job in the program," said Brad.

Odelle smiled. "Learned a lot, don't you know?"

Brad and I looked at each other and grinned. Odelle might not be aware of it, but she'd sounded a bit like Becky. That went a long way with us.

"After you're through feeding Silas, can you meet with Brad and me?" I said. "There's something we want to discuss with you."

Odelle's expression brightened. "Of course." She looked to Alice.

Alice merely smiled and reached out her arms to take Silas from her.

Moments later, the three of us sat in my office.

Brad took the chair behind my desk. Odelle and I each sat in a chair opposite him. He studied Odelle and cleared his throat.

"Marissa has spoken to me about you possibly taking Gracie's place—working here during the day and returning to your home at night with Silas. Is that something you're interested in doing?"

Odelle nodded emphatically. "Oh yes. I don't have my certificate yet, but I will. And I will stay straight—for Silas, for me, for you."

Brad smiled. "All right then. I've drawn up a few questions to discuss with you."

I turned to Odelle and gave her a comforting pat on the arm. "He's a lawyer. It's his way of doing things."

The creases that had appeared across Odelle's brow softened. "Okay."

I shifted uncomfortably in my seat as Brad asked Odelle about police records and health issues that might prevent her from doing the work around the house.

Satisfied with her answers, Brad leaned back in his chair. "So what do you have planned for your future?"

Odelle smiled. "I'm going to take care of my baby boy the best way I can by learning as many things as I can. No disrespect, but I probably won't want to be working here beyond ... let's say twenty years or so."

At her teasing tone and the sparkle in her dark eyes, Brad and I burst out laughing. If we were going to follow through with our plans of taking in children, we'd need someone with a good sense of humor.

"Alice has given you a wonderful recommendation," I said.

"And I'll follow through with the references you gave us," said Brad.

"There's just one more thing," I added. "Becky our housekeeper and Henry, our caretaker, are away on a cruise. We will want to make sure you all can work together. Is that all right?"

"Sure. And I'll want to make sure she'll be fine with Silas."

I grinned. "No worries there. She's already seen him. The worst problem you'll have with Becky is her wanting to hold him all the time."

Odelle visibly relaxed her shoulders. "I'll do anything to

make this work. It's like an answer to all my prayers. Thank you so much."

"Going from working in a hospital to our home is a big change," said Brad.

Odelle's smile held a bit of impishness. "A healthy change."

Brad stood. "Okay, we'll get back to you as soon as possible. Thanks, Odelle."

She turned to me and gave me a big hug. "You've got the heart of a good mama, Marissa."

Tears stung my eyes. She couldn't have given me a bigger compliment. I couldn't wait to prove it to Kaylie.

CHAPTER EIGHTEEN

We all gathered around Alice's car as Odelle settled Silas in his car seat. I held Kaylie. Brad held Summer. Gracie stood by, trying not to cry. She wouldn't see Silas again before leaving for school.

Alice stood outside the driver's side door, leaning against its frame. "I'll be in touch."

I waved, and she climbed in behind the wheel. I'd been so nervous when I'd first met Alice. Now I knew her as a kind, caring woman who trusted me to be the kind of mother I'd always wanted for myself.

"See you soon, I hope," I said to Odelle.

She patted a hand over her heart. "God willin'." She slid into the passenger's seat and waved as Alice turned the car around and drove away.

I put an arm around Gracie. "Silas is going to be just fine with his mother. And Brad and I interviewed Odelle to take over your job, so we may have him here with us during the day."

Gracie's face brightened. "Do you mean it? That would be wonderful!"

"I think so too. Come on! We've got two little ones to take care of. And I want to hear more about the letter you got from school."

We turned to walk inside and caught sight of Courtney running toward us, waving her arms. "Am I too late? Did I miss him?"

Puzzled, I glanced at Gracie.

"I told her Silas was leaving." She gave me an apologetic look. "I thought she might like to know."

Courtney approached us, a little out of breath. "Whew! I tried to make it over here sooner, but you-know-who was watching me like a hawk."

"How are things going with you, Courtney?" I hadn't made contact with either her or her mother. I had no intention of ruffling quiet waters.

"Mother's seeing a new doctor. I think it might help. And for once she's happy with me. I've promised to go to Europe with her before finding a job." Courtney smiled. "She actually wants to do things together."

"How nice," I said, inwardly wishing her the best of luck. This sudden change seemed too good to be true.

Gracie privately rolled her eyes at me.

"And who's this little girl?" Courtney asked in a high, little voice she used when talking to the babies.

Turning my hip toward her, I lifted the little girl up for her to see. "This is Kaylie."

Courtney leaned closer. "What a pretty little thing. But why isn't she smiling?"

"She will in time. Won't you, Kaylie?"

Kaylie studied me for a moment before turning away and gazing at Courtney curiously.

"Can you stay for a while?" Gracie asked, checking for my reaction.

"Sure," I said, nodding toward the house. "Come on inside."

"I can't stay. My mother and I are going shopping for our trip. I just wanted to see Silas one more time. And, Gracie, you and I are going to meet up tonight. Right?"

"Yeah, I've only got a couple weeks left in Maine. I've decided to go back to school after all. That's what I was going to tell you tonight."

"Oh, wow! So I won't be seeing you after that?"

Gracie shrugged. "Maybe not. That's up to you."

A frown crossed Courtney's face. "Maybe I can get a job in New York after I come back from our trip." Her lips formed a pout. "I thought you and I would hang around Maine for a while, have a little fun."

Gracie shook her head. "That's not going to work out. But we'll stay friends. I'm so grateful to you for helping me get this job. It's changed my life. I'm going into family counseling."

"Well, I'd better go." Courtney's voice held none of her earlier excitement. "I'll see you tonight, Gracie. Bye, Marissa."

After she left, Gracie turned to me. "I don't think things are going to work out the way Courtney wants. I've been through this with her before. Everything's terrible with her mother, and then everything's wonderful!"

"Yes. I can see why you're worried."

We went inside. Gracie left me and returned a few minutes later to hand me an envelope. "This is my acceptance to the program." She grinned. "My parents are thrilled."

"They should be, Gracie." I meant it.

I gazed at Summer in her baby seat and Kaylie sitting in the swing, where I'd placed her. If these girls turned out to be half as wonderful, kind, and caring as Gracie, I'd be thrilled too.

Brad and I were sitting in the kitchen eating a late, quiet lunch. Gracie, taking advantage of a day off, had borrowed my car to go shopping at the outlet stores along Route 1. Both babies were down for afternoon naps.

"It feels so good to have time alone with you," I said, rising from my seat and giving him a kiss on the lips.

He grinned and pulled me onto his lap. "Guess we have to

take advantage of every chance we get, huh?"

At the sexy look he gave me, I laughed.

I moistened my lips and smiled. "We could finish lunch later."

He helped me up and got to his feet. "Come with me to the casbah," he said, holding out his hand to me.

His pseudo-accent was terrible, but that didn't stop me from grabbing onto his hand and hurrying out of the room with him.

We raced upstairs to our bedroom. I paused for a minute outside the door to my room to listen for any sounds from the girls. We'd put Kaylie in Silas' room temporarily. All was quiet.

Gleeful, I went into our bedroom and closed the door behind me with excitement.

Brad tugged his shirt and jeans off and stood before me in his new, blue boxer shorts. From the bulge in front, it was apparent he was ready for some action.

Smiling, I stepped out of my jeans and lifted my shirt over my shoulders. Standing in front of him in only my pink, lacy bikini panties and matching bra, my heart pounded with anticipation. Making love in the afternoon was something I'd missed.

Lying on our bed with the sun shining down on us through the windows, I inhaled Brad's scent and stroked his body. He kicked off his shorts, freeing himself. He unhooked my bra and I wiggled out of my panties. I smiled as our eyes met. My gaze traveled the length of him. The familiar ache of desire settled in my lower body as I awaited the pleasure that was sure to come.

We took advantage of our time together, giving and receiving love in a carefree way. It was amazing to me that after a couple years of discovering what we most liked, there was always something new to add to the enjoyment.

A sound of crying woke me from my nap following our lovemaking. I rose to an elbow and checked the bedside clock. Four o'clock. I scrambled to my feet.

"Wha ..." Brad lifted his head and gazed at me sleepily.

"Sounds like both babies are up. I'll get one. You get the other, okay?"

He got to his feet and started putting on his clothes.

I finished dressing and left to go to Kaylie.

When I entered her room, I found her sitting in the middle of the crib, staring at the Winnie the Pooh decals. She was playing with her toes and making soft little sounds.

"Hi, Kaylie! I'm here," I said, going over to the crib.

She held up her arms and I lifted her into mine, feeling enormously proud that she'd reacted to my presence. As I changed her, she stared at me before turning her attention to the decals. I wondered then what kind of stimulation she'd received growing up without much adult attention. She was unusually quiet for a baby her age, probably a result of being left alone.

I carried her over to the wall and patted the picture of the Pooh. "That's a bear. That's Winnie the Pooh." I tapped the picture again. "Bear. Winnie."

Though she remained quiet, she seemed to take it all in.

"Okay, come on, we'll go downstairs, but first, let's stop in Summer's room."

I carried her into Summer's room.

"What's up?" Brad asked as he finished changing Summer's diaper.

"I want to get a book from the shelf here. I think Kaylie might respond to a good picture book. She really liked the pictures of Winnie the Pooh on the walls."

"Puh," Kaylie said.

I could feel my eyes widen. "Can you say that again, Kaylie?"

She remained silent.

"You heard it, right, Brad?"

"Looks like that one word will have to hold us for a while." He lifted Summer up. "Chow time, girls. Let's go."

Downstairs, while Brad and I worked together to get the bottles ready, the girls fussed, waiting for us to finish.

As I sat in the rocking chair with Kaylie, I watched Brad give Summer her bottle. His gentle manner was so pleasing to me. He'd shown the same behavior with Aunt Doris and even Lady when I'd seen him during my first visit to Barnham after my mother's death.

Kaylie finished her bottle first. I burped her and placed her in the swing while I got out a teething biscuit for her. Earlier, I'd checked her teeth. She had four— two on top, two on the bottom and more coming in.

Summer finished her bottle. While Brad burped her in his lap, she pointed to the swing and started to cry.

"Oh, dear, it looks like we might need another swing. Kaylie loves it. Now Summer wants to be in it."

Brad gave me a knowing look. "Why do I feel another shopping trip coming up?"

"Well, we haven't been back to the store for a couple of weeks. And I want to get Kaylie some outfits of her own. And maybe an outfit for Summer. Right, girls?"

Both girls turned their gazes to us as if to say yes.

Brad and I laughed together.

"Shouldn't we wait for Gracie to come back?" said Brad. "Might be easier."

I shook my head. "With all the colors and shapes in the

store, taking them there would be a good adventure for each of them." The state had given us a second car seat when we took Silas, so putting them both in the car would be no problem.

He shrugged. "Okay, I'm game if you are. But if there's a lot of fussing, we're leaving."

"Agreed."

The weather was warm and wonderful as we loaded the girls into my car. Seeing them in their seats, I smiled. This first road trip would be an adventure for me too. I wondered how many more trips like this we'd take. I hadn't dared to ask Alice about adopting Kaylie. Not yet. And we still had no word on Summer's mother.

Brad straightened from buckling Summer in. "Okay, they're set. Ready?"

I placed the diaper bag on the floor in front of the backseat before climbing into the car.

Brad slid behind the driver's wheel, and we took off.

It was quiet as we rode along. I turned to look at the girls. They were busy looking out the back window.

When we arrived at the store, we propped up the girls in the little seats on the shopping carts. Facing me, Kaylie's eyes rounded as we entered what must have seemed like a fantasy land to her. Brad and Summer followed behind us.

As we checked baby swings and car seats, I tried to keep up a stream of talk with Kaylie, pointing out objects and colors. She studied everything around her. Once in a while, she'd point at something and look up at me with those dark eyes of hers. I had the feeling she was assessing me, like Summer once had done. Then, I'd been scared I wouldn't measure up. Now, I was more confident.

In the clothing department, I went a little crazy. I figured whatever Kaylie outgrew would soon fit Summer. They were almost the same size. If we got to keep both of them, like I'd begun to hope, I guessed they could pretty much share clothes.

Brad and I looked at cribs but decided not to buy one. We'd keep Kaylie in Silas' old room and give him the blue guest room, along with one of the portable cribs we had. As I told Brad, we'd probably be playing "musical cribs" for some time if we kept taking in more babies.

Brad loaded up the car with our purchases, and we headed home.

Both girls fell asleep along the way.

I checked them and turned to Brad. "Did you notice how attentive Kaylie was in the store? I think she's very smart."

He smiled. "Yeah, both Summer and Kaylie seemed to enjoy all the sights."

I sat back in my seat, making a mental note to ask Gracie for suggestions about how best to work with the girls and Silas. I wanted to teach them as much as I could. Every child needed a fair chance at learning. And behind those cute faces of theirs were brains eager to learn.

We were nearing home when Brad turned to me. "We never did finish lunch. I'm hungry. Why don't we stop at The Lobster Trap? A lobster roll and a mug of beer sound perfect to me. Then you wouldn't have to cook."

I smiled. "Sounds perfect. I even have bottles for the girls."

"Great." He took a detour into New Hope. Passing the crowds of tourists meandering across the street, we pulled into the parking lot of The Lobster Trap.

"Hmm," Brad said, studying the full lot. "Stay here. I'll go inside and see if they can get us a table."

I sat in the car waiting for Brad to come back, wondering if I should tell him about my meeting with Cherie. If she was working, I wouldn't be able to avoid it. I had the feeling Brad would see my curiosity as meddling.

Brad appeared at the car. He opened a door to the backseat and said, "We're all set. They'll give us a corner booth out of the way."

I swallowed hard. "Okay." We unhooked the car seats and carried the girls inside.

The hostess, whose name tag read Sharon, recognized me. "How are you today? Did you ever get hold of Cherie?"

Ignoring Brad's look of interest, I said, "Is she here?"

The hostess shook her head. "No. She up and quit on me. Nice girl and a good worker, but she had some family problems. It was a shame to lose her."

The tension that had been building inside me in anticipation of seeing her evaporated. "Do you know where she went?"

The hostess shook her head. "No idea."

I took Kaylie over to the table and set her on the seat beside me. Then, in an effort to get over my disappointment, I silently studied my surroundings.

"What was that all about, Marissa? Why were you asking about that waitress?" His tawny gaze pierced me.

I couldn't lie to him, but I was pretty certain he wouldn't understand my pressing need to find Summer's mother. Not wanting to disappoint him, I said simply, "Cherie was so curious about Summer, I wanted to know why. And since she'd asked about babysitting for us, I thought we might be able to use her in the future."

Summer began kicking and fussing. Brad turned to her, ending our conversation.

As I withdrew two baby bottles from the diaper bag he'd carried in, Brad said, "I know what I'm having. How about you?"

"A lobster roll sounds good. I'll take that and a glass of lemonade. I'll have my glass of wine later after the girls have gone to bed."

We were able to start our meal before the girls started fussing. Between snacks of fries and bites of food, we fed the girls their bottles. We'd just finished our food when it became apparent that a dirty diaper from Kaylie was in process.

"Let's just take them home. We can change Kaylie there."

I started to say yes, then, stopped. "No, I want Kaylie to know I'm here to take care of her. Let me quickly change her, and we'll be on our way."

I took Kaylie into the ladies room, where a baby changing area had been set up. As I finished changing her diaper, I felt a presence behind me. I turned to see who it was.

"What a cute little girl," said the hostess. "Is this the one Cherie told me about?"

My jaw loosened. "What are you talking about?"

The hostess shrugged. "All I know is what she told me. She was worried about your baby. She wanted to make sure she was okay staying with you. She said she might even babysit for you. Then, she suddenly went away."

I frowned. "And you don't know where she lives? Do you know what address she used when she applied for the job?"

"An old one from Maine. I checked when we set up the schedule. When I questioned her, she said she hadn't changed it from before she moved away. She still had a driver's license with that old address in Riverton."

I picked up Kaylie. "This may seem a little unusual, but is there any way you can give me that address? It's important or I wouldn't ask."

"All right. I knew something was bothering her about the situation. As I said, she's a good girl and we became friendly. I'll do it for her."

When she turned to go, I stopped her. "Could you do a favor for me and wait until Monday for me to get it? I'll stop by at lunch time."

At her quizzical look, I grimaced. "I don't want my husband to know about this. Not yet."

She nodded thoughtfully. "Okay."

I didn't ordinarily keep things from Brad but this was one time I needed to do something he might not like.

CHAPTER NINETEEN

B rad pulled out of the driveway Monday morning. Waving good-bye, I felt a little guilty knowing I was about to go ahead with my secret plan. But that wouldn't stop me. If Summer's mother could be found and she was willing to sign away her parental rights, Summer could stay with us.

I studied the tall pines and listened to the slap, slapping of the water in the distance meeting the beach. It sounded like a playful game. I wondered if my mother had ever stood in this exact spot, thinking these same thoughts. Had she ever felt the maternal instinct that had risen inside of me like a giant, engulfing wave? I hoped so.

The sound of a baby's cry broke into the quiet around me. I hurried inside. Mothering was an exhausting business.

Gracie and I went through our Monday morning routine of changing the bed linens and settling the house into a tidier situation. As I loaded the washing machine, I thought of Becky and wondered how she and Henry were doing. We'd received one postcard from a port in Spain. I was thrilled for them but couldn't wait for them to return home. In the short time since Summer had arrived on our doorstep, they'd become more like stand-in grandparents than help around the house.

Summer's babbling noises in the sunroom drew me to her. I set down the laundry basket at the bottom of the stairs and followed the sweet chatter. She was lying on her play mat, kicking happily. Kaylie was sitting beside her. As I watched, Kaylie rolled to her side and stretched out on her stomach.

Gracie, who'd been playing with them, glanced at me and

held a finger to her lips. Together we quietly observed Kaylie as she drew her knees up, then pushed herself forward. Her look of satisfaction brought a chuckle out of me.

Gracie grinned at me. "You're in trouble now. She looks like she's going to be a speed demon."

I turned to Kaylie. "Good job, baby!"

Kaylie moved forward again. This time, Summer noticed. She kicked and managed to roll onto her side and watch Kaylie's every movement.

"Summer's going to be right behind Kaylie," added Gracie.

I felt better about seeking out Cherie. We might need her, even if Odelle came to work for us. I checked my watch. Noon. I hastily bid Gracie good-bye to make the quick trip to town.

As I drove toward New Hope, I studied the trees. Soon it would be fall. Then, "summer people" would turn into "leaf peepers" who came here to enjoy the red, orange, and yellow colors of the trees in New England.

In New Hope, I parked the car outside The Lobster Trap and went inside. Sharon was busy with a customer, so I wandered over to the lobster tank which sat behind the receptionist's desk. A number of good-size lobsters, their claws banded, were piled in the salt water. Before coming to live in Maine, I'd never eaten a whole lobster. Now, they were a treat I often couldn't resist.

"Oh, there you are!" said Sharon, returning to her post. She glanced around and signaled me to come closer.

She slipped a piece of paper into my hand. "I wouldn't do this for anyone else but Cherie. It's against all policy. But I don't believe she would've told me about you and the baby if she didn't trust me or you."

"Thank you very much. It could make a huge difference to one little girl." I refused to let the sting in my eyes produce any tears.

She studied me. "Good luck!"

New customers appeared at her desk. I waved my appreciation and left.

Outside, I climbed into my car and sat behind the wheel staring down at the piece of paper. A shiver crossed my shoulder as I studied the written letters. Riverton was the town listed on the address.

I left New Hope with a new hope of my own.

.

At home, I sat in my office, holding the phone in my hand, trying to guess who might be my best help in trying to track Cherie or her sister down. I decided on Susan Reynolds. Since she'd given me the lead on Celeste, I figured she would be discreet about my trying to find them.

When Susan answered the phone, I tensed. This information meant so much to me.

I told her what I had in mind. She promised to swing by Celeste's old house to see if, by chance, anyone was still there.

"I'll let you know as soon as I can," Susan promised. "If things remain quiet here, I'll take a break sometime this afternoon."

"Thanks." That one simple word might not ever be enough if Cherie or her sister were found. Call it women's intuition, but I felt they were somehow connected to Summer.

As the hours passed, I checked the clock time and time again. Still, Susan didn't call. Five o'clock came and went. I was about to call her when my cell rang.

"Marissa? It's Susan. I drove by the address you gave me. As I mentioned to you earlier, Celeste's father moved out of town. I checked with the people living there. They don't know anything about Cherie, Celeste, or her father's whereabouts. Sorry. It seems it's a dead end."

"Thank you for checking." Disappointed, I hung up. Through the office doorway to the kitchen, I observed Summer happily kicking her feet and waving her hands as she sat in the swing.

"I've done my best, baby girl," I whispered to her, wondering where all this was going to end.

The next couple of days were busy. Setting aside my worries about Cherie, I concentrated on doing what I could to help the girls. With Gracie's tutoring, I learned a few new exercises to perform with the two of them. The movements were made to provide strength to their limbs and the words to stimulate their minds. While interacting with them, I noticed that though Kaylie was quiet, she obviously loved the attention.

One afternoon, while I was trying to catch up with the laundry, I got a phone call from Alice. "My boss Lisa and I would like to stop by sometime tomorrow morning. Is that all right?"

"Is everything okay?" I asked, unable to hide my worry. The last time Lisa wanted to visit, it hadn't been for a good reason.

"She wants to see Kaylie. How's she doing?"

"Really well," I responded proudly. "She loves the attention she's getting." In little more than a week, Kaylie had become a different baby—a much happier, more outgoing little girl.

"Great. See you then."

Left with the feeling Alice wasn't telling me everything, I disconnected the call.

That night, talking to Brad, I asked him what he thought about the upcoming visit from Alice.

"It's probably nothing. Don't worry about it."

I remained quiet, but I knew he didn't understand the extent of my concern. We talked of other things before hanging up. But later, lying in bed, I wondered again why Lisa wanted to see me. I knew from her last visit that she was a busy woman. It had to be something important.

The sun was rising when I got up. The house was quiet. I put on a robe and led Lady down the stairs and out to the front of the house. The cooler night had formed a low-lying fog above the water that made me want to reach through it to touch the nautical treasures floating on the water beyond the shore.

I took a seat on one of the rockers and wrapped the robe closer around me. In the distance, a foghorn sounded as boats moved about on the water. It was eerie to be unable to view much around me—it made me feel so isolated. At one time I would've enjoyed such a feeling. But with babies upstairs, it made me a little uneasy. I got up and went inside where my new family would soon join me.

I'd finished a cup of coffee before I heard the sounds of Kaylie in her room. She was a lighter sleeper than Summer. I hurried upstairs to her before she awakened Summer. It didn't always work out, but I tried to have some alone time with each girl. This morning, I wanted that extra time with Kaylie.

As I entered the room, Kaylie held her arms up to me.

I went to her and lifted her up, snuggling her neck as I did. The refreshing smell of lemon and lavender met my nose. Her skin, which had at first seemed dry to me, was now moist and soft under our care. And more importantly, her arms and legs wrapped around me—a sign of connection to me.

I laid her on the changing table. Making the buzzing sound of a bee, I swirled my hand above her, preparing for a tickling session. Her eyes brightened. She pulled her arms close to her body, to cover her chest.

Laughing, I said, "Here it comes! Buzzzzzz!"

She let out a sound that was a lot like a giggle. I gasped with surprise.

"Good girl." I lifted her to me and hugged her tight.

When I laid her back down to change her diaper, she looked up at me and said something like "zzz."

"Yes, bees go buzz," I said, talking to her as I pulled her wet diaper off, washed off her skin and applied lotion.

Studying me quietly, she listened as I talked to her about bees.

As I finished dressing Kaylie, Summer awoke. I carried Kaylie into Summer's room, and over to her crib.

Summer held up her arms for me. I leaned over and gave her a kiss. "Hold on, honey. Gracie will be here soon."

Gracie promptly came into the room. "I'm here."

I smiled at her. "Just in time. I'll meet you downstairs."

By the time the girls had been given their morning bottles, snacks, and baths, it was time to get them dressed for company. Dressing up a little girl was still a thrill for me. Gracie and I decided to put matching dresses on them. While Gracie tried to put a bow in Summer's hair, I gently brushed Kaylie's dark hair, which was straight and surprisingly thick. It would one day be beautiful, I guessed. Looking at her tan skin tone, I wondered at her heritage.

I stood her up on the dressing table and held onto her. The ruffles of her flower-patterned dress met her knees. She looked adorable.

I took her over to the mirror above the bureau. "See, Kaylie. That's you. Pretty girl. Sweet girl."

Kaylie lifted a hand to her head and patted it. Then she patted my cheeks.

I drew her hand to my lips and kissed the soft skin. "Love you, Kaylie."

The corner of her lips curved slightly. But her small smile was no match for mine as I hugged her close.

Downstairs, I grabbed my cell phone. "Let's get a picture of the girls together. We can put them side by side on the couch in the sunroom."

Lady followed us into the sunroom, watching us carefully as Gracie and I placed the girls on the couch.

Standing back, I quickly took several shots of them. They could have been models for baby clothing, they were that cute—one smiling blond baby and one solemn dark-eyed one.

We were returning to the kitchen with the girls when Alice's car came down the driveway.

"Let's go meet them while the girls are still dressed nicely," I suggested.

Gracie and I walked outdoors with the two babies as Alice was stepping out of the car. Lisa opened the passenger side door and watched me carefully as I approached her.

"So this is Kaylie," she said. She eyed Gracie and turned to me. "Where's Courtney?"

"Her mother insisted she come back home. She and her mother are now going to Europe." I couldn't hide the disrespect in my voice.

"I see. So how's this little girl doing?" Lisa asked, indicating Kaylie with a nod of her head.

Before I could respond, Alice finished greeting Gracie and Summer and rushed over to me. "Marissa, I can't believe this is the same little girl. I see such a difference. And what an adorable dress!" She put an arm around me and gave me a quick squeeze.

Kaylie stared at Alice and laid her head against my shoulder.

"Nice," said Lisa. "She's already beginning to trust you."

I smiled. "Yes, I've spent most of my time with Kaylie, but, of course, I can't and won't ignore Summer. She needs my attention too."

"Of course," said Alice. "I told Lisa it's a good idea for Kaylie to be around other children close to her age."

"You ought to see the two of them," said Gracie. "They're beginning to interact with one another."

I smiled at her and turned to Alice and Lisa. "Gracie's been teaching me some of the exercises for babies she learned at school. I think it's making a big difference in getting Kaylie to react to us and to Summer."

"Very good," said Lisa. "Shall we go inside? There's something I want to discuss with you, Marissa."

A shiver darted across my shoulder.

We entered the house and walked into the sunroom, where we'd moved both swings. The play mat lay in the center of the floor.

I placed Kaylie on the mat. Gracie immediately sat down beside her with Summer. Lisa and Alice took seats on the couch.

"What can I get you? Coffee? Sodas? Water?"

"Diet coke for me," said Alice.

I smiled. I'd learned to have some around when I knew Alice was going to make a visit.

"A glass of water for me," Lisa said. "Thanks."

"Gracie? Anything?"

She shook her head. "No, thanks."

I left the room, worried about the grim expression on Alice's face. I'd been concerned from the beginning. Now I was terrified.

When I returned with the drinks, Alice was down on the floor beside Gracie, watching the two little girls.

I laughed with the others at the look of glee on Kaylie's face when she rolled to her knees and scooted forward.

Alice got to her feet with a groan. "Wish I could be that nimble."

Lisa checked her watch and looked at me. "Is there some place we can talk in private?"

"We can go into my office." I turned to Gracie. "You'll stay here with the babies?"

"Sure. They should be fine for a while."

Carrying their drinks, Alice and Lisa followed me into the office. I closed the door, offered them seats in the leather chairs in front of my desk, and then settled in my desk chair, facing them. The framed picture of Brad on top of my desk did nothing to take away my nervousness.

"Is this about Summer?" I asked, my throat dry.

"Yes ..."Alice began.

Lisa gave Alice a sharp look and cut her off. "No. It's about Kaylie."

I straightened in my chair, waiting for her to continue.

"As you know, Kaylie's mother has signed away her rights. This week, one of our social workers was able to pay a visit to Kaylie's father. He's in prison in Massachusetts, doing a life sentence for a particularly heinous murder. Our social worker was able to get him to sign away his rights on Kaylie. That means she's free for adoption."

I stared at their intent expressions, glad I was sitting down. If I hadn't been, I would've hit the floor for sure. "Are you saying we can adopt her?" My heart pounded so fast my words came out in a gasp.

Alice's smile lit her face. "Yes. I told Lisa this would be a perfect place for Kaylie. You and Brad are so caring." She indicated our surroundings with a wave of her arm. "And you have this wonderful place for children. It would be a blessing for this child. And you would have a baby, after all."

"What about Summer? Is she available for adoption?"

Alice and Lisa exchanged troubled glances.

My heart sank. "What's wrong?"

Lisa looked at me and sighed. "The office received an anonymous phone tip a couple of days ago. The caller said she knew who Summer's mother was and that she might want her baby back."

The cup of coffee I had earlier bubbled like acid in my stomach. "Want her back? But she specifically asked us to take care of her. Didn't she know what taking her back would do to us?" My voice rose in a tortured cry.

"I'm sorry," Alice began. "This is exactly why it's so important to have termination of parental rights. In so many ways, not having those rights terminated isn't fair to those who take in children only to have them taken away."

"Our goal at the Office of Child and Family Services is to keep families together as much as possible. I'm sure you understand that," said Lisa.

It made sense but why, oh why, did the thought of losing Summer hurt so much? My mind worked around the issue. "Wait! The caller said the mother *might* want the baby back? Do you know where the person was calling from?"

Alice shook her head.

I persisted. "Okay, then. Was the caller male or female?"

"A woman. I suspect a young one," said Lisa.

"What do we do now?" My lips shook.

"For the moment, we sit tight," said Lisa. "This might even be a practical joke, a mean one at that. Or it could be a means of trying to make you pay for the baby. We don't know at this point."

"I'm sorry," said Alice, looking contrite. "This type of thing isn't typical. But your case has been unusual from the beginning."

I clutched my hands together, trying to hold back tears. I was being given the chance to adopt one little girl I was just beginning to know, while the one I'd grown to think of as my own was about to be taken away from me.

An understanding expression filled Lisa's face as she studied me. She reached over and patted my hand. "I know this is all such a surprise. No doubt you'll want to talk this over with your husband."

Feeling as if the life had been kicked out of me, I nodded. "Yes, there's so much to think about." I turned to Alice. "I've read that children like Kaylie, coming from violent backgrounds, sometimes have problems of their own later in life."

Alice's smile was sad. "Most of the children we get in foster care come from problematic situations."

"Yes," said Lisa. "After working in this field for a number of years, it's been my experience that the majority of children respond well to love and structure and guidance. There are exceptions, of course, but we all need love and care."

"Yes, of course," I said. "I'm sorry for asking, it's just that I'm a little overwhelmed with all the recent changes and want to be sure I can do my best as Kaylie's mother."

Lisa's features brightened. "I understand Odelle and Silas might be back in your life."

"I'm hoping so. It was hard to let Silas go." I lowered my face into my hands, trying to hide the tears that I could no longer hold back. When I got my breath, I managed to get out, "Maybe I'm not cut out to be a foster parent. It's been sort of dumped into my lap."

The silence in the room finally forced me to look up.

Expecting to find disapproval stamped on Alice and Lisa's faces, I was surprised to see tears in their eyes.

"You, my dear, are a perfect foster mother," said Lisa. "And heaven knows we need them. We have so many children who need the help you can give them."

"You can do it, Marissa," said Alice. "Think what you've done for Kaylie already. And Summer is so happy here ..." Her voice trailed off.

I drew a deep breath to steady myself. "Brad and I will talk everything over and get back to you. Thank you for your support."

A solemn group, we all stood and left the office.

Gracie was in the kitchen with the girls, fixing bottles.

"Good to see you again, Gracie. When do you leave for school?" said Alice, halting Lisa's exit. "Remember, Gracie is going into counseling and is taking courses at NYU."

Lisa smiled. "We need good people like you, Gracie. I hope you'll come back to Maine."

"I just might," Gracie said. "This summer has been a fabulous experience for me, getting to know a bit about the Office of Child and Family Services and how things work for those in foster care."

"Maaaa," said Kaylie.

Shocked, we all turned to look at her. She was holding her arms out to me.

My emotions in a whirling mass, I picked her up and kissed her cheek. Tears of joy pooled in my eyes.

Alice and Lisa exchanged looks of satisfaction. "We'll wait to hear from you," said Lisa. "It's a golden opportunity."

I hugged Kaylie closer even as I focused on the little girl we called Summer. I wanted them both.

CHAPTER TWENTY

After Alice and Lisa left, I handed Kaylie to Gracie. "Can you take her for a minute? I need to make a phone call."

Gracie frowned. "Are you all right?"

I let out a laugh that held no humor. "I hope so."

Inside my office, I took a moment to settle my emotions. Joy and sorrow were doing a wild tango inside me. Summer was the little girl who'd taught me about becoming a mother. How could I let her go? Thank goodness, the risk was over with Kaylie. The threat of losing one was bad enough.

The room spun in slow motion. Resting my head against the back of my chair, I closed my eyes. Thoughts of Aunt Doris comforting me as a child entered the dance. I knew then what I'd say to Brad and lifted the phone to call him.

After punching in his number, I waited for him to pick up. The phone rang and rang. Concerned I shifted in my chair.

Finally, the receptionist's voice came through. "Crawford and Crawford. May I help you?"

"Jenna? Hi, this is Marissa. Is Brad there?"

"Oh, Marissa, he just left in the ambulance with his father."

My heart stuttered. "What? Is he hurt? What's going on?"

"It's Jim. A heart attack."

"Oh, my God! Is there anything I can do? Should I come?"

"You'd better talk to Brad," said Jenna. "It doesn't look good."

"I'll call his cell now. Thanks." Jim had already had one heart attack. A second one seemed ominous.

I drew a deep breath and punched in the numbers for Brad's cell. But it also rang and rang before Brad's voice came on telling me to leave a message. After leaving word with him, I clicked off. I was sickened by the idea that Jim's life might be in jeopardy. He was a big man with a booming voice and a kind heart. Though he hadn't wanted Brad to move to Maine, he'd been supportive of me and our marriage.

I went into the kitchen and sank down on a chair at the table. "Where are the girls?"

"Down for a nap. I think this rainy weather helped make them sleepy." Gracie studied me. "What's the matter?"

I explained the situation to her. "I'm going to try to get a flight to Syracuse. Do you know when Courtney is leaving on her trip to Europe?"

Gracie made a face. "It's been called off. Courtney and her mother had an awful fight. I can't say I'm surprised, but I do feel sorry for her."

"Do you think she could come and babysit with you for a couple of days? Would you feel comfortable staying with the girls, or would that be too much for you?"

"I can handle them myself if I have to," said Gracie calmly.

I studied her. "What about Courtney? Would she be a help to you?"

Gracie smiled. "Oh yes. She'd be good with Summer. I'll concentrate on Kaylie because she's new to us."

Relieved, I said, "Okay, let's call her."

Gracie left the room to make the call, and I went back into my office to try Brad again.

This time, he picked up.

"Marissa? Thank God. It's Dad. He had another heart attack and ..." his voice caught. "He's gone. My dad's gone."

Tears came to my eyes. "Oh, Brad. I'm so sorry. He was

such a good man and he loved you so much."

I heard Brad's shaky intake of air. "Yeah."

"Look, I'm coming to Barnham. I'm making arrangements to fly into Syracuse as soon as possible. I'll let you know what flight I'm on."

"Thanks," Brad said softly, and my heart clutched at the sound of tears in his voice. After we hung up, I immediately went to work on finding the best way to get to Barnham.

Gracie knocked on the door and entered the office. "Courtney says she's glad to help us out. It will give her a reason to get out of the house. She's going to tell her mother there's been an emergency. Courtney doesn't feel there will be a problem with her staying here. Not if she's being a good neighbor and all."

"You're okay with all this, Gracie? I trust you with the girls. You've been the one teaching me a lot of stuff."

"Don't worry, Marissa. We can take care of everything here while you're gone."

"Great. I'm booking a flight now. I'll drive to Portland and leave my car at the airport so I can get back home without bothering you."

"The guest room is all ready, so Courtney can move in anytime. She said she'd come right away."

After Gracie left the room, I booked flights on the internet and texted my schedule to Brad.

Upstairs, I sorted through my clothes and selected a simple black sleeveless dress to wear to the funeral, along with black heels and the string of Mikimoto pearls Brad had given me as a wedding gift. As I put on a pair of nice slacks and a blouse, I realized I hadn't been this dressed up since Summer had arrived at the house. Burping babies and changing them had altered me in so many ways.

I finished packing and carried my suitcase downstairs.

While I waited for Courtney to appear, I went over all the emergency numbers with Gracie and talked to her about the protocol with each one. Though we'd spoken about this often before, Gracie kindly let me go through it again, aware it was making me feel better about leaving the girls.

Courtney arrived, and I greeted her with a hug. "Thank you for coming. I really appreciate it."

She smiled. "I'm the one who's grateful." She shook her head. "Guess it was too much to hope for, this trip to Europe with my mother."

"I'm sorry ..."

She cut me off. "No, it's for the best. I'm now seeing a counselor regularly to deal with my mother's rejection and her abusive behavior. I've learned I have to go on with my own life."

Gracie and I exchanged hopeful looks.

"It sounds good, Courtney." I gave her a quick hug. "I'm happy you're working on that. I've had to deal with similar issues myself."

"Thanks." She smiled at me. "So, Gracie told me it's just the two girls now. That should be easy for the two of us."

"Yes, I think you girls can handle everything. Gracie, you'll be in charge, like we discussed. Does everyone agree?"

Gracie and Courtney bobbed their heads in unison.

"Okay, I'm off. It will give me plenty of time to get to the airport in this rainy weather. I'll make some calls from there. When I arrive in New York, I'll call here to see how things are going."

Gracie gave me a pat on the back. "It'll be fine."

I hurried to my car, loaded the suitcase inside, and drove away. Glancing in the rearview mirror, I saw Gracie and Courtney standing at the doorway, waving me off.

I hated leaving Summer and Kaylie, but my husband

needed me. I'd be there for him like we'd promised each other at our wedding. Besides, I'd be gone for only a couple of days.

After an afternoon of delayed flights caused by major storms along the coast, my plane finally landed in Syracuse around seven o'clock that evening.

Tears filled my eyes when I saw Brad waiting for me at the Hancock Airport. With his hunched shoulders and defeated stance, he was obviously suffering.

I ran to him, dropped my overnight bag on the floor, and threw my arms around him. "I'm sorry, babe. So sorry."

He nestled against my neck, and I felt his body tremble. When we finally pulled apart, his eyes were wet with tears.

I took hold of his hand. "How's your mother? I talked to Doris. She said Ellen isn't doing well at all."

"It's such a shock. We weren't ready for this." Brad shook his head. "Things are up in the air. We've decided to put off a funeral until a later date. I don't think my mother can handle one now."

I hadn't realized things were so bad. "What can I do to help?"

He hugged me to him. "Just be here with me and Mom."

Brad picked up my suitcase. As I walked with him to his Jeep, parked in the short-term lot, my thoughts remained on Ellen. I was especially grateful for her visit to Maine. It had produced a friendship that had been lacking in the earlier months of my marriage to Brad. Maybe, now, I could be a real help to her. I wanted to try.

On the way to Barnham, I called Gracie. "How are things with the girls?"

She laughed. "Just fine. We're following our normal routine. Don't worry about us. Just take care of things there."

Behind the wheel, Brad turned to me. "Everything all right?"

I smiled. "Fine. Gracie and Courtney have everything under control, but I miss those little babies. Who knew I'd get so attached?"

He grinned. "It's only been a few months since Summer came."

"I know. But it doesn't take long to make a connection. Silas was with us for only a short time, but I still miss him."

When we walked into Jim and Ellen's house, I entered a gray atmosphere that reeked of sorrow. The blinds were drawn, the house silent. Doris greeted me with a hug and held on tight. She'd always loved her brother. She led me into the kitchen. The counters were covered with casseroles and other food brought in by friends and neighbors—a sweet, small-town gesture.

"Where's Ellen?" I asked Doris.

"Upstairs in her room. She won't leave it. Not yet." Doris gave Brad a worried look. "She's devastated."

"Give her time," Brad said gently. "She'll come around. Right now, she's coping the best way she knows how. And I'll be right here to see that she does."

"You're right, dear boy. She just needs time." Doris turned to me. "How about a cup of coffee?"

"Sounds wonderful," I said, sitting at the round kitchen table.

Brad left with my suitcase.

"Such a shock," said Doris, handing me my coffee. "I couldn't believe it when I got the call from Ellen this morning. Poor thing was hysterical. But then, she'd just lost her best friend."

I took a sip of the hot liquid, feeling the adrenaline leave my body. I'd been so anxious to get to Brad, I'd forgotten to grab lunch before I left. My stomach growled. I clamped a hand to my abdomen.

"Oh my!" said Doris. "Let me get you something to eat. Brad and I have already sampled some of the food. I'll fix you a plate. What would you like?"

"Just something light," I responded. Saddened by the reality of Jim's death, I wasn't sure I could choke down much food.

Brad sat with me for a few moments, then he gave me an apologetic look. "I hope you don't mind, but I'm going up to bed. This has been an awful day."

He left, and Doris and I talked for a while. She'd received the latest pictures of the girls and she wanted to know how they were doing. I told her how well Summer was growing and about Kaylie learning to crawl. The news of Kaylie's adoption was something I was saving for Brad when we had a quiet moment together.

Brad had already arisen when I awoke in the morning. He must have realized how exhausted I was and quietly let me sleep. I lay in bed watching the morning light sift through the blinds on the window, wondering what I should do. Brad had said the funeral wouldn't be for a while and I had two little girls at home who needed me. I decided to talk it over with Brad, got up, and went into the guest bathroom for a quick shower.

Later, standing in front of the mirror in the bedroom, I studied my image—classic features coated with a new sadness. I slipped pearl earrings into my earlobes and brushed my hair. Its auburn color had faded a bit, and I realized I needed a haircut. It was way overdue. I guessed trips to the beauty parlor were one of the sacrifices a mother was forced to make when having to meet babies' schedules.

At the sound of a knock at the guest room door, I went to open it and stepped back. Ellen stood there looking older and more fragile, like a toy lamb that's suddenly lost its stuffing.

"Ellen! I'm so sorry about Jim." I threw my arms around her. "I came as soon as I could."

She patted my back and stepped away. Her normal vivaciousness was gone. Her cheeks were drawn, her eyes blue pools of sadness.

"What happened?" I asked. "Jim seemed to be doing so well."

"Last week we found out he had an electrical problem with his heart, causing some arrhythmia. He was scheduled to go in for a pacemaker, but he put it off because of a golf tournament he was to play in." She wrung her hands together. "I should have insisted on having the procedure done, but I didn't realize how dangerous his situation could be. I wish Jim had explained it better."

"Oh, Ellen! You can't blame yourself." I squeezed her hands.

"That's what everyone says, but I do."

She sat down on the bed. I lowered myself beside her and put my arms around her. After a few moments of silence, I said, "It's far too easy to blame ourselves. But you shouldn't. Honestly, I don't think Jim would want you to."

She smiled her gratitude and rose. "Well, I'd better leave you to your day. Did Brad tell you we're putting off the funeral for now?"

"Yes. When the time comes, I'll be here for you, Ellen."

Her eyes filled with tears. "Yes, I know. Thank you, dear. There are so many things to think about. I want to sell this big house. I can't imagine living here with Jim's ghost."

After she left the room, I got to my feet and wandered

over to the window. Looking out at the side lawn, I studied the spread of green grass, the carefully manicured bushes. Ellen would have no trouble selling her home. It was one of the beautiful, old houses lining the town square. Well-maintained and modernized, it would be a wonderful place for a large family. I left the room and went downstairs.

Brad was sitting at the kitchen table, sipping a cup of coffee. I helped myself to a cup and sat down beside him.

"How are you?" I asked softly, well aware of the pain I saw in his eyes.

He shrugged. "Okay. I'm going to try to sell the practice as soon as possible. And I'll stay here for a while to help my mom." He took a deep breath. "So how are things at home? We didn't get a chance to talk much last night."

I took hold of his hand. "Let's go for a walk. I'll give you the latest update."

The morning air was crisp but not too cold as we stepped outside. Silently, we walked around the edge of the town square, holding hands. Then we took a seat on one of the wooden benches sporadically placed on the grass.

"Want to tell me what's happening?" Brad said, and waited for me to answer.

I gave him the news on Kaylie and told him about the anonymous phone call regarding Summer. Predictably, his happiness at having the chance to adopt Kaylie quickly eroded at the news of possibly losing Summer.

"The only thing we can do about Summer is to sit tight like Lisa said." Brad shook his head. "I sure would hate to lose that little girl. She's the one who started this whole fostering thing rolling."

I studied him. "If we could adopt them, these girls would be your children. Right?"

"Yes, of course. Why?"

"I need to know that if we never have children naturally, you're okay with it. I don't want to go ahead with adoption if you're not as committed as I am." I knew what he would say. But I needed to hear his words. Once we said yes to adoption, we could never take it back.

He took both my hands in his. "Do you remember my promising to chase your ghosts away?"

My lips curved at the memory. Without his patience, his support, I never would have been able to share intimacy, to have a full life.

"This time, I promise to be not only the husband you need me to be but the father our children deserve." His gaze on me, he lifted my hands to his lips and kissed each one.

The warmth of his kiss sent a shiver of pleasure through me. I looked into those light brown eyes and saw the truth of his words. Leaning forward, I met his lips with mine, sure of our commitment to each other.

We pulled apart. "So what are you going to do?" Brad asked me.

"If you and Ellen don't need me, I'll go home tomorrow to be with the girls."

A look of amazement crossed Brad's face. "Kaylie is really going to be ours?"

At his excitement, I filled with happiness. "Yes. It's hard to believe it's all happening so quickly, but Alice and Lisa think she's perfect for us."

"We'll try to keep Summer too, won't we?"

"Oh yes. I'm going to do everything I can to see that it happens." I hadn't given up on making Summer our own. And with luck, there'd be other children too.

"There's one thing I should mention," said Brad. "I'll be busy setting up a practice in Portland, so I won't be around as much as you might like. Maybe we should limit the foster children we take in until I get my feet under me with a new practice."

"I guess there's never an easy time to expand a family," I said, trying not to sound too disappointed. Things were in such a quandary. I had my commitment to Rivers Papers, and I didn't yet know about getting proper help.

"And I'll have to oversee my mother's affairs, too," Brad added, shaking his head. "I still can't believe Dad is gone."

"Life definitely is uncertain," I commiserated. My life before the arrival of Summer and all that had happened to us now seemed a breeze.

CHAPTER TWENTY-ONE

The sun shone down on Ellen and me, warming us as we sipped our coffee on her patio. Our friendship was warm too. Together Brad and I had told her about adopting Kaylie. She was thrilled for us. Now, with Brad at the office taking care of things, the two of us were discussing the situation in both New York and Maine.

"Before all this happened, I was thinking of getting a place near New Hope for the summer months." Ellen glanced at me, looking uncertain.

Not long ago, I might've felt differently. Now, gladness filled me. "That would be wonderful! It would mean so much for Kaylie to have a grandmother close by. For Summer, too, if we're able to adopt her."

Relief coated her face. She smiled. "After my visit, I realized how much I wanted to be a part of the lives of any children you may have. Men don't understand how it is with us women. It can be a child of your body or a child of your heart. You love them all the same."

I liked Ellen more in that moment than I'd ever thought possible.

"Maybe you'd even consider moving to Maine permanently. Brad's talking about setting up his own law office in Portland. I'm worried about his having enough time to be with the girls."

Ellen studied me. "Let me see how the next few months go. There's so much to think about. And I couldn't leave Doris behind."

"Leave me behind where?" came Doris's voice behind us. We turned and smiled at her.

"Come sit," said Ellen. "I was telling Marissa that I might consider getting a little place in Maine for the summer months."

Doris grinned. "Really? Then most definitely you can't leave me behind. It's something fun to think about, huh?"

Ellen shrugged. "It's just a thought. There's so much to be done before I could consider anything like that. But, as I told Brad and Marissa, I want to sell this house. I can't imagine living here alone."

"Don't move too quickly," warned Doris.

"Marissa, you'd better tell her your news," Ellen said, changing the subject.

Doris beamed at me. "Tell me what?"

"You're about to become a great-aunt for real," I said, becoming teary. "Brad and I are going to adopt Kaylie."

"Hooray!" cried Doris. "I'm so happy for you. I loved the pictures you sent. But what about Summer?"

I let out a long breath and told her about the phone call. "We don't know what it means yet."

"It'll work out. You'll see," said Doris with a conviction I wished I had.

A short while later, Brad returned to the house and joined us. We traded our coffee cups for glasses of lovely red wine.

Sitting together outside, we sipped companionably.

Ellen raised her glass. "Here's to Jim Crawford. May he rest in peace."

I lifted my glass in a toast to the man who, with Ellen, had raised a wonderful son.

That night, I lay in bed waiting for Brad to finish brushing his teeth and join me. I wiggled my toes, reveling in the comfort of the soft bed. It had been a tumultuous two days emotionally. Tomorrow, I'd go home. We'd agreed there wasn't anything for me to do for Ellen at this point.

Brad slid into bed beside me and drew me to him. I let out a sigh of contentment at his nearness. In his arms, I felt safe, secure. It had always been that way.

We made love quietly. With death still a part of the scene around us, the joy of being alive, of being loved, felt so very good.

Sunlight streamed through the blinds, warming my face, urging me to wake up. I rolled over and lay still, gathering my thoughts as I stared at the striped pattern the sunlight made on the carpet. Careful not to disturb Brad, I inched my way to the edge of the bed.

A hand grabbed my arm. "Where are you going?"

I laughed at his playfulness. "I've got to get up. It's late. I have to get ready to go home."

He sat up and ran a hand through his hair. "Yeah, I guess so. You sure you don't mind my staying here for a while? It could even be longer. Sometime in the night, I thought of a friend of mine who might be interested in buying the practice."

"Really? That would be wonderful if you could make a sale so quickly."

"He's a good guy, associated with a law firm in Syracuse. He once mentioned to me that he's interested in moving to a small town. He's got a number of kids and he wants them to experience what he did, growing up here in Barnham."

I grew excited at the idea. "You might want to mention this house. It's perfect for a large family."

Brad frowned. "I agree, but that's pushing my mother quite a bit."

"It's just something to think about." I left him to go to the bathroom.

When I emerged from the shower, hair dripping, he stood in the bathroom before me, naked.

He embraced me and rubbed my back. "Mmm. Wish you had a later flight."

I reached up to touch his stubbly cheek. "Me too, but I need to get home."

He nodded. "I'm hoping to be able to drive to Maine in a couple of days for a quick visit."

"Good. I told Ellen she's welcome anytime. She might need a break before she puts the house on the market."

Brad kissed me. "I'm glad you and she are getting along so well. It means a lot to me."

"And to me," I said truthfully.

I left him to get dressed.

I'd finished putting on my makeup when Brad walked into the room. "All set?"

"Almost. I have to call Gracie. Then, I'll be downstairs."

Gracie answered after several rings, sounding breathless.

"Is everything all right?" I asked, feeling my body grow taut with worry.

"Fine," said Gracie. "Summer and Kaylie are out on the porch with Courtney. They got up early, so Courtney and I decided to watch the sunrise. It's such a nice day we set up their swings out there. Don't worry. It's all good."

I let out a sigh of relief. "Great. That's what I needed to hear. I should be home sometime after lunch. I'll let you know."

We hung up and I paused, wondering what I was going to do without Gracie. Her help was invaluable to me. Courtney might be a possibility as a replacement now that she was home, but I'd have to see if she'd be willing. Becky wouldn't be home for another couple of weeks. And Odelle would need a little more time before she was available.

Downstairs, I grabbed a cup of coffee and sat with Brad. We held hands.

Ellen walked into the room, looking smaller and more delicate than normal. As much as she might think she could easily change her life around, I wasn't so sure. She and Jim had been close. While we might want her to be part of our family, it would be a very different existence for her.

She accepted a cup of coffee from me and took a seat at the table with us. After sipping her coffee, she set the cup down on the table's surface with a sad sigh. "I wake up thinking Jim is down here making coffee like he used to. Then I remember it's Brad, and Jim is gone." Her eyes filled with tears.

"I'm sorry," I said simply.

She dabbed at her eyes with a tissue. "I was thinking, if it's all right with you, I'd come to Maine with Brad when he leaves here. I think I need a break before tackling things here." She gave me a hopeful look. "Is that all right with you, Marissa?"

"Of course. That will give you an idea of what areas you might like in Maine if that's still your plan."

"I don't know what my plan is," she said sadly. "I just know I have to get away from here."

I rose and gave her a quick hug. "You're always welcome at Briar Cliff."

She grabbed onto my hand. "Thank you, Marissa. You've become such a dear daughter to me."

This time, it was my eyes that welled with tears.

Later that day, when I walked into my house, I heard

laughter coming from the sunroom. I hurried toward the room, wondering what was going on. I paused in the entranceway. Lady lumbered to her feet and, tail wagging, trotted over to me.

Startled, Gracie and Courtney jumped to their feet. Swim goggles covered a good portion of Courtney's face. A party hat sat atop Gracie's curls. Summer and Kaylie were sitting in their swings.

Seeing me, Summer made an indistinguishable sound and laughed. Kaylie raised her arms and clearly said, "Maaa."

Thinking of her as mine now, I rushed over to her and lifted her in my arms. "Hi, Kaylie! It's me. Mama." It was the first time I'd used that word with her and it felt good.

I carried Kaylie over to Summer. "Hi, sweet girl. It's me." I leaned down and gave her a kiss.

Kaylie tapped Summer's head. "Ssss."

"Yes, Kaylie. That's Summer."

Gracie smiled. "We've been working with her on some words."

"And I've been making them laugh with these goggles I found in the hall closet," said Courtney. "We've been having fun with them."

I smiled. It was such a happy foursome, I felt foolish for having worried.

I hugged Kaylie and handed her to Gracie so I could pick up Summer. Wrapping my arms around her, I wished I could say "I'm Mama" to her too. But I wouldn't do that. Not until I was sure I could.

CHAPTER TWENTY-TWO

Life continued in a bittersweet way, with my mourning Jim and worrying about Summer, while at the same time rejoicing at the idea of Kaylie being ours.

Brad called to say that while things looked good for the sale of the practice, he'd be delayed in getting home because of the meeting he'd set up with the prospective buyer. Though I was disappointed, I assured him I understood. He sounded so pleased to be free of the office, I was happy for him.

He went on to explain that, in Jim's will, he'd been given the practice in its entirety. He'd also been given Jim's fancy little Mercedes, along with all his personal items. As expected, the rest had been given to Ellen.

"It'll take me awhile to sort through everything," said Brad. "The receptionist is going to help me clear out the office of all personal items."

"Good luck with it. Don't worry, I'll keep things running here. By the time you get home, we'll be more settled here.

"Gotta go. Love you, woman."

I heard the love in his voice and smiled. "Love you, man."

We hung up, and I sat back in my desk chair musing about the stress Brad was under. While it was possible, with Gracie still here, I wanted to do something fun for him—something that would be healing for both of us.

Hearing cries from the kitchen, I rose to my feet, my mind spinning with ideas.

###

Later that week, Alice brought more paperwork for us to fill out and made an official inspection of the house. Because we'd cleared so many hurdles earlier to become foster parents, adoption seemed a simple deal. Seeing all the changes in Kaylie, Alice was thrilled she was coming to us.

As excited as I was about adopting Kaylie, the uncertainty of Summer's future tore at my heart. Every chance I had, I picked her up and hugged her to me, whispering a silent prayer she'd be able to stay with us.

At night, when Brad and I had the chance to talk quietly on the phone, he kept me up to date on what was evolving in New York. His lawyer friend was interested in buying Ellen's house and wanted to settle quickly so his kids could start school on time in Barnham. That meant a whole lot of work for everyone. I wished I could help, but I agreed with Brad that my place was home with the girls.

I felt better about staying in Maine when Doris called to tell me she and Ellen were working with a professional estate buyer to make a quick move possible.

I talked to Ellen as often as possible. As time went by, she seemed more able to deal with the future as a widow. She talked once more of coming to Maine. Now that the idea of her living close by had come up, I hoped it would happen soon. The girls would love her.

When he realized settling things in New York was going to take longer than he'd wanted, Brad decided to come home for a long weekend. I couldn't wait to see him.

As he drove up the driveway, I didn't know who was happier to see him—me or Lady.

He emerged from his Jeep and rubbed Lady's ears. She wiggled and leaped around Brad like a puppy, not the aging Lab she was. Then, grinning at me, he swept me up into his arms and gave me a lingering kiss. I hugged him to me.

When we pulled apart, he sighed with contentment. He wrapped an arm around my shoulder and stood looking at the house. "It's so good to be home. Where are the girls?"

"Inside with Gracie and Courtney."

We went into the house and headed to the sunroom. With sun streaming through the long windows into the room on most days, it had become a favorite place to play with Summer and Kaylie.

At the doorway, we paused.

Gracie and Courtney were sitting on the floor with the girls. Seeing us, they looked up and smiled. Rising to their feet, they exchanged greetings with Brad before leaving the room, giving us our needed privacy.

"Watch," I said quietly to Brad, holding him back.

Kaylie scooted our way, doing her knee and push routine.

"Wow! She can really crawl now." Brad went to her and picked her up.

At the uncertain look that crossed her face at being in his arms, I hurried over to them. "Kaylie, this is Daddy. Can you say Daaadee?"

Her dark gaze lifted to his face. "Da ..."

A smile of pleasure crossed Brad's face, brightening his strong features. His eyes widened and then grew watery. "My God, it's real. She's gonna be ours."

I beamed at him. "It's all but done."

Kaylie held out her arms to me. I took her, and Brad went over to Summer, propped upright in her little plastic seat. At seeing Brad, she waved her arms and kicked her feet with excitement. He lifted her into his arms and turned to me. "Still no word?"

I shook my head. "Maybe, like Alice said, it's some kind of joke."

Brad hugged Summer to him. "I hope so."

I set Kaylie down on the floor. "Will you watch her? I'll fix some snacks. Then we can sit on the porch and relax a bit before dinner."

"Sounds good." He chuckled when Kaylie crawled after me as I left the room, then cried, "Help! How can I keep track of both of them at the same time?"

I turned back and grinned at the helpless look he gave me. "That's what life's like with the two of them. I'll send Gracie and Courtney in to help you."

After dinner, Brad and I sat on the porch with Gracie and Courtney and the babies. The darkening sky embraced the colors of a spectacular sunset, spreading color around us like an overflowing paint box. With the water calmly meeting the shore in comforting embraces, it all seemed so peaceful.

Studying Gracie sitting on the porch steps holding Summer, I wondered if she knew how much I'd miss her when she left after the weekend. She'd been at my side as I took baby steps into motherhood. Her calm manner and the knowledge she'd received getting her degree at school had been a tremendous help to me.

My gaze settled on Courtney. She was sitting next to Gracie, holding onto one of Summer's hands. Courtney had grown up a lot over the past weeks. She'd lost that air of entitlement that had been a little off-putting at the beginning. I liked her better now than I had back at the start of summer. She'd also turned into a good worker, willing to take on most anything. She'd even agreed to move in with us until Becky and Odelle were able to take over. Best of all, both Kaylie and Summer liked her.

"It sure feels good to be home," said Brad, giving me a smile as he sat in the rocking chair with Kaylie.

I returned his smile. The little getaway I'd planned would be the perfect time alone we needed.

"I've got a surprise for you. I've arranged for us to go away tomorrow to one of our favorite Bed and Breakfasts down east. You need a break, and so do I. Gracie and Courtney have agreed to stay with the girls so we can get away."

"B&B down east? Do you mean The Harbor Inn?" The grin Brad gave me could only be described as sexy.

As he continued to stare at me suggestively, my body heated with expectation. Yes, indeed, this was going to be a wonderful little trip.

It was late the next morning when we were finally able to pack up and get ready to leave.

Brad stood by, watching me with an amused expression as I went over schedules, phone numbers, and every little detail I could think of so Gracie and Courtney could take care of the girls.

"C'mon, Mom, let's go," he teased.

Comfortable that I'd covered everything, I gave each baby one last kiss, thanked Gracie and Courtney, and went outside to the car. It was remarkable how much things had changed for me. At first, I'd been so scared to take on the care of a baby. Now, it seemed almost natural.

We headed up the coast or "down east" as Mainers say. Following the rocky coastline, I felt as if I were off on an adventure. The thought of being alone with Brad made my body bubble with excitement.

Brad reached over and clasped my hand. "Good to get away, huh?"

I smiled into his gaze. "Oh yes!"

It had been a while since Brad and I had taken such a trip, and it was important to me to have time for old-fashioned romance with my man. With the arrival of Summer and the other babies, our spontaneity for making love had all but vanished. We needed this time together.

Studying Brad's face, noting the circles under his eyes, I hoped it would be a relaxing, healing time for him.

The Harbor Inn was one of his favorite places. We'd discovered it shortly after we became engaged. It was a lovely Victorian waterfront home that had been beautifully restored. But the attraction to this place, for us, was the Four Diamond rating and the pleasant owner, who loved to prepare specially-ordered dinners. And too, the setting was lovely, allowing privacy to the guests. We'd considered having our wedding there, but transportation to New Hope was easier for our guests.

After a two-hour drive, we pulled up to the Inn. I felt a little like the younger person I'd been when I first saw it, wondering what my life would be like with the newly-engaged man beside me. Now, I smiled at him. I had no more knowledge of what the future would bring, but I knew it would be the two of us facing the future together.

One of the young attendants from the Inn hurried to open the car door for me. I stepped out onto the brick walkway in front of the building and breathed in the clean air. The aroma of garlic and blended spices drifted in my direction from the back of the house. I happily realized the owner had already begun his early preps for tonight's dinner.

We were led to the Captain's Suite, a room that had become our favorite. It contained a high, four-poster king bed, a brick fireplace and, best of all, a modern bathroom with a huge spa tub for two.

Inside our room, a welcome card and a basket of fruit, cookies, cheese and crackers sat on the small coffee table in the living area of the suite. I smiled at the touch of hospitality and walked over to the sliding doors leading to the private patio outside the room. With an abundance of colorful flowers, the garden beyond the patio looked like something one might see at an English country estate.

The attendant made sure our ice bucket was filled and that we had everything we needed before leaving.

Brad walked over and stood beside me, gazing outside. "So nice," he murmured.

"Yes," I said, turning and wrapping my arms around him. I laid my head against his chest and, feeling his arms come around me, sighed with pleasure. Looking back over the last few months, I realized how difficult they must have been for him. I reached up and gave him a kiss.

He smiled. "Want to take a walk into town? We can have lunch there."

"Sure. It will feel good to stretch my legs."

The Inn sat about a mile outside the small picturesque town of Redmond. The town, like New Hope, had been built up around a small harbor that served as a haven for power boaters and sailors. In places, the rugged coastline jutted out into the blue-gray water—rocky reminders of ancient history when glaciers had formed the land.

We started out at a brisk pace. I moved my arms freely. It felt good to travel along without holding a child or carrying a bundle of soiled baby clothes.

Brad clasped my hand and we easily walked in step. Peace and happiness wrapped around me like a soft, warm cloak. Above us, the sun played a game of peekaboo with the white puffy clouds that raced across the sky.

"I'm glad to have some time alone with you," I said.

Brad smiled. "I needed this too."

We soon entered the heart of the town. We walked up and down the streets, peeking into intriguing store windows. When we came to the bookstore, I couldn't resist.

"I'll only be a minute," I told Brad.

"A minute?" He laughed. "Not a chance. But I'll go in with you."

Close to an hour later, we left with a number of children's books. It was such fun for me to imagine all the reading adventures that might lie ahead for Kaylie and Summer.

We turned into The Chowder House, a favorite of ours. The small, rustic restaurant was known as having the best clam chowder on the Maine coast.

The hostess seated us at a corner table. "You'll have privacy here," she said with a smile. "Are you on your honeymoon?"

Brad and I looked at each other and laughed. He winked at me and said to her, "It's that obvious?"

In a way, it felt like a honeymoon. But unlike the newlywed I'd once been, I was well acquainted with all the ways Brad could make me happy since I'd married him.

The hostess gave me a smile and moved away.

Brad took hold of my hand. "You're still my beautiful bride, you know."

I shook my head, knowing it wasn't true, but pleased that he said it. I still hadn't had time to get my hair styled or to fuss with myself the way I used to.

"Shall we order a nice crisp, white wine to go with the mussels I know you're going to order as an appetizer?".

I hesitated, then nodded. "Sure. I don't have to worry about taking care of babies. This is our time to be... wild." I gave him a look that suggested what I had in mind.

His eyebrows lifted in mock surprise. "Well then, I guess we'd better order quickly."

I laughed. It felt so good to flirt with him.

Looking out through the window at the scene, I sighed happily. The sight of the lighthouse in the distance was like a beacon to me, reminding me to leave my worries behind and simply enjoy this time.

We ordered, and as we sipped wine, we talked about his dad. Brad had come to terms with his decision to leave the law practice in Barnham and set up practice in Portland. I supported him but knew we'd have to decide what we wanted to do about help for me. He would be too busy setting up his practice to devote much time to us at home. We talked about hiring new people to slowly take Becky and Henry's places, giving them more time to travel, then decided to wait until they returned before making any decisions.

After our leisurely meal, we strolled back to the Inn, hand in hand. As we approached the beautiful old house, my anticipation grew. Making love in the afternoon always seemed so exciting to me, as if I should be doing something more mundane and had decided instead to indulge myself.

We crossed the broad sweep of the front porch, avoiding the temptation to sit for a moment in one of the bench swings, and entered the building. As we approached our room, I began to unzip my cardigan sweater, preparing to get out of my clothes as rapidly as possible. Maybe, after making love, we'd soak in the spa. Remembering where that could lead, my lower body tightened with desire.

Brad unlocked the door and we stepped inside our room. Leering at me, Brad eased his sweater over his head. "Better hurry up," he teased, noticeably ready for some fun.

Following his lead, I unzipped my pants and stepped out of them. Rolling back the quilted covers, I tossed my shirt aside and climbed up on the high bed.

Naked, Brad threw himself across the sheets and growling playfully, gripped me. "Okay, woman. You asked for it."

I clung to him as he unhooked my bra, freeing my breasts

for his inspection.

He lowered his lips to one nipple, then the other, sending frissons of electricity through me. My body hummed with pleasure before registering the fact that a phone was ringing.

Brad suddenly stopped and lifted his head. "What? Who'd be calling us now?"

At the sound of my cell ringing, I sat up, alert as only a mother can be. I jumped off the bed and ran over to the table where I'd left the phone.

My stomach knotted as I read the caller name. Gracie.

Picking up the phone, my hands shook. "Yes? Is everything all right?"

"You'd better come home right away. There's trouble," said Gracie, her voice strained.

"What's happened?" I choked on the words, imagining all sorts of things.

"Summer's mother is here. Oops. Gotta go."

I dropped the dead phone on the floor and collapsed in a chair.

Brad picked up my cell. "Hello? Hello?"

I shook my head. "She hung up."

"My god! Look at you! What's wrong?"

"It's Summer's mother. She's at our house. Gracie said we have to come home right away. There's trouble."

"Hold on! I'm calling her back," said Brad, punching in the numbers.

Pacing the floor, he grilled Gracie. The words I heard through a fog added to my worry. "Legal rights. Alice. Office of Child and Family Services. Police."

While Brad continued to calm Gracie, I scrambled back into my clothes. Looking around the room, I gathered our things together, packing as quickly as I could.

When Brad finally hung up, he looked as worried as I felt.

"We've got to get there quickly. It seems Summer's mother and her new boyfriend are at Briar Cliff, threatening to take Summer away. I told Gracie to call Alice immediately and to call the police to come to the house. I told her we'd be there as soon as we could."

"I've laid your clothes out and packed the rest of our stuff," I said, feeling as if I was going to throw up the lunch I'd enjoyed a short while ago.

Brad laid a hand on my shoulder. "Summer has legal rights too. We'll do everything we can to see that she's protected."

I wanted more than protection for her. I wanted her to be ours forever.

CHAPTER TWENTY-THREE

The two hours it took to return home felt like twenty-four. We raced down the highway at speeds I might've reprimanded Brad for on a usual trip. This time, he couldn't go fast enough.

At last, we reached New Hope and the entrance to our driveway. Traveling down it, I strained forward trying to guess what was happening inside. Outside the house, the only sign of visitors was a beat-up, red sedan sitting in the driveway.

Brad pulled up beside it and slammed to a stop. We each opened our car door, hit the ground, and began running toward the house. Holding Summer, Gracie met us at the door. Her face filled with relief at the sight of us.

"Thank God you're here," she said. "I think they're both high on something."

Brad straightened to his full height of six-two. "Have you called the police?"

""Yes. I had to leave a message for Alice, and Courtney is upstairs with Kaylie," said Gracie. "One officer came and talked to them but had no reason to arrest them. I agreed to let them stay here until you came home. I was afraid they'd fight me for the baby if I didn't."

Brad's jaw worked in an angry rhythm. "Okay, let's go talk to them."

Gracie handed Summer to me. I hugged her so tightly, she squirmed. "Okay, baby. We're here. You'll be all right," I murmured, wondering if I'd just told a lie.

When we walked into the kitchen, a girl sat at the kitchen

table. She had long, blonde hair that looked like it hadn't been washed in some time. She wore no makeup on features that looked unclean. Her face was a thin version of Summer's, with a few different twists. She looked very young to me, or maybe her baggy clothes made her seem so small.

My gaze fell on the boy sitting beside her at the kitchen table. He had long black hair, dark eyes that glared at me belligerently and a lazy posture that made me want to shake him. If there was trouble, I guessed he'd be at the root of it.

Brad faced the girl. "I understand you are saying you're the mother of this child," he said in lawyer mode, indicating Summer with a nod of his head.

"I'm not just saying it," the girl said. "I had her. If you'd had a baby you'd know it." Her eyes flashed angrily at him.

"What's your name?" Brad continued smoothly.

"Celeste. Celeste Durant. What about it?"

"You're Cherie's sister, aren't you?" I said, hoping to catch her off guard.

Her eyes widened. "Yeah? Why? Has she been in touch with you?" She narrowed her eyes. "Is she trying to get money out of you too?"

Brad and I exchanged worried glances. Were we entering a game of blackmail?

My knees felt weak. I wanted to sit but didn't want to be near Celeste or the rough-looking boy with her.

Brad turned on him. "What's your name? Are you the father?"

"Hell no," the boy said. "I ain't that stupid."

"I asked for your name," Brad said, giving him a commanding stare.

"Billy Mueller. Don't blame me for the trouble *she* got into with some rich kid named Harry or one of his friends."

My heart faltered for a beat. I turned to Celeste. "Who's

this Harry? And is he Summer's father?"

She shrugged. "I'm not sure. All I know is it happened when I got high with him and his friends at his fancy schmancy garden party."

My mind clicked along with the few facts she'd given us—facts I didn't like at all. Harry, garden party, sister Cherie, it all added up to a possibility I dreaded.

Gracie left the room.

"What garden party are you talking about?" I asked Celeste.

Celeste waved her hand. "You know, the one down the beach, the one all you rich folks go to every year. Cherie told me all about it. I met up with her there."

Gracie returned to the kitchen with Courtney. I gave them an inquiring glance.

"Kaylie's asleep in her crib," Gracie said quietly to me, coming to my side. "I thought Courtney should hear this."

I nodded. It would all come out anyway.

"Let me get this straight," said Brad, facing Celeste. "You met your sister at this garden party, got high with a boy named Harry and his friends, and one of them, you're not sure which one, got you pregnant. Is that about it?"

"I guess." She shrugged as if none of it mattered.

"Why did you choose us to take your baby?" Brad asked.

"I'd seen you and Marissa at the party. You looked real nice. Then I found out you didn't have any kids. I wanted Summer to have a nice life, you know? I thought you'd give her one." Her gaze turned from Brad to the baby I held in my arms and down to the floor.

"Why are you here then?" Brad said.

Celeste glanced at Billy.

"Go on, tell them," he said to her.

She took a deep breath. "Billy says that people pay a lot of money for babies. I know you're rich. He says it's only fair that you pay me for her. Cherie said if I couldn't take care of her, I should put her up for adoption. But I wanted to choose the parents. So I chose you." She glanced at Billy, hesitated, then, turned to me. "I'll take her away if you don't pay me."

"You say Harry might be the father of the child. Why wouldn't you go to him or to his parents?"

Celeste shook her head. "He's an asshole and that mother of his is weird. A crazy bitch, the catering staff called her. Why would I do that to my baby?"

I handed Summer to Gracie. "Please take her upstairs."

"You can't take her away," said Billy. "That's Celeste's baby!"

"Right now, the law has given her care to us," said Brad firmly. "This is where she'll stay until it's ruled otherwise."

I barely held onto my temper as I turned my attention to Billy. "How long have you and Celeste been together?"

"Just a couple of months." He shot Celeste a look of disgust. "I didn't know she had a baby, but then I thought maybe that could help us."

Brad shook his head. "So, it was you who came up with the idea of making us pay for the baby." He turned to Celeste. "But you were happy with the arrangement for Summer until Billy came up with this plan. Right?"

She wouldn't answer or look at him.

"Did you do drugs while you were pregnant with Summer?" I asked. Summer hadn't shown signs of it, but I had to know.

Her eyes widened. "No. Cherie would never let me do anything like that. That's the reason things got so bad at the garden party thing. It was coke or some kind of date drug, I don't know which. It could've been both. Everything turned into a fog. That's why I don't know who got me pregnant."

"But you think it might be a boy named Harry?" Courtney said in a deceptively innocent voice.

Celeste shrugged. "It was somebody."

"What drugs have you taken today?" Brad asked.

"You don't have to tell him," said Billy. "We're not on some fucking trial here. Get your bag, Celeste, and let's get out of here." He got to his feet and shook a finger at us. "Don't think this is over. She has rights. If you want that baby, you'll pay."

The ferocious look he gave me was frightening. The strength in my legs left. I leaned back against the kitchen counter for support. I turned to Celeste. "Does Cherie know you're doing this?"

"God no," she said, emitting a sound of disgust. "She kicked me out of her place when I started up with Billy."

"How old are you?" Brad said to her.

She drew herself up. "Old enough to have a baby."

"I'm guessing you're not even eighteen." He whipped around to Billy. "Guess where that leaves you, boy?" Brad's voice shook with anger. "I'm calling the police. Contributing to the delinquency of a minor is just one of the things they'll throw at you."

Fists at his side, Brad loomed above the boy.

Billy's eyes widened. Then his body appeared to collapse. "Fuck it," he said. "I'm outta here." He turned and hurried toward the door, all cockiness gone.

"Wait!" cried Celeste. "What about me?"

He stopped and faced her. "You're nothing but trouble. Screw you!"

He stormed out of the kitchen.

I took hold of Celeste's arm to hold her back, expecting her to fight me. Instead, she merely stood beside me. We watched Billy turn his car around and head down the driveway away from the house.

"I've got his license number," said Brad, going to the pad of paper I kept by the phone and writing it down.

Celeste burst into tears. "I'm sorry. He made me do it."

She collapsed in my arms. I let her cry. She wasn't much more than a baby herself.

"When's the last time you had something to eat," Gracie said to her.

Celeste shrugged. "I can't remember."

"Sit down," I said. "We'll get you something to eat and then we'd better call Cherie. After that, we'll handle one thing at a time."

Like a puppet whose strings had been cut, Celeste sank into a chair at the table and laid her head down on it.

Brad gave me a grim look. "There are a lot of legal matters involved in this case—possible rape, delinquency, drug use, possible distribution of drugs and then the threats made on us."

"And one sound asleep screwed-up girl," I said, indicating Celeste with a wave of my hand.

I went over to the small cloth bag which Celeste had used like a purse, drew out a cell phone and handed it to Brad. "See if you find a listing for Cherie Finnell."

"Celeste? Come with me," I said, shaking her gently. "You can sleep on one of the couches in the sunroom."

Her head shot up. She blinked at me sleepily and allowed me to lead her out of the kitchen into the sunroom.

"Go ahead, lie down," I urged. "Nothing's going to be resolved anytime soon, so get some rest."

As she lay back on the couch, her facial features relaxed. Seeing her face like that, I guessed she was younger than I'd first thought. When Susan Reynolds had called me from Maine, she'd told me Celeste's father had kicked her out of the house when he'd learned she was pregnant. I knew now that Cherie must have taken her in, giving up her schooling to do so. It was a sad situation, but it wouldn't change my determination to keep Summer. There had to be a way to make everyone happy.

When I returned to the kitchen, I found Courtney in tears. "What am I going to do? Summer might be my niece and Harry, that jerk, might be a father." Her eyes widened as her jaw dropped. "Oh, my God! My mother might be Summer's grandmother!"

I staggered back. What I'd feared earlier hit me all over again. If it was so, I was sure that Eleanor in all her meanness would not let us keep Summer.

I sank into a chair and looked up at Brad helplessly.

His lips spread into a thin line. "We'll have a DNA test done." He turned to Courtney. "Before we go all crazy with this idea, let's make sure it's true. We don't want to raise undue alarm."

"All this worry about Harry might not mean anything, anyway," I said in a dull voice. "If Celeste doesn't want us to keep Summer, it won't matter. The Office's policy is to try and keep families together."

Brad shook his head. "Anyone can see how young Celeste is, how many problems she has ..."

"She hasn't given away her parental rights. That counts for a lot." Saying the words, worry pierced me like a sharp-edged sword. "While I was with Celeste, did you get hold of Cherie? She might be a voice of reason for us."

"I left a message for her. That's the best I could do," Brad said. "I'm going to take a few moments to write down exactly what took place and what was said here. It might help us in the future."

He went into my office.

I turned to Courtney. "If it turns out Summer is Harry's baby, do you think your mother would want to take Summer away from us?"

Courtney shook her head. "I don't know. Like everyone thinks, she's a crazy bitch."

Gracie appeared in the kitchen holding Kaylie.

I rose to my feet and went over to her. "Here, I'll take her."

Hugging Kaylie to me, I wondered if she would have the sister I wanted to give her.

Gracie was helping me in the kitchen when Celeste appeared in the doorway.

"Have a good sleep?" I asked. Brad and I had agreed to keep things on a friendly basis if at all possible. We really didn't know what Celeste's true feelings were about Summer staying with us. If we could work out an amicable solution, it might be easiest.

"Where's a bathroom?"

I indicated the one off the laundry room. "You're welcome to use that one. It's closest."

When Celeste reappeared, she'd washed her face and combed her hair. I could better see where Summer got her bright blue eyes, her long lashes.

"Are you hungry?" I asked.

At her nod, I fixed her a sliced chicken sandwich. "Brad has called your sister. We're waiting to hear from her."

"Oh, God!" Celeste sank her face into her hands and mumbled, "She's gonna be so pissed with me."

"Yes, I'm sure she won't be happy with you. I've talked to her on occasion and she seems like such a nice person and a very caring sister. It sounded to me like she's given up a lot to take care of you."

When Celeste raised her face, tears were streaming down her face. "My father kicked me out of the house. She had to take me in. She didn't want to."

"But she did," I reminded her. "That says a whole lot."

"Yeah, well now she thinks she's some sort of saint, telling me what I can and cannot do."

Listening to her, I realized Celeste was, in some ways, simply a young adolescent who had yet to learn a lot.

The sound of a car drawing near brought me to my feet.

Alice's blue Ford came to a stop next to my Land Rover.

I went outside to meet her.

"What's going on?" Alice asked as she climbed out of the car. "I got an urgent message from Gracie, asking me to come right away."

I filled her in the best I could.

Alice gave me a troubled look. "Have you talked to Celeste about signing her rights over?"

I shook my head. "No, Brad warned me not to say a word about it. He thinks it should come from the Office of Child and Family Services, not us."

"Good. I want our lawyers to advise us as to how best to go forward." She took hold of my arm. "Why don't we go in and see what, if any help I can be?"

We walked together toward the house, uncertain what lay ahead.

CHAPTER TWENTY-FOUR

Brad met us at the kitchen door. "Thank you for coming, Alice. We all have a lot of sorting out to do." He held the door open, and Alice and I walked into the kitchen.

She gave him a grim smile. "As I told Marissa, our lawyers will want to be advised. I'm here to protect the interests of Summer."

Celeste looked up from the sandwich she'd all but gobbled down and gave Alice a dubious look. "Who's *she*?"

"This is Alice Tremblay from the Office of Child and Family Services," I explained. "Summer's case is assigned to her."

Celeste's eyes widened. "Case? She's not supposed to be anybody's case. She's supposed to be your baby."

"That's what we all are trying to make happen," said Alice calmly. "We want to make sure your wishes are met and that Summer will be Marissa's and Brad's child like you wanted."

Celeste's jaw jutted out like a stubborn child's. "Well, maybe things have changed. My boyfriend says that people like them should pay for a baby."

"I see," Alice said calmly. "Do you think he's right? You, yourself, left Summer with Brad and Marissa. For these past months, they've done everything they could to make sure she's happy and healthy and well-loved—exactly like you wanted."

Alice took a seat at the table opposite Celeste. "I've met with many adoptive parents and I have to tell you that Brad and Marissa are among the nicest and most capable. With them, you have an opportunity to see that your baby has the best home possible."

Celeste turned away from Alice's gaze. She indicated Brad with a nod of her head. "He chased my boyfriend away. Now, what am I going to do?"

Alice reached over and took hold of one of Celeste's hands. "That's one of the reasons I'm here. I may be able to help you."

Celeste sneered. "Yeah? I know what kind of help you state people do. I was in foster care for a year after my mother died—a whole, terrible year before my father got me out of there." She snorted. "Some father he is. He kicked me out when I got pregnant."

"There's a lot that can be done to help you," Alice said in a controlled manner I admired. "Give us a chance to make your life better."

The sound of a car coming down the driveway stopped the conversation.

I rose. "I believe that might be Cherie," I said, seeing a young girl get out of the small gray car.

Celeste's face tightened. She jumped to her feet. "Oh no! Let me out of here."

"Calm down. We didn't send for her to have you punished," explained Brad. "We wanted her here to help work things out for you. Besides, she has a right to know what you've been up to."

Celeste sank down on her seat and shot an apprehensive look at the door.

I went to the door as Cherie approached. She hurried up to me. "Is she still here?"

"Yes. Come on inside."

Cherie let out a long sigh and walked into the kitchen.

I introduced Alice and stepped aside as Cherie faced her sister. "What in the fuck are you doing here?" Her lips thinned with anger. "Did that awful guy Billy bring you here? The same guy I told you to stay away from?"

"You can't keep bossing me around," snapped Celeste, jumping to her feet. "I can be on my own. You're not my mother."

"Obviously," Cherie said coldly. "But as long as you're in my care, I can and will keep tabs on you. That's my job. Now you'd better tell me what's going on. Why are you here?"

Remaining silent, Celeste looked down at the floor.

"Both of you have a seat and I'll fill you in," said Brad quietly.

Cherie sat down next to Alice and glared at her sister.

From across the table, Celeste cast uneasy glances at them.

Celeste and Cherie looked nothing alike. Celeste's blond hair and blue eyes accented features that were small and delicate. Cherie had dark hair, darker skin and larger features that were in contrast to Celeste's. With their different names and appearances, it seemed obvious they had different fathers. I wondered why Cherie, as young as she was, appeared to be on her own.

Reading from his notes, Brad told the assembled group what had happened—from Celeste's arrival at the house with Billy to Billy storming off. When he was finished talking, the room was filled with a charged silence.

Gripping the edge of the table, Cherie stared with dismay at her sister. "Do you know how many of my rules ... how many laws you broke?"

Celeste's lips puffed out in a pout any two-year-old would be proud of. "I told you, I don't want to live with you anymore. Billy was going to let me live with him. Now he's gone." Her shoulders slumped. "What am I going to do? We had it all planned out."

Cherie studied her sister with a look of horror and turned to Alice. "I've done my best with her, but ever since she started taking drugs, nothing I say or do matters. Billy's the one who's been supplying her. I don't even want to think about how she's paying him back." She lowered her face into her hands and sobbed. "I don't know what to do anymore. I don't know what to do."

Alice patted her back. "We're going to get help for both of you."

Celeste leaned back in her chair and crossed her arms in front of her. "I don't need help. I'm getting outta here." She started to rise.

"Sit down," I said firmly. "We need to get some things settled."

Reluctantly, she returned to her seat.

"Let's address one thing at a time," said Alice, staring at Celeste. "The continued use of drugs would prohibit you from getting your daughter back. I'm recommending that in lieu of any legal actions against you, Celeste, you enter a rehabilitation program. That will give you time to get your body and your mind straight. Then you can make a reasonable decision about your baby."

Alice turned to Cherie. "You have the option of participating in a support group for relatives of addicts. I'm guessing you've been under a financial strain, as well."

Cherie wiped the tears from her face and nodded.

"If you take in your sister after she completes the program, the state may be able to assist you."

I cleared my throat to get attention. "Before this happened, Cherie and I talked about the possibility of her babysitting here. But I have an even better thought. She told me she dropped out of beautician's school in Portland to take care of Celeste. I'd like to pay for her schooling so she can graduate from there and get a good job."

"Let me make it clear that this would in no way be payment for Summer," interjected Brad.

"Right," I added. "It's just a way for me to thank you for taking care of Summer's mother."

Alice gave me a thoughtful look. "It's a generous gift to be sure. I think our staff would heartily approve. It will give Cherie a chance to maintain her independence, which we all would want for her."

"Yeah? Well, what about me?" Celeste said. "I want to be independent too."

Alice dismissed Celeste's words with a wave of her hand. "First things first. You'll learn all about that in the weeks ahead."

Celeste's chin jutted forward. "What if I don't want to go to rehab? Huh?"

"Do you want a life on the streets?" Brad asked quietly, giving her a piercing gaze. "You've seen what kind of loyalty you'd find." His voice softened. "I think you deserve much, much better."

Tears filled Celeste's eyes. She lowered her face.

I walked over to her and patted her back. "We want you to be well and happy."

Alice stood. "I think we have a good plan. Celeste, you're coming with me. I'll drop you off at the center." She turned to Cherie. "Follow me there. Afterward, you'll need to go home and bring Celeste's things to the center. Monday morning, we'll work out the details of her stay and what we can do to help you."

"Let me know about the school. Brad and I will see that you can get into their program," I added, relieved to have such quick, firm actions in place.

Alice came over and gave me a hug. "I want to get going

before any minds are changed," she whispered in my ear.

"Thank you," I whispered back to her. She'd done a fantastic job of making order out of painful chaos.

"We'll be in touch," said Brad, showing them to the door.

Standing outside, the two of us held hands. His fingers were as cold as mine as we watched their cars leave. We still had no idea if we'd be able to keep Summer.

Monday morning, Brad gave me a kiss good-bye before climbing into his Jeep.

I stood by feeling unusually unsteady about being on my own. After the confrontation with Celeste, I was still shaken by the thought of how easily we could lose Summer. Her future was in the hands of a young teenager who might not realize what losing her would do to us.

"I hate to leave you with so much hanging in the air," said Brad through the open car window beside him. "I'll come back as soon as I can. And maybe, this time, Mom will be with me."

"That would be nice. I'd love to see her. Perhaps, she can help out here. I have a board meeting coming up at the paper mill sometime soon."

He waved good-bye and pulled out of the driveway, leaving me to wonder what we could do to help convince Celeste that it would be best if her daughter became our child.

I went inside to more heartache. Gracie had her bags packed and was sitting at the kitchen table watching Kaylie in the swing. Summer sat in her infant seat on the floor beside the swing, watching its movement.

"Where's Courtney?" I asked. "She's taking you to the airport. Right?"

"Yes. She'll be right back. She went to her house to see if she can get a sample from Harry for the DNA test Brad wants to have run."

I couldn't hide my dismay. "I don't think that's what Brad had in mind. He probably wanted a sample voluntarily given." I shook my head and sank down in a chair next to Gracie. Turning to her, I said, "Have you any idea how much I'm going to miss you?"

Her eyes filled. "This has been a fabulous summer for me, Marissa. I've learned so much. Best of all, I've decided what I want to do for my career. My parents are so happy." Her lips curved. "My father, the politician that he is, says that if you ever need anything done for you in New York State, he'll handle it for you."

I smiled a bit sadly. "Wish he could do something for us here in the State of Maine."

Gracie nodded. "I do too."

I turned at the sound of Courtney running up the porch steps to the kitchen door.

At the look on her face, my insides shrank. "What happened?"

Tears spilled from Courtney's eyes. "I'm sorry. I'm sorry. I didn't know she was there. Oh, my God! She's gonna ruin everything."

Finding strength I didn't know I had, I rose and went to her. "Tell us what's going on."

She sniffled and drew in a shaky breath. "My mother usually goes to one of her meetings on Monday mornings. I was in Harry's room, trying to get a hair from his brush when my mother barged in and demanded to know what I was doing back at the house. I tried to make up something, but before I could, she grabbed the brush out of my hand."

The room began to spin. I gripped the table and waited for her to go on.

"And then Harry came into the room, yelling at me for

being there. Between the two of them screaming at me, I lost it and told them about Summer maybe being Harry's kid."

Courtney took a steadying breath. "All hell broke loose between my mother and Harry. I got out of there as fast as I could." She held up a small plastic bag. "But I got these—about six strands of hair. Maybe that will make up for me blabbing the news."

Gracie and I exchanged looks of anguish. I'd hope to avoid any contact with Eleanor Worthington regarding Harry and Summer. Now it was inevitable.

"Should I stay?" asked Gracie with concern.

"No, you'd better go or you'll miss your plane." I gave her a hug that couldn't begin to convey how much I wished she didn't have to leave. Forcing a calm demeanor— a calm I didn't feel— I watched her lift her suitcases.

Courtney knotted her hands together and gave me a hopeful look. "Maybe we can get the DNA test done right away. Wouldn't that make things easier?"

"We can only hope," I responded, feeling hopeless.

"I'll be back as soon as I can," said Courtney. She took a suitcase from Gracie's hand and lugged it out of the house, to her car.

I stood at the door, watching them pack the luggage in the car. After the girls finished loading up, they climbed into the car, and with a final wave, took off down the driveway. Watching the car pull away, I felt more alone than I had in years.

Summer started to cry. I checked the clock. It was time for her morning nap.

Kaylie watched from the swing as I picked up Summer. As I walked away, she began to whimper.

"One at a time," I said to Kaylie. "I'll be right back."

I raced up the stairs with Summer, checked her diaper

and laid her down in her crib. Yawning, she drew her stuffed lamb to her body and closed her eyes. Unlike her mother, she was an easy child.

Hurrying downstairs to Kaylie, I heard the phone ring. Thinking it might be important, I dashed into my office.

"Hello?" I said at the same time I noticed the call was from Eleanor Worthington. Too late to hang up, I said, "Yes?"

"I understand you have my granddaughter." Eleanor's voice was cold, demanding an answer I didn't want to face.

"That remains uncertain," I replied, unwilling to give her the benefit of the doubt when we had no proof.

"Nevertheless, I'd like to come over and see her."

"I'm sorry, Eleanor, she just went down for her nap. Perhaps another time?"

"Perhaps," she said icily, "you will call me when she awakens. I need to see her."

"I'll make arrangements with her case worker to meet with you. Under the circumstances, that's the best I can do, Eleanor."

"You little shit," she murmured before slamming down the phone.

Even if Harry proved to be the father, I'd fight her and everyone else to keep Summer from going to that household. The mere thought made me feel ill.

Kaylie let out a wail. Anxious for her not to disturb Summer's nap, I hurried to her.

"Okay, here I am, baby girl," I said, my words choking in my throat.

Carrying Kaylie upstairs, I decided to call Brad. I wasn't the lawyer in the family, but I thought it was time to get one. Summer had rights and so might we. Celeste had mentioned she hadn't wanted to place Summer with the Worthingtons. Neither did I.

As soon as I'd rocked Kaylie to the point of sleep, I laid her in her crib and tiptoed out of the room.

Brad was still on the road when he took my call. Quietly, he listened to what I had to say.

"Let me get some recommendations from Alice as to whom we should talk to. I'll get right back to you," he said grimly.

As I waited for his call, I busied myself getting Gracie's room ready for Ellen's visit. If she was going to stay with us for any length of time, it was the most comfortable guest room we had, with a small sitting area and a view of the water.

When Brad finally called back, it was with the news that Alice had already heard from Eleanor Worthington . "Alice is going to call you to make arrangements for Eleanor to pay you a visit. Probably this afternoon."

My heart sank. "It won't go well. She's already sworn at me."

"All right," said Brad. "I'm turning around and coming home. This is too important for me to miss."

"Thanks," I said. "I don't think I could handle her alone." She'd always undermined my self-confidence and this was a battle I couldn't lose.

"When I get home, I'll call one of the lawyers Alice suggested. After talking to Eleanor, Alice agrees we need legal representation."

After we hung up, I went upstairs and tiptoed into Summer's room and over to her crib. Gazing down at that little cherub sound asleep, I was glad she had no idea she was about to become the center of a terrible storm.

CHAPTER TWENTY-FIVE

When the phone rang, I clicked onto the call from the Office of Child and Family Services. I wished the problem with Eleanor would magically go away, but I knew it wouldn't, and our meetings would not be pleasant.

Alice's normally cheery hello held a tenseness I understood. "I think you know why I'm calling, Marissa. As I told Brad earlier, Eleanor Worthington's request to see Summer seems reasonable, considering her son was accused of being her father."

"Yes, Brad told me you were trying to set up a visit for this afternoon. If you don't mind, I'd rather not meet with her here."

"That's absolutely understandable. I suggest bringing Summer to my office. How does three o'clock sound?"

"Fine. Summer should be up from her nap by then." I took a deep breath but was unable to hold back my deepest fear. "No matter what happens, I wouldn't want Summer to live with the Worthingtons. I've heard and seen too much about life in that home to let her go there."

"One day at a time. One step at a time," Alice said in a voice I now found irritatingly calm. *Didn't she understand what I was going through?*

"Take a deep breath, Marissa," Alice said. "We're here to protect Summer's interest, along with her mother's."

"Thanks," I managed to get out. I felt like collapsing in a heap. "Is Celeste in the rehab program?"

"Yes," said Alice. "You know, I think she was a bit relieved that others were going to take care of her. She's only sixteen. Her life has been hard. Sometimes these programs have remarkable recoveries."

"I hope she's one of them," I said, wondering what her recovery might mean for Brad and me.

"I'm sorry, Marissa. I have to take another call. We can talk later," Alice said.

We said good-bye, and I clicked off the call. Sitting alone in the kitchen, I felt so lost, so afraid. What at first seemed a miracle with Summer's arrival was now turning into the nightmare I'd dreaded.

Seeing Brad's Jeep head down the driveway toward me, I burst into tears. His presence was so precious to me. I left the house and ran to greet him.

He stepped out of the car and met me with open arms. I rushed into them, letting all my emotions overflow in a tearful wail.

"Hey, what's this?" he said, lifting my tear-streaked face.

"I know I'm an emotional mess, but I can't bear the thought of losing Summer, especially if it means she's going to be around the Worthingtons. This whole thing is so unfair. Summer was given to us, not them."

"Whoa," said Brad. "Before worrying unnecessarily, let's see where all this is leading. We'll meet with Eleanor this afternoon. Then I'm guessing it will be a matter of waiting for DNA testing to be done and for Celeste to complete her program before any major decisions are made."

I drew a trembling breath. "You're right. Like everyone says, I should relax. But, Brad, this is so hard for me."

He put an arm around me. "Yeah, it's hard on all of us. How about making some lunch? I didn't take the time to stop."

"Sure. Come in. We don't have to meet with Eleanor until three. I didn't want Eleanor to come here, so we're meeting her at Alice's office."

"Good thinking. It's going to be hard enough having her live a few doors down from us."

With my hand in Brad's, I walked inside the house. I was more in control, but I had no idea how I'd be after our meeting with Eleanor.

In the kitchen, Courtney was supervising Kaylie's and Summer's lunch. They were almost finished. Kaylie was in her high chair, smearing applesauce all over her tray, playing happily. She looked up at Brad and me and smiled.

"Hello, little love," I said, going to her and kissing the top of her head, avoiding her dripping hands while inhaling the sweetness of the apples.

Summer was in her seat, gobbling down an organic fruit mixture from a squeeze pack I'd recently bought. I chuckled. She loved to eat.

I went over to her. "Guess who's here?" I pointed to Brad.

She turned to him and gave him a food-dripping smile.

He laughed. "That's my girl." He kissed both girls on the top of their heads, pausing an extra moment with Summer. We exchanged glances, and I knew he was thinking about her leaving us.

While Brad ate the sandwich I made him, I cleaned up Kaylie and put her down on the floor. She crawled over to the drawer where I kept plastic containers and wooden spoons especially for her and pulled them out. Lady went and lay down beneath the table at Brad's feet, watching warily as Kaylie pounded a spoon on the floor with a loud tap-tap.

As I did the dishes, Courtney cleaned up Summer and put her in the swing. Listening to the light music as her swing went back and forth, I hoped she'd get sleepy so we could put her down for an early nap. I wanted at least one of us to be well-rested for the visit at Alice's office.

Later, just before we were to leave for Alice's office, she called. "Instead of meeting at the office, I've arranged for us to get together at Dr. Smithson's office. She's one of the child psychologists we use. She has a small, private room where it will be easier to talk. And it's closer for you than Portland."

"That sounds good," I said. Whenever I'd been to the Office of Child and Family Services, it had been chaotic.

"Excellent." Alice gave me the directions and I hung up, feeling hopeful. Surely Eleanor wouldn't make a scene in the doctor's office.

A short while later, Brad and I said good-bye to Courtney and Kaylie and left the house with Summer. I'd put a bow in her hair and dressed her in one of my favorite outfits. With or without such "window dressing", she was a beautiful little girl.

The drive to Dr. Smithson's office was a silent one. I worked on preparing myself to be pleasant and helpful. Brad seemed as focused as I.

We pulled up to a small, yellow, wooden building that resembled a little country cottage. I admired it, thinking it wouldn't be as frightening to a child as a large, medical or office building.

Wishing I didn't have to, I removed Summer from her car seat and straightened her dress. In the parking area, I noticed Eleanor's Cadillac parked nearby. I followed Brad inside the building.

A gray-haired woman greeted us. "You're the Crawfords?" At our nods, the pleasant, grandmotherly woman rose. "I'll take you to the small conference room. They're waiting for you there." She led us down a short hallway to a room at the end of it.

Alice rose as we entered the conference room. "Thank you

for coming. I'm sorry to disturb your day."

Eleanor stood near the doorway, her eyes glued on Summer.

I tensed, wanting to turn around and run from the room.

Sensing my reaction, Brad put a hand around my shoulder and urged me forward.

A huge smile crossed Eleanor's face as she stared at Summer. She clapped her hands together. "Oh, she's wonderful! I see so much of Harry in her, it's remarkable."

I couldn't hide my surprise. "Really? I think she looks a lot like her mother."

Eleanor shook her head. "No, no. Those ears, the nose, the mouth—they're all like Harry." She held out her arms. "May I hold this little Worthington?"

At Alice's nod, I reluctantly handed Summer over to Eleanor.

Watching Eleanor caress Summer's ears and run her fingers over Summer's nose, I felt queasy.

"Why don't we all take a seat?" said Alice in her usual calm manner.

I sat at the table in the chair closest to Eleanor and next to Brad. Facing Alice, we were lined up like three children sitting in front of the principal.

"Before you arrived, Eleanor and I discussed the situation," said Alice. "I've explained to her that a DNA test will be done on Harry to determine if he is indeed the father."

"Humph, that won't be necessary," sniffed Eleanor. "Just look at this child! She's her daddy's girl, all right."

"If she is," I said, working hard to keep my voice from trembling, "I don't see how Harry would be in any position to raise her alone."

"That wouldn't be a problem. I would do that until he was old enough to take over. I'd consider her my own." She gave

Summer a squeeze that made Summer's face crumple. She let out a wail.

I automatically held out my arms to take her.

Eleanor stiffened and pulled her away.

I glanced at Alice. "May I please take her now?" My words were forcibly calm, though my pulse had begun to race. Summer quieted, but she continued to keep a pleading gaze on me.

"Until a final outcome is determined for Summer, she's under our care and supervision," Brad said. "Isn't that correct, Alice?"

"Correct," said Alice. "But it's also reasonable for Eleanor to have supervised visits from time to time."

"Here at the office," said Brad in a tone that brooked no argument.

Alice bobbed her head. "That seems fair."

"But I only live a few doors away. I should be able to see my granddaughter more often than that." Eleanor's voice was an irritating whine.

"Those will be the rules for now," said Alice, and I appreciated her firmness. "My schedule is full. We'll all have to be flexible."

Summer held out her arms to me, and I took her.

"I've saved most of Courtney's sweet little dresses. They're going to fit Summer just fine. She has the same body build that Courtney had."

I hid my disbelief, unsure where Eleanor was going with all this emphasis on Summer's physique and her features. I didn't see the comparison myself.

Eleanor pulled out a photograph and handed it to me. "Here's Harry at nine months. Don't you think the resemblance is uncanny?"

This time, I couldn't hold back. "I'm sorry, but I don't."

"Of course, you don't," huffed Eleanor. "I wouldn't expect you to."

I handed the photograph to Brad. He looked at it and shrugged. "I can't tell."

Eleanor turned to Alice. "Well, I insist my rights be honored." She checked her watch. "And now, I have another twenty minutes with this baby."

Alice checked her watch and rose. "Don't worry, Marissa. We'll be right here. Why don't you and Brad go get a cup of coffee."

I glanced at Brad. He slowly got to his feet. "Okay, we'll see you in twenty minutes."

Wanting to cry, I handed Summer to Eleanor and turned to leave.

Brad put an arm around me and we left the room.

Outside the building, I climbed into the car and sank down into the passenger's seat, trying to sort out my feelings. The memory of Summer crying in Eleanor's arms haunted me.

Brad got in behind the wheel. "Where do you want to go?"

"Nowhere," I said. "I don't trust Eleanor. Something's going on with her. Summer doesn't look like Harry to me. Do they look the same to you?"

Brad shrugged his shoulders. "Sorry, but all small babies look mostly alike to me. Summer and Harry both have blue eyes and a small mouth, but that doesn't make her Harry's daughter."

"Can we urge Alice's office to rush the DNA test?"

Brad gave me a thoughtful look. "I might have a connection in New York. Next time I go there, I'll take a sample, if Harry is willing to give one."

"Courtney took hairs without his permission, but if he's willing to give us a sample on his own that might be very helpful. I just don't believe Summer's a Worthington. She doesn't look like Eleanor or Courtney. I don't know Harrison very well, but as I recall, he has very large features."

Brad reached for my hand. "We'll get through this, Marissa."

I bowed my head so he wouldn't see the tears welling in my eyes. He had a lot on his plate taking care of his father's estate and helping his mother. I didn't want to add to his difficulties.

When the twenty minutes were up, Brad and I got out of the car and went inside.

Summer's eyes lit up at the sight of me. She held out her arms. I hugged her to me.

"Once again, thank you for meeting us here," said Alice. "I'll let you know when the next meeting is to take place. Sorry, but I have to run." She picked up her things and made a hasty exit.

"Good-bye," I called to her and turned to leave.

Eleanor tapped me on the shoulder. She gave me a smile that didn't quite melt the ice in her voice. "Being neighbors, we can arrange our own meetings."

I shook my head. "I don't think so. We don't want it to be confusing for Summer."

Eleanor pressed her lips together. "We'll see about that. I have rights too."

Brad stepped between us. "A lot of things will be resolved over time. Until then, she's ours."

We all went out to the parking area.

As I was getting Summer settled into her seat, Eleanor opened the back door of her Cadillac. I was startled to see a baby's carseat inside. A shiver did a dance on my shoulders. Something was very wrong with this whole situation, but I didn't know how I could prove it.

CHAPTER TWENTY-SIX

When we drove into our driveway, I was surprised to see Courtney outside holding Kaylie in her arms and talking to her brother.

Harry shot us a startled look and took off, racing around the side of the house and out of sight.

"I wonder what he's doing here?" Brad asked as he parked the car.

I kept my eyes on Courtney as I got out of the car. She didn't seem particularly upset. Still, it didn't seem quite right.

She hurried over to me and stood by while I got Summer out of her car seat. Handing Summer over to Brad, I turned to her and took Kaylie in my arms.

"What was that all about?" I asked her.

Shaking her head, Courtney grimaced. "You won't believe it. My mother thinks that if Summer really is her granddaughter, it will improve things between her and my father. She was furious with Harry at first, but now she thinks it might be a wonderful thing if he really is the father."

"And what does Harry think?" asked Brad, hugging Summer to him.

Courtney let out a sigh. "He's really upset. He said it was one crazy party that night, but he's pretty sure he's not Summer's father. Even if he is, he wants no part of raising her. My father's been away, but Harry's scared stiff at what will happen to him when my father gets back home."

"I suspect the fact that Celeste doesn't want her raised by your family will have an impact on things," said Brad. He turned to me and then studied Courtney. "Let's try to keep things going smoothly here. Things will sort themselves out in time."

Courtney nodded. "Harry offered to give a sample for a DNA test. In fact, he cut a big lock of hair off his head and carefully put it inside a baggie, keeping it as safe as possible. Like I said, he's really upset about the whole thing."

"I can understand why," said Brad. "At his age, no one should have to take on the role of parent—something kids don't always think about when they're having unplanned sex."

"If it comes down to it, I think Harry will give away his rights whether my mother wants Summer or not."

I lifted my gaze hopefully to Brad.

He shook his head. "It might not mean much. We just have to wait to see what Celeste wants."

All the hope I'd felt evaporated in a cloud of gloom. There would be nothing simple about anyone's decision in this matter.

"C'mon," said Brad, giving me an encouraging smile. "Let's take these little girls inside."

Following Brad into the house, I lifted Kaylie's hand and kissed her fingers.

Brad left for New York promising to come home as soon as possible. I forced myself to forget the worries that had kept me up at night—worries about keeping Summer, worries I could do nothing about. He'd taken Harry's hair sample with him, but we'd have to wait for decisions about Summer's future until Celeste finished rehab. That could take a number of weeks.

As days went by, Courtney and I fell into a compatible routine with the girls. After witnessing the way she cuddled and played with them, I was pleased to see she genuinely seemed to love them. Though we worked well together, I wondered how I could continue with board meetings and other work at Rivers Papers without more help. And spoiled as I was, I wanted a cleaning service to take care of the large house that had proved to be more than I could handle. Courtney had never been trained to properly clean, and I was feeling exhausted by all the time the girls were taking.

I was mopping the kitchen floor when the ringing of the phone interrupted me. I washed off my hands and picked up my cell.

"Hi," said Alice. "Good news. Odelle is being released from her program. She's now available for baby care."

I let out a puff of breath. "What I really need is someone to keep this house clean. I haven't been able to do any work for the paper mill in weeks."

"Funny you should say that," said Alice. "Someone in the program told Odelle she should offer to do that, along with the baby care, for a whole lot more money—money she really needs. She was going to talk to you about it. Would that be of interest to you?"

"Is she good?"

Alice chuckled. "Apparently, she drove everyone at the center crazy, wanting to keep it tidy and clean. So I would guess she's probably very good."

"If she's willing to do both, that would be an answer to my prayers. When can I talk to her?"

"She's free today. I'll have her give you a call. If you two can make such an arrangement, that would give Odelle enough pay to stay in her apartment. Let me know what you decide."

We hung up, and my thoughts turned to Courtney. She'd promised to stay until Odelle or Becky took over, but if I was going to work on paper mill projects and continue to do online courses, I'd need her continued help with the two girls and Silas.

As I tried to decide what I'd do if she wanted to leave, I went back to mopping the floor.

When Odelle appeared at the kitchen door, I hurried over to her.

"Hi, there!" I said, pleased to see her. She looked fabulous. There was a new glow to her face and she'd lost some weight. But it was the little boy in her arms I wanted to see.

Odelle stepped inside.

I reached for Silas. "Hi, little guy," I murmured.

He looked up at me with those big brown eyes of his and then, magically, his lips curled into a smile.

Tears filled my eyes. I hugged him to me. "Oh, baby boy, I've missed you!"

Odelle looked on, beaming at the two of us. "He recognizes you!"

"He'd better," I teased. "Do you know how many really messy diapers of his I've changed?"

She laughed.

I held Silas up before me. His body dangled in my arms, exposing his long limbs. "I can't believe how much he's grown. It's amazing!"

A smile spread across Odelle's face. "Yeah, he's gonna be a big boy like his dad. Not short like me."

"Good thing. Tall and handsome."

We smiled together.

Courtney came over to us, carrying Summer. Kaylie crawled behind her like a puppy dog.

"Wow!" said Courtney. "Look at Silas! I can't believe it's

the same baby. He looks so big."

Odelle giggled softly and removed him from my arms. The love for him that shined in her eyes made her face beautiful.

I picked up Kaylie from the floor and turned so Odelle could see her. "This is Kaylie. She's about to become our little girl." I reached over and took hold of Summer's hand. "And, Odelle, do you remember Summer? She's still with us, thankfully."

"Yes, when I asked how many children you had now, Alice told me the situation."

I was happy I wouldn't have to explain the sensitive circumstances. "Would you like a cup of coffee before we talk business?" I asked Odelle and turned to Courtney.

Courtney shook her head. "No, thanks."

"Sounds good," said Odelle. She glanced around. "Where can I put Silas? In the swing?"

"Sure. Courtney can take the girls into the sunroom. We can keep an eye on him here."

"I'll go put Summer in the swing and be back for Kaylie," Courtney said helpfully.

I fixed two cups of coffee and sat down with Odelle at the kitchen table.

Pouring a package of sweetener into her coffee, Odelle stirred it around and around in her cup. Looking up, she gave me an impish grin. "I've lost some weight, but I can't give up a little sugar in my life."

I smiled and took a sip of coffee, letting the warm liquid slide down my throat, wondering how best to approach the situation. After speaking with Brad last night, I wanted to make sure we covered everything.

"Have you thought more about what you're able to do and how much you're asking for in salary? Brad wanted me to let you know we'll take out social security from your pay. Later, if it all works out and he sets up his practice like he wants, he might be able to put you on his business insurance program."

Odelle's eyes, so like her son's, brightened. "That would be huge."

"Yes, I agree. He's looking into setting up a new practice here in Maine, so it may take time for that to happen."

We talked about other small details, and then I waited for Odelle to state her price. I was surprised at the hefty sum but pleased that she valued her work. Dealing with personnel issues at the mill, I'd learned how important that was.

We made the deal.

Afterward, I gathered up Silas and walked Odelle through the house, room by room, explaining what Becky usually did. Though Becky liked to cook, Odelle would do child care instead. In Becky's absence, I was beginning to enjoy cooking. When I wasn't too tired to come up with something new, I thought of it as a creative outlet.

We agreed Silas should sleep in his own room and set up a port-a-crib in a guest room with a blue décor. Odelle fed him and put him down for his morning nap.

It felt good to have that little boy back in my household. I'd learned so much from taking care of him. I'd realized how a mother's activities during pregnancy could affect her baby and how many babies needed special care because of it. Having grown up with an alcoholic mother and an abusive step-father, I myself was careful around alcohol and had never even tried drugs. For most of my life, I'd seen the ugly side of it.

Over the next few days, Odelle easily fit into her own routine. As I'd done with Becky, I turned the house over to her. Between Courtney's help and Odelle's supervision, I was soon able to get back to work in my office. But when the babies were awake, I tried to spend as much time with them as possible. They were all growing so fast.

I tried not to think of Summer leaving. At the same time, I was embracing the joyful thought that Kaylie was about to become our own. She was a bright little girl with a growing sense of confidence. With it, came an adorable sense of playfulness. Observing her, I felt as if she'd blossomed from a recalcitrant rosebud into a spectacular blooming flower. She now called me mama, which gave me a joy I'd never known.

Summer watched Kaylie's every move, trying to imitate everything she did. One day, playing with Kaylie, she looked up at me and said, "Maaa".

I knelt beside her. "What did you say?"

"Maaa!"

I hugged her to me and burst into tears. Wiping the moisture away, I chided myself for being so emotional lately, but I couldn't seem to shrug off any little thing.

Brad called later to say he and Ellen were going to head to Maine the next day. I grinned at the excitement I heard in his voice. It almost matched my own. It would be wonderful to have my husband home beside me as we continued to go through so much turmoil.

"I can't wait to see you!" I gushed. "The girls are growing fast. Wait until you see Silas. He's one big boy."

"Yeah, I'll be happy to get home. Things are more or less settled here—nothing I can't take care of from Maine for a while."

"How's Ellen?" I hadn't been able to talk to her for a couple of days.

Brad hesitated. "Dad's death, the quick move—it's all taken a toll on her. That's one reason I decided not to wait any longer to come home. I think a visit to Maine might lift her spirits."

"Her room is all ready for her. And tell her we can't wait to see her."

"Thanks, I will. Mom will be happy to hear it," Brad said. "There's nothing new on the home front with the girls?"

"No. Alice has been too busy to set up another meeting with Eleanor, so I haven't had to deal with that. The girls love Odelle. I can't tell you what a difference it makes to have her here with us."

"Glad to hear it. Gotta go. Love you, woman. When I get there, I'm going to show you exactly how much!"

I laughed. "Love you, man! Come on home!"

Going into my office, I took a seat, deep in thought. I really didn't want to make the call, but I knew, with Ellen in her fragile condition, it was the right thing to do.

When I finally got hold of Samantha, she was very understanding. "Of course, I'll come to the board meeting next week in your place. We can't let Ted think motherhood is a way to eliminate us from serving on the board at Rivers Papers. He doesn't understand all the things we do. He wouldn't get it, even if he were a mother himself."

We laughed at that idea.

After chatting with her for a while longer, I hung up the phone, feeling more comfortable about neglecting my duties at the mill lately. Sam and Allison were more than cousins; they were the sisters I'd never had.

"I think your man is here!" said Odelle, looking out through the kitchen window.

Grinning happily, I wiped the flour off my hands onto the kitchen cloth and hurried outside.

A little red convertible was making its way down the driveway, followed by Brad's Jeep.

Brad waved from the open window of the little car and pulled it up next to me. "What do you think of this?"

I laughed at the little boy excitement on his face. "It's perfect for you."

While he unfolded himself from the car and stepped onto the driveway, I hurried to greet Ellen, who'd been driving Brad's Jeep.

"Hi! Welcome back to Maine!" I enfolded her in my arms, noting a new thinness. Pulling back, I studied her. Dark circles ringed her eyes. There was a hollowness to her cheeks that hadn't been there before Jim's death. My heart went out to her.

I took hold of her elbow and led her toward the house. "Wait until you see the girls and Silas. You won't believe how much he's grown since you held him last."

Brad stopped us.

"Isn't this cool?" he said, indicating the car with a sweep of his hand. "Dad bought this 2000 SLK recently. Sort of a toy for him."

Ellen's eyes moistened as she smiled at me. "Jim was so proud of it. I'm glad Brad decided to keep it."

"Yes, that's nice. I'm sure Brad will have fun with it."

He gave me a kiss and said, "Later, I'll find a place in the garage for it. Now, I want to see the kids."

Odelle greeted us at the door holding Kaylie. "Someone wants to see her Grandmother." She grinned at Ellen. "Hi, I'm Odelle."

"And this is Ellen Crawford," I added quickly. "Better known, perhaps, as Grammy, the name Ellen has chosen for herself."

Ellen said hello to Odelle, and reached for Kaylie. I watched anxiously, wondering if Kaylie would make a fuss at being in a stranger's arms. She stared at Ellen for a moment and then patted Ellen's cheek as if to say hello.

Ellen and I smiled at each other, and I relaxed.

Brad leaned over and gave Kaylie a kiss on her head, then straightened. "Where are the other two?"

"Outside on the porch with Courtney. We've set up both swings there so they can get lots of fresh air," said Odelle.

Brad and I headed to the front of the house. Before we reached the screen door leading to the porch, I heard angry voices. I pulled Brad to a halt and held a finger to my lips. Tiptoeing toward the door, I strained to listen.

"I want you to bring Summer to me," said a voice I recognized as Eleanor's. "It's not enough to simply hold her."

Tensing, I waited for Courtney's reply. "You know I can't do that, Mother. I work for the Crawfords. You have to make arrangements with Alice. Marissa told me all about it."

"You ungrateful child!" said Eleanor in a harsh whisper. "After all I've done for you, you owe me."

"I don't owe you this," said Courtney.

At the trembling in her voice, I heard how hard it was for Courtney to defy her mother.

When Brad and I opened the screen door, the squeak of its hinges sent a warning.

Eleanor shot to her feet and quickly handed Summer back to Courtney.

"What are you doing here, Eleanor?" Brad's voice was calm, but I knew him well enough to know how angry he was. He gathered Summer into his arms protectively.

Eleanor lifted her chin and stared at him defiantly. "I'm here to see my granddaughter."

"You know as well as I do it may be proved that she's not your granddaughter. You think she looks exactly like Harry. I don't think so. And neither does Alice nor Marissa." Brad's voice tightened. "We're trying our best to be understanding, but finding you here with her is not acceptable."

"I'm sorry," said Courtney, coming to stand by me. "I tried to get her to leave."

Eleanor gave Courtney such a venomous look, I shuddered. No wonder she was afraid of her mother.

"I knew the moment you moved into this house, you were going to be trouble," snarled Eleanor to me. "You're a...a nobody!"

"Don't ever talk to my wife that way!" Brad stood directly in front of her and pointed a finger to the lawn. "Leave now, Eleanor. Don't make it more difficult than it is."

She shifted away from him and walked down the porch steps. Turning back to us, she said, "This isn't over. And when Summer is declared mine, you will never be allowed to be near her. Never! Never!"

She turned, walked across the grass, and headed down the beach away from us.

In the silence that followed, Courtney gave us an apologetic look. "My mother needs help. She's becoming delusional. I don't think Summer looks like Harry, either. But she thinks having Summer is going to bring the family together. I tried to tell her it's too late. My father is sending Harry to a military school and he wants a divorce." She let out a snort of disgust. "He told me he's waiting for the right moment to tell her. As if that's going to happen in our household."

Brad and I exchanged silent looks of concern. Eleanor had the makings of a woman about to become undone.

I decided not to let Summer out of my sight.

CHAPTER TWENTY-SEVEN

With Kaylie in her arms, Ellen joined us on the porch. Her eyes lit when she saw Summer in Brad's arms. She went over to them and kissed Summer's cheek. "Hi, precious girl!"

Ellen noticed Silas in the swing and, grinning, went over to him. "My, what a big boy!" She turned back to me. "I can't believe how much he's grown!"

Seeing the sadness fade from Ellen's eyes when she was with the children, I was delighted. I hoped this visit would be good for her.

I smiled. "We figure he's going to be tall. Odelle says he's like his father that way."

Brad put Summer back in her swing. "I'll go get the suitcases."

"If you'd like to unpack and get settled, I'll take Kaylie," Courtney said to Ellen.

Ellen handed Kaylie to her. I was touched by her reluctance to do so.

I led Ellen up to her room in the corner of the house, overlooking the lawn and the big maple tree that had been dubbed The Talking Tree in my mother's day. Beyond, the water moved rhythmically. Originally my mother's room, then mine for a short while, I'd changed the décor from a girlish pink to a soothing pale gray-green. The four-poster bed was gone. In its place was a king bed that fit nicely in the large room. A matching bureau hugged a wall. I'd replaced the rocking chair with an overstuffed chair and footstool, which sat by the small fireplace. With its cozy warmth, the room had become a favorite room of guests.

"This is so lovely," Ellen exclaimed as she looked around the room and sank into the chair. She leaned over and sniffed the fresh flowers I'd placed in a vase on the table next to the chair. "Thank you for making me feel so welcome."

"Would you like help unpacking?" I asked.

Ellen shook her head. "Thanks anyway, I'll do it myself." She gave me an apologetic look. "I brought a lot of things because I didn't know how long I'd be staying."

I hugged her. "Stay as long as you want, Ellen." I chuckled. "I should say, stay as long as you can stand all the confusion around here."

She smiled, "It's such a change in this house with the babies here, but it's good."

It *was* wonderful. The elegant house had become a lived-in home.

I thought of what the house had been like when my grandmother and her companion had lived here—two old women with a horrible history between them. The sound of babies echoing in the house had chased those ghosts away permanently, I hoped.

I left Ellen and went into my bedroom where Brad was unpacking his suitcase.

He grinned at me. "Never did get to say hello properly." Drawing me into his arms, he gave me a lingering kiss.

I inched closer to him, wanting him, needing him.

He quickly responded.

I marveled at the instant chemistry between us. It had always been there.

When we pulled our lips apart, I lay my head against his chest, listening to the rapid beat of his heart. I took a few calming breaths. Not many months ago, a greeting like that would have us in bed, making up for lost moments. Now all I could do was sigh. To make love, we'd have to steal a few quiet moments in the night—if I was still awake. Sweet talk had become baby talk.

As I descended the stairs, Odelle waved me over. "While you were upstairs, your cell rang. I didn't answer it, but I heard the signal for a message. You might want to check it."

"Thanks." I was waiting for a call from Alice. The judge was to have signed the paperwork for Kaylie's adoption. I'd been keeping that information to myself as a surprise for Brad.

The message was from Samantha, asking me to give her a call.

Disappointed not to hear from Alice, I punched in Sam's number. She picked up right away.

"What's up?" I asked, hearing the sounds of her children in the background.

"Hang on! I'll go to another room."

I waited, imagining her life was as busy as mine.

"You there?" she asked. "I got a call from Jake Weatherbee at the mill. The board meeting next week has been postponed for a few weeks. So Allie and I have decided we'll both come and then have a family reunion at my mother's house. Mark it down on your calendar. It's about time we got the families together again."

"That sounds wonderful." This time, I'd have my own family.

"Any reason the board meeting was postponed?" I asked her.

Samantha's laugh was edgy. "You won't believe it. Ted Beers is getting married and taking a long honeymoon."

Stunned by the news, I sank down into my office chair. "You've got to be kidding me! Who's the unlucky girl?"

"Someone named Therese Houghton. Jake told me he's

met her and she's a real ball buster."

A laugh rolled out of me. Samantha joined in. It couldn't happen to a better man.

"I was curious about her so I looked her up on the internet," said Samantha. "She's an only child in a wealthy family. She's young and beautiful, but I swear in every picture I saw of her, she was pouting."

I grinned. "Perfect." Ted deserved someone like that.

There was a sound of crying in the background. "Guess I better go," Sam said. "The twins are fighting. Allie and I will send details as we get them worked out. I can't wait to see you and those babies!"

"It should be a lot of fun!"

I disconnected the call and sat a moment, realizing how fast things change. By the time Sam and Allie and I were together again, my life should be more settled. I certainly hoped so.

As I rose to leave the office, my cell rang. Alice.

I quickly clicked on the call. "Hello?" I crossed my fingers for good news.

"Just wanted you to know, it's official," said Alice. "Kaylie's yours. I've got all the papers for your records here. I'll bring them out sometime later this week when we set up another meeting with Eleanor."

"Thank you! Thank you! We're so thrilled to have Kaylie. But, Alice, I need to talk to you about something." I got up and quietly shut the office door. Then I told her of my fears concerning Eleanor.

Alice listened to me and said, "It may be that the state will have to step in and forbid such meetings with Summer until Eleanor gets help. It's a very tricky situation. My personal opinion is that the family should intervene and insist that she gets the help she needs."

"That's just it. The family is in turmoil. Harry is being sent away to military school and, according to Courtney, her father wants to divorce her mother. Actually, I feel sorry for Eleanor. Still, I don't want her alone with Summer."

"It's understandable. Let's see where the next few days lead us. In the meantime, enjoy being Kaylie's official parents. She's one lucky little girl."

We ended the call. I fell back against my chair, clasped my hands together and whispered, "Thank you" to the heavens above. Then, holding back excited screams, I hurried into the kitchen, feeling as if I were flying. "Quick! Where's Brad?"

Startled, Odelle looked up at me from fixing a baby bottle. "He's on the porch with his mother, Courtney, and the babies. I'm getting ready to feed Silas."

"Hurry and join us! Happy news!"

I dashed through the house, slammed the screen door behind me, and stepped onto the porch. Brad was rocking Silas. Ellen was sitting on the porch steps, holding Summer. Courtney was sitting on a blanket on the lawn with Kaylie, helping her stack plastic rings on a short post.

I rushed over to Brad and gave him a kiss.

"We just got the call. Kaylie's ours! She's really ours!"

Brad's face flushed with emotion, then a huge smile spread across his face. "Here! Take him!"

He handed me Silas and rose from the chair. He rushed down the porch stairs to Kaylie. Lifting her into his arms, he tossed her up in the air.

She shrieked with delight.

"You're ours, Baby Girl!" he said, tossing her in the air again.

He caught her and hugged her to him.

Watching him, tears came to my eyes. He was a natural

father. It didn't matter that Kaylie wasn't ours by blood; she was ours by heart.

I sat down on the steps beside Ellen and put an arm around her. "It's official. You're Grammy now."

She wiped her eyes. "It's wonderful!"

"This calls for a celebration," said Brad, joining us. "I've been saving a bottle of bubbly for just this occasion."

Odelle appeared and beamed at us. "Congratulations! Great news!"

"Yes, it is. I'll get out the champagne glasses and we can each toast Kaylie." I handed Silas to her and went inside to the dining room. Opening the sideboard I removed five delicate champagne tulips. Beautifully etched, they'd been my grandmother's.

I carried them carefully into the kitchen to be washed.

As I placed the clean glasses on a tray, I felt a strong sense of family. I didn't know for what occasions they'd been used in the past, but I knew none would equal the joy of today's celebration.

I carried the tray of glasses onto the porch and set it down on a table.

Brad stood by, waiting for me with a chilled bottle of champagne. With a flourish, he uncorked the bottle correctly, so it made only a soft pop.

From her place on Ellen's nap, Kaylie watched our every move. I had the uncanny notion she knew the celebration was in her honor.

Brad poured a small amount of bubbly liquid into each glass. I handed them out, warning Courtney that this was a special occasion and we wouldn't be offering alcohol on a regular basis. Odelle opted for water.

When we'd all been served, Brad lifted his glass in a toast. "To Kaylie, our...daughter." He cleared his throat. "May she have a full, happy, and healthy life!"

"We love you, Baby Girl!" I added, before taking a tiny sip. The cool liquid bubbled in my mouth. My heart bubbled with joy.

I looked at the people around me. Only Ellen and Brad had been known to me a few months ago. Courtney and Odelle and all three babies had entered my life in ways I hadn't thought possible back then.

My gaze rested on Summer. If only I knew what the future held for her.

Brad spent most of the next days away from the house investigating how best and where to set up his new law practice. At home, Ellen spent a lot of time alone in her room or walking the beach. I understood the grieving process and gave her all the space she needed.

Odelle continued to settle in. As she became more comfortable with us and our routines, her voice—a pleasant alto— filled the place with her singing. Her sense of fun was contagious.

I was busy in the kitchen one morning when Courtney approached me. "Can I talk to you about something? Privately?"

Surprised by the wariness in her voice, I said, "Sure. Let's go into my office."

I led her into my private space and lowered myself into my desk chair. Courtney sat in one of the leather chairs facing me.

"What is it, Courtney?" I asked gently, concerned by the troubled look she wore. Her blue eyes had turned gray. Her lips curved downward.

She took a trembling breath. "I need to take some time

off. This afternoon, my father and I are going to try to convince my mother she needs help. He's arranged for her to go into a rehab program in Connecticut. If all goes well, we'll take her there tomorrow."

"Is this part of the divorce agreement?" If so, I couldn't see Eleanor agreeing to it.

Courtney's eyes widened. "No! She has no idea my dad wants to ask for a divorce. I tried to tell him to keep that quiet until she's stronger." A gleam came to her eyes. "It may be that when's she stronger, she'll want to divorce him for all the fooling around he does." She let out a sigh. "It's all such a mess."

"Take whatever time you need, Courtney."

"That's not all." She gave me a pleading look. "May I live here while things get sorted out?" Her eyes welled. "I love it here with you and all the babies. It feels so safe, you know?"

I felt the sting of tears. As a child, I'd known very well how it was to feel unsafe. It was one of the reasons I'd already made up my mind about Courtney living here. It would be like taking in a foster child. And when circumstances were right, she'd leave.

"You can stay as long as you need," I told her, feeling protective toward her.

Courtney rose and gave me a hug, holding onto me longer than expected.

"It's going to be all right, Courtney," I murmured, patting her back. She quietly began to sob. Knowing she was in pain, I held her and let her cry.

She finally pulled away. "Thanks. I guess I needed that." She wiped her eyes and gave me a shaky smile.

"One day at a time. Remember?"

She nodded, and giving me a little wave, left the room.

Watching her go, I was reminded of how many times

Doris had taken me in. Maybe that's why, after learning to have faith in myself as a mother, the whole idea of fostering babies and children seemed so right to me.

I lifted the phone to call Brad. When I got hold of him, he sounded out of breath. "Hey, what's up?"

After I told him the situation with Courtney, he agreed Courtney could stay. "But, Marissa, we have to have enough time and space for some alone time together. It never seems to happen anymore."

"That only works if you're home," I teased. "We hardly ever see you."

"That's how it's going to be for a while," Brad said. "I tried to warn you. If I'm going to build a practice here, I have to get it set up and then fill it with clients."

Though I knew he was right, it didn't make it any easier to accept. There were times I needed him around. And I was beginning to feel stifled by the lack of time to myself. I'd been doing some reading online about stay-at-home mothers and the personal problems they encountered. I hoped with all the help I had, I could become more active in the Rivers Papers business. At one time reading through business reports had seemed boring—all those numbers and facts and figures— now, it made me seem part of a bigger world outside the walls of my chaotic home.

Odelle knocked on the door and peered into the office. "Can you watch Summer while I put Silas down for a nap? Ellen has taken Kaylie for a walk along the beach."

I grinned and got to my feet. "Sure."

This was, after all, life with babies. Wasn't it exactly what I said I wanted?

CHAPTER TWENTY-EIGHT

As I was reading in the sunroom, I heard sirens coming closer and closer. It was unusual for them to be in our neighborhood, especially after the summer people had gone home.

"That sounds pretty close," said Ellen, giving me a worried look.

A chill crossed my shoulders. I set my book down, got to my feet, and turned to Ellen. "I'll be right back."

I hurried to the kitchen and turned on the outside lights. I saw flashing red lights coming down the road toward the cluster of homes around me. Dread enveloped me.

"Lady, stay."

I slipped out the kitchen door and began running. I knew in my heart who was ill before the ambulance even headed down the Worthingtons' driveway. Heart pounding, I sprinted across the back yards of the three houses nearest mine.

Maude Miller met me outside the Worthingtons' home.

I grabbed hold of her elbow. "What happened?"

She shook her head. "I'm not sure. Harrison came home this afternoon. I saw Courtney outside talking to him. Since then, it's been quiet."

Together, we approached the ambulance. It was empty.

"Courtney told me they were going to do an intervention for Eleanor," I said. "I hope nothing went wrong."

Maude nudged me. "Here they come now."

Two EMTs lifted a stretcher down the back stairs. I strained to see who they were carrying.

Courtney emerged from the house, followed by Harrison. Seeing her, I let out a sigh of relief. She noticed me and ran over to my side.

"What happened?" I put an arm around her shivering shoulders.

"It's my mother. After our talk with her, Dad and I thought everything was fine. She ate dinner with us, then she said she was going upstairs to pack. She told us she wanted to go to bed early so she'd be ready for tomorrow." Courtney let out a shuddering sigh. "When I went in to say goodnight to her, I couldn't wake her up. I tried, but she didn't move."

"I'm so sorry," I murmured.

Courtney lifted a tear-streaked face to me. "Marissa, she tried to kill herself. What if I hadn't found her?"

"It's a good thing you were there or she might not have made it," I said honestly. "Maybe now, she'll be forced to see she needs help."

Harrison came over to Maude. Courtney and I listened as he spoke to her.

"They pumped her stomach. I'm told she'll live." He wrapped an arm around his daughter. "Thank God, Courtney found her and called 911. We didn't want anything like this to happen to Eleanor. Did we, hon?"

Courtney sniffled and shook her head.

"We should have pushed for help earlier," said Harrison. "I had no idea things had gotten so bad."

Maude and I exchanged glances. If Harrison had been home more, he might've known.

"I'll go to the hospital and stay with her." He looked at me. "You're Marissa, right?"

"Yes. Marissa Crawford," I answered.

"Courtney's staying with you. Why doesn't she go home with you now? She's had enough to deal with tonight and she's comfortable with you."

"Good idea. She knows she can stay with me for as long as necessary."

"Is there anything I can do?" asked Maude.

Harrison shook his head. "At the moment, I can't think of anything. Once Eleanor recovers from this, I'll make sure she enters the rehab program she agreed earlier to attend. This time, we'll take her directly there. They have excellent counseling at the center—counseling I've tried to get her into for years."

Standing there, talking about his wife like that, I realized he was a lonely man. I turned to go.

Harrison held me back. "One more thing. That baby you have, Summer, do you really think she's Harry's?"

"No, I don't. I don't see any common features. DNA tests will provide the answer, of course. We're waiting to hear the results." I hesitated, wondering how much to say, then I blurted out, "It was a dream of Eleanor's that Summer was Harry's child, that as her grandparents, you two would become closer."

Harrison shook his head. "My God! She's crazier than I thought."

"Some women find the idea of having her children gone from home overwhelming," said Maude sympathetically. "Maybe that's how she felt—too lonely to cope."

There was a moment of silence, then, Harrison said, "Whatever the reason, we're going to get help for Eleanor. She deserves that."

"Maybe then she will go back to being the mother I used to know—the nice one," said Courtney woefully.

Harrison's forehead creased with worry. "Maybe," he said in such a hesitant way I knew he didn't believe it.

A man wearing a white EMT shirt approached Harrison.

"You can follow us into Portland."

Harrison gave Courtney a quick hug. "I'll be in touch. Don't call Harry until we know how things are working out."

"Text me as soon as you can," said Courtney.

He nodded and walked toward his car.

I wrapped my arm around Courtney's shoulder. "Let's go home."

She gave Maude a hug and allowed me to lead her to Briar Cliff. As we approached, the light by the back door sent a comforting beam of light into the dark, like a hand outstretched to greet us. I gave Courtney an encouraging pat on the back.

Brad arrived home a short while later. I filled him in with the news of Eleanor's attempted suicide.

He shook his head. "It's too bad. I heard someone at the Kiwanis meeting say something about it. Apparently, a friend of this man works at the hospital. But hearing it from you makes it all too real. How's Courtney holding up?"

"She's a bit of a mess. She and Ellen sat and talked on the porch for a while and then they took a walk on the beach before she went up to bed. But it's a frightful thing to see someone like that. She's finding it difficult to deal with."

"Mom will be a big help to her," said Brad. "I hate to admit it, but I'm glad the threat of Eleanor stealing Summer away is over. I doubt she'll be out of that facility for some time."

"I know." I looped my arm through his. "Let's go to bed ourselves. The girls get up early."

We turned off the lights downstairs and climbed the stairway.

Upstairs, I tapped on Courtney's door. Not hearing an answer, I cracked it open. The bedside lamp was on, making it easy to see the tears still wet on Courtney's face. The sound of soft snoring met my ears.

I quietly closed her door. For all the material things she had, Courtney lacked the one thing all kids needed—a stable, loving home.

I arose early and tiptoed downstairs, eager to have a few moments to myself. With all that was going on around me, I felt as if I was constantly riding a roller coaster, my emotions creeping high and swooping quickly to low. Though I was exhausted from lack of sleep and sheer fatigue, I now knew a mother had no time to baby herself—she had to keep a steady hand on her household.

Going into the kitchen to fix a cup of coffee, I came to a surprised stop. "Good morning, Ellen. What are you doing up so early?"

She smiled. "Hi, Marissa. I couldn't sleep, so I thought I'd get up and see the sunrise this morning."

"Want to join me out on the porch?" I said. "It's my favorite place to see one."

"That would be nice."

As I got my coffee, Lady came over to me and nudged my leg. I bent over to rub her head and straightened, feeling a little dizzy. The feeling quickly passed. I told myself I had to do a better job of eating. I grabbed a couple of saltines from the cupboard before walking out to the porch with Ellen.

We each chose one of the rockers and sat quietly. The slow, gentle movement of the water and the brightening skies calmed my racing thoughts.

"Thank you for spending some time with Courtney last night," I said to Ellen. "She really needed that attention."

Ellen smiled at me. "Actually, it was good for both of us. After talking for a little while on the porch, we walked along the beach and discussed many things. Life can be so confusing for someone her age in that type of home environment." She gave me a steady look.

"Yes, it's taken me years to figure out a lot of stuff about myself and others."

"The strange thing is, when we talk to others about them, we can resolve things about ourselves. That's exactly what happened to me last night," said Ellen.

I straightened in my chair and turned to her. "It did?"

"After knowing Courtney's mother tried to take her life, I've done a lot of thinking. I miss Jim terribly, of course, but I realize more than ever that life is short and I should live it fully. Although I'm alone, I should go ahead and do some of the things Jim and I talked about."

"You mean you want to come to Maine? Right?" I prayed it was true.

Ellen chuckled softly. "Don't look so worried, dear girl. Yes, I want to live here in Maine close to you and Brad and those babies." Her expression turned to one of concern. "You understand I won't intrude, don't you?"

"Oh, Ellen, I want you to intrude like a real mother would!" I exclaimed, and then laughed at how awful that sounded. "You know what I mean, don't you?"

She smiled warmly at me. "Thank you, Marissa, for wanting me here. It means so much to me. I'd like to start looking at real estate right away. Then I won't be a burden on Doris."

"What about Doris? If you leave New York, will she be all alone?" The thought made my stomach knot with sympathy.

Ellen grinned. "I have a feeling she'll want to come to Maine too. In fact, I intend to look at houses that have in-law suites or apartments attached to them. We'll see how it works out."

The thought of Ellen and Doris being nearby filled me

with joy. It meant adding to the rapidly growing family I called mine.

We sat in companionable silence and watched the gray sky turn a pale pink with the promise of another nice, autumn day. It had been unusually warm but after living in New Hope for a couple of years, I understood this summer-like weather was merely a seasonal tease. Autumn would soon settle into crisp days that would lead into winter.

From above us, through an open window, I heard a baby's cry.

"That's Kaylie. I'd better get her before she wakes the others." I took the last sip of coffee and got to my feet, content that another busy day was about to begin in the Crawford household.

I hurried up the stairs and into Kaylie's room. She stood inside her crib, waiting for me. Seeing how tall she'd grown, how nicely she'd filled out, I filled with pride. I loved best of all the happy smile that crossed her face at the sight of me.

"Good morning, Miss Sunshine," I said, picking her up in my arms.

"Mama." She laid her head on my shoulder. I rocked her back and forth in my arms. Once she'd gotten used to a lot of physical contacts, Kaylie had become a real cuddler. I laid her down on the changing table and swept a hand through her dark hair, which had become tangled from sleep. She gazed up at me with dark brown eyes which seemed to see so much.

"Sweet baby," I whispered. "That's what you are—a sweet baby."

Her whole face lit up. She kicked her feet happily, and I felt sure she understood exactly what I'd said. As she continued to kick and squirm, I worked quickly to exchange her wet diaper for a dry one.

As we were leaving Kaylie's room, Brad came down the

hallway carrying Summer. "Here's another one."

I kissed Summer on her pink cheek. "Hi, Baby! Love you!"

She smiled and grabbed a lock of my hair. Laughing, I freed myself. "I've got to get my hair cut!"

Brad followed me down the stairs and into the kitchen. Even though they still took bottles, we'd lined two highchairs for the girls against the wall of the eating area. Summer loved eating with Kaylie. Sitting next to each other, the two of them looked adorable—one blond-haired, blue-eyed baby; the other, a combination of browns.

Summer was growing well and was now able to sit up comfortably for long periods of time. It wouldn't be long before she started crawling. It was very cute to see how she constantly watched Kaylie and tried to do everything she did.

Brad put Summer in her little seat and helped get Kaylie in the highchair, while I fixed Summer's bottle. When she was hungry, that little girl wanted her bottle in a hurry.

As Brad fed Summer, I gave Kaylie a slice of soft cheese to nibble on while I prepared a scrambled egg and toast for her. She'd graduated into foods with more substance and liked to eat by herself. I'd read the tactile experience was good for her, even if it made a mess.

Ellen joined us in the kitchen. "Good morning, Brad! It's going to be a beautiful day!"

At her chipper tone, his eyebrows lifted in surprise.

"Ellen's made some exciting decisions," I said to him.

Brad smiled at his mother. "Really? Let me grab a coffee and we can go out on the porch to talk. It's a lot quieter there."

He placed Summer in her highchair. "She gobbled down the bottle. I'll give her a teething biscuit to chew on."

"Thanks." As always, it was interesting to see how quickly Brad had adapted to fatherhood.

I was cleaning up the mess Summer and Kaylie had made

when Courtney appeared.

"Hi. How are you?" I said. "Were you able to get much sleep?"

She shook her head. "I had terrible nightmares. I probably will for a while."

"Aw, hon, I'm sorry. Is there anything I can do for you?"

Again, she shook her head. "After Odelle comes, I'm going to go to the hospital. I got a text from my father. He came home sometime late last night. I'll ride down there with him."

"Okay. I suggest you get something to eat. It might be a long day."

She smiled. "Thanks. I think I will."

Ellen came into the kitchen. "Can I help?"

I nodded. "Let's get the girls into the sunroom. They can play there for a while."

She picked up Kaylie, and I got Summer, and we carried them into the sunroom. Two swings edged a large square of a blanket that held a number of toys. We'd done our best at baby-proofing the room. The tables, which had once held attractive decorative pieces, were now bare. The fountain in the corner of the room, a favorite of my grandmother's, was temporarily turned off. It had proved too much of an attraction for Kaylie.

Ellen took a seat on one of the couches edging the blanket. "I'll watch them for a while. You go do what you need to."

I smiled. Maybe I'd have time to pop into the shower.

I left her and raced up the stairs. After Odelle came, I wanted to help Ellen with her research on real estate for sale.

When I reached the bathroom, the door was closed. Grinning, I opened it slowly. Brad was in the shower, shampooing his hair. I tossed my pajamas aside and stealthily walked into the open-entrance shower.

I reached my arms around his waist and hugged him. He

chuckled and whipped around.

"Playing games, are we?"

I laughed. "This might be the only way we have any time together."

He drew me into the warm water streaming down on him. Standing so close to him, feeling the water cover my body with warmth, desire flared inside me. Brad evidently felt the same way.

I held a finger to my lips. "We have to be quiet," I whispered.

His lips came down on mine. His kiss was sweet, lingering, hungry. But it wasn't enough for either of us.

He lifted me into his arms.

I wrapped my legs around him, taking him inside. We moved together in a familiar pattern known to all lovers. Sensation after sensation rolled through me, and I lost all sense of time and place.

When we finally stilled, I let out a soft sigh of satisfaction and gazed up into his face. He smiled at me and gently swept my hair away from my face.

With the water pouring down on us, he kissed me. "That's the best shower I've had in a long time."

"Too long a time," I said, standing and leaning against his strong body.

"Nice to meet you, Mrs. Crawford. We should do this again," he said teasingly. "Maybe tomorrow?"

I pushed at him playfully. "You'd better go."

Before leaving, he gave my derriere a pat. "Love you, woman."

With Odelle in charge and the babies down for morning naps, Ellen and I took off for the Coastal Real Estate office.

Though the main office was in Portland, a tiny branch office was located in New Hope. Mindy Snowden, one of their realtors, was a friend of Adrienne Hartwell's. I'd met her at the luncheon I'd attended with her and Samantha at the country club a few months ago. I'd liked her. After calling and telling her Ellen's circumstances, her sympathy made me like her even more.

From the passenger seat in my car, Ellen stared with interest at the properties along the coast-hugging road. "With the sale of the house, I should be able to move forward," she said, "but I don't want to jump into anything too quickly. As it is, people won't believe I'm doing this so soon after Jim's death."

"I agree. Take your time. You're welcome to stay with us for as long as you want. And I know Doris feels the same way about you staying with her."

Ellen gave me a thoughtful look. "I think Jim would want me to move ahead. We'd already talked about buying a little place here."

"Mindy is a good agent. Tell her exactly what you have in mind. I'm sure she'll come up with something—if not right away, sometime in the near future."

I pulled up to the small, clapboard building containing the real estate agency. It sat on the edge of the busy downtown area of New Hope. Painted gray and trimmed in white, it was classic in appearance except for the deep purple door that set it apart from the surrounding buildings.

We got out of the car and stood a moment. The trees lining the street had turned yellow—a precursor to the display of oranges and reds that would follow.

"Ready?" I said, hoping for a miracle. Property in this area didn't stay on the market for long.

Ellen grinned. "Let's do it!"

We entered a small room that held an old-fashioned wooden desk, a small Oriental rug, and four leather-covered chairs.

At the sound of us making our entrance, Mindy appeared. A tall, spare, woman dressed in a navy linen business suit, Mindy gave the appearance of a no-nonsense business woman. But the smile she gave us was warm and friendly.

"Hello again, Marissa. And you must be Ellen Crawford," she said, reaching out to shake Ellen's hand. "I was sorry to hear of your recent loss. I'm sure we can find something suitable for you. However, I'm certain you've been advised not to move too fast after such a sudden change in your circumstances."

Ellen visibly relaxed. "Yes, I don't want to rush into anything."

"Come into my office," Mindy said. "After talking to Marissa, I've come up with some properties you might be interested in."

Mindy's office was a larger version of the reception area. Ellen and I took seats in front of Mindy's large desk. A large-screen computer was set up there, facing us.

"I'll show you pictures of the properties and tell you a bit about them. We'll note what interests you and go from there."

Forty minutes later, Ellen and I climbed into Mindy's Cadillac. Sitting in the back, I listened to Ellen talk about what she was hoping for in the future. It pleased me that Brad and I would play a part in it. But I knew from past experience Ellen would need to have activities of her own. She'd been a leader in Barnham society and would need to find a new place in a new community.

We looked at properties that were too big or too small. Other properties were too old, too untended. Still, others were too contemporary, too cold.

Ellen sighed. "Do you have any other suggestions?"

Mindy shook her head. "Not at the moment. But I'll call you if I think of anything."

We'd just pulled away from an aging Victorian when Mindy suddenly slammed on her brakes. She turned to Ellen. "How would you feel about living in a recently built cottage on a summer estate? It's farther north, but it's in a lovely new area."

Ellen turned to me sitting in the backseat. "What do you think?"

I shrugged. "We've looked at everything else."

"Okay, let's take a look at it," said Ellen.

We drove along the beach road north of New Hope. Off to the right, on a hill overlooking the beach, a long road led into a tiny neighborhood of recently built cottages. A sign posted at the entrance to these homes indicated a company called Maine Line Development had done the work. A second sign read, "Welcome to Seaside Place".

A total of three, two-story homes were placed on sizeable lots. Each was distinctive in design. All had clapboard siding painted in earth tones, stone chimneys and plenty of windows.

"They're deceptively small from the outside," said Mindy. Two of them have master bedrooms on the first floor. All have modern kitchens with huge family rooms, dens, everything you've mentioned, Ellen. I don't know why I didn't think of this before."

We went inside a home and discovered finishing touches were still being done. I stayed in the kitchen, marveling at the kitchen appliances while Mindy took Ellen on a quick tour.

"What do you think?" I asked Ellen when they returned to the kitchen.

Ellen grinned. "If I can choose some of the finishes, I'm buying it. Mindy thinks there's going to be one more house, a smaller one, built on the last lot. That might be something Doris is interested in. Come see."

She took my elbow and led me outside. "The lot's over there." She indicated an area fairly close to the lot we were standing on. If Doris wants to buy the little house, we'd be neighbors and able to watch out for one another." Ellen's eyes lit with excitement. "Wouldn't that be wonderful? And I think Jim would be so pleased if he knew we were still close."

Grinning happily, I agreed it would be perfect. If, and it was a big 'if', Doris would leave her hometown and follow her sister-in-law to Maine.

CHAPTER TWENTY-NINE

Ellen and I returned to Briar Cliff mid-afternoon.

"Glad to see you," Odelle said, greeting us at the door with Kaylie. "All three babies are just getting up from their afternoon naps. Silas is upstairs crying and Summer is stirring."

While Ellen offered to take Kaylie from Odelle, I went to get Silas.

I eagerly climbed the stairs, glad for the opportunity to spend some time with him. Each baby had a separate room. When the time came to take in more children, it would be wonderful to have this much space.

Silas was lying on his side, looking out through the rungs of the crib's side when I entered his room. Seeing me, his eyes brightened.

"Hi, big boy," I said, lifting him out of the crib and giving him a hug. I pretended to nibble at his neck with little kisses. He kicked and squealed happily. When I sang a little song to him while changing his diaper, he made little noises as if he'd joined in.

"You're going to be musical," I said, laughing when he made another high-pitched sound. I marveled at the changes in him. Gone were the days when he'd been so fussy.

"C'mon, Silas, let's go eat," I said.

Hooked over my hip, he kicked and waved his hands, doing what I thought of as a hilarious pantomime of someone running.

Downstairs, the babies fussed and cried and cooed while

waiting for their meal. Odelle fixed Kaylie a sippy cup of milk and several snacks, while I gave Silas a bottle and Ellen fed Summer her bottle.

The scene was of domestic calm when Brad burst into the kitchen from outside. Courtney followed him. "Look who I found in Portland!"

Courtney gave me a weak smile. "He gave me a ride from the hospital."

Surprised, I said to Brad, "You went to see Eleanor?"

He shook his head. "Not exactly. I wanted to talk to Harrison. I got the DNA report back from my friend in New York."

I held my breath. "And?"

"And Harry is not the father." He glanced at Courtney and back to me. "I thought it only right that Harrison knows, considering the circumstances surrounding Eleanor."

"Now, maybe my mother will give up on that crazy idea of hers," said Courtney in a wobbly voice.

"Oh, hon, I hope it will help her sort through things," I said sympathetically. "But, Brad, what does it mean for Summer? Will the authorities go after the other boys at the party?"

He shook his head. "I don't think so. Celeste can't name anyone, and at this point, she probably won't want to take it any further. I put in a call to Alice. We'll know more about what Celeste wants to do in a couple of weeks."

My gaze turned to Summer. She was such a beautiful, bright baby, what mother wouldn't want her? My stomach, which had been acting up lately, tightened. Another emotional roller coaster ride.

"On another note, how did things go today?" Brad said to his mother.

She lifted Summer to her shoulder to burp her and

smiled. "I've found a place I want you to look at. If the price is right and I can choose some of the interior finishes, I would like to buy it. Marissa liked it."

"Liked it? I *loved* it! It's a new cottage built on one of the summer estates in Seaside Place," I explained to Brad. "And they're about to build a smaller one in the same little development. We think it would be perfect for Doris."

He laughed. "You two have it all figured out, huh?"

I grinned. "It would be so wonderful if she could join us too."

He glanced around the room. "If all this baby stuff continues, we'll need all the help we can get."

Courtney gave me an apologetic look. "This might be a bad time to tell you, but I'm leaving Maine for New York right away. My father and I have been talking more than we ever have. He wants me to get a job for a few months and then go back to school. I called Gracie. She and her roommate have enough room for me in their apartment. Sharing the space will help them with their expenses. So it's all sorta working out."

I studied her face. Her earlier innocence was gone. And though I saw sadness coating her features, I noticed a new inner strength behind it. I rose to my feet, shifting Silas to my hip, and gave her a squeeze. "I'm pleased for you. I really am."

"It's a good idea. I don't know what's going to happen to my parents. And Harry is okay with everything. He says he's glad to be away from all of it."

"Does he know he's not the father?" I said.

She grinned. "Yeah, Brad and I told him."

"He's one happy, relieved kid," said Brad. "I would be too."

"So now Summer's future rests with Celeste," I said, wondering how I could endure more of that kind of suspense for another couple of weeks.

#

Ellen's project with her new house redirected my attention away from Summer and my constant worrying about her future. Ellen and I spent hours looking at rug samples, wooden floor colors, and ideas for window treatments. We were trying to come up with an overall color scheme that would coordinate with the furniture Ellen intended to keep. She had a couple of lovely old pieces of furniture and other items that were too sentimental to her to sell or give away.

More than once, we traveled to the outlet shops on Route 1, looking at everything from kitchen items to glassware and crystal. And, of course, we did a little clothes shopping there as well.

Those trips with her were spiritual journeys for me. Ellen and I had become so close, I knew now what it must feel like to have a mother with whom a woman like me could do simple, fun things. I vowed to be the same sort of mother to Kaylie and prayed I'd have the chance to be a real mother to Summer too.

While we were happily pulling things together for Ellen, getting Doris to commit to the idea of moving away from long-time friends into an entirely new area proved to be harder than either Ellen or I had thought. Finally, Doris agreed to come take a look.

When Brad left Maine to check on things in New York, he promised to return with Doris.

Seeing him off, I stood in the driveway with Kaylie, clutching one of her hands, waving it up and down to say good-bye.

"Bye, bye, Daddy," I coaxed her to say.

"Da."

I gave her a squeeze and headed toward the house. Courtney was inside, packing up to leave for the city. I'd miss her like crazy. She'd turned out to be a big help to me. But with Becky and Henry due to return, and Odelle working full-time, the timing couldn't be better.

Becky's upcoming return made me a little nervous. I wondered how she would feel when I told her Odelle had taken over the care of the house and would continue to do so. Becky would, no doubt, consider it an insult. But it eased my conscience to know that Odelle, young and energetic, would carry on with those duties.

As I entered the kitchen, Courtney was pulling her suitcase behind her, heading for the door. No one else was in the kitchen.

"All set?" I asked.

Her eyes moistened. "As ready as I'll ever be. I've said good-bye to everyone else." She dropped the handle to her suitcase and gave me a hard hug. "Thanks so much for everything, Marissa. It's been the best and worst summer of my life." She straightened and covered her mouth with her hand. "Oh, I didn't mean it quite like that. You've been the best part. That's what I meant by it."

I smiled. "You've helped make my summer the best, too. I really appreciated all your help, especially after Gracie was gone. It was pretty much just the two of us for a while."

"I'll miss everyone." Courtney took hold of one of Kaylie's hands and shook it gently, sadly. "Good-bye, baby girl." Turning, Courtney picked up the handle of her suitcase and rolled it toward the door.

I hurried to hold the door open for her, then I followed her outside and walked her to her car.

"Keep in touch," I told her, as she lifted the suitcase into the car. She straightened and turned to me. "Dad says he's going to sell the house, so I don't know if or when I'll see you again." Tears spilled onto her cheeks.

I tried for a bright note. "I bet you and Gracie end up here for at least a visit. You know you're always welcome here."

She wiped her eyes. "Thanks. I'm going now. Goodbye."

She got into the car and started up the engine.

Kaylie and I stood aside and watched as she turned the car around and pull away from us.

"Wave bye-bye," I said to Kaylie.

She lifted her hand. "Bah."

I chuckled as she continued saying it, though my heart was sad. The summer had been full of so many surprises, so many heartaches.

The family reunion rapidly approached. Though Sam and Allie's mother Adrienne agreed to host a big dinner at her house, I invited everyone for a family picnic luncheon.

Ellen offered to provide decorations and tableware for the party. I immediately took her up on it. With Samantha's three toddlers and Allison's two children, I had no illusions about how hectic it would be. Ellen's help would be enormous. As Odelle helped with the kids, I'd be busy in the kitchen. Hopefully, Becky would be back by then, so she and I could work together on the meal.

Thinking of Becky's return, I grinned. We'd received several postcards from exotic ports filled with news of all they'd seen. But in each one, Becky had written that she couldn't wait to see us again. We hadn't heard a word from Henry, but Becky had told us he was loving all of it. Becky had written that quiet, taciturn Henry had even taken to dancing. I couldn't wait to have them back.

Brad called from New York to say he would be delayed in

returning to Maine. "Doris has decided to put her house on the market to see how fast it would sell before making any decisions about moving."

Though I was happy with the idea that Doris was serious about coming to Maine, it saddened me to think of her Cape Cod house leaving her hands. It was a darling house, filled with her love and special attention. To me, it symbolized all the good I'd had in my life growing up. Even as an adult, I'd loved spending time there.

"How is your lawyer friend doing, setting up the office in Barnham?" I asked.

"He's holding a reception for me tomorrow, inviting all of our old clients to meet him and to say good-bye to me. It's a real nice gesture on his part."

"A smart business move, too. Are you going to miss it, Brad?"

"I'll miss the people, but like I told Dad before he died, I want to be home with you and our family. So, no, I won't miss it for those reasons."

"Good." It had been a big decision for Brad to move to Maine to begin our marriage here at Briar Cliff, where my responsibilities lay. I'd always been grateful to him for that. Now, with a child, maybe two, he had even more reason to be here.

I awoke to the sound of someone moving around downstairs. Thinking it was Ellen unable to sleep, I rolled over. When I heard different noises, I sat up. I listened for and heard the sound of the coffee machine being turned on. Then I heard the sliding of not one chair, but two, moving away from the kitchen table and being pulled in again.

"Lady, come with me," I whispered, throwing on a robe

over my pajamas.

I headed down the stairs with my faithful dog.

Ahead of me, Lady let out a soft yip and galloped down the stairway.

I trotted after her sleepily. Coming to the kitchen doorway, I stopped short. Blinking rapidly, I chased the sleep from my eyes.

"Becky? Henry? Is that really you?"

Becky beamed and got to her feet. "We couldn't stay away another minute, don'tcha know. We've been up for hours, still on European time."

"Sure did miss this place," said Henry, rising and facing me with a beaming smile. "But that trip was a dream of mine."

I rushed into Becky's arms and hugged her again and again.

Henry's face flushed as I turned my attention to him, giving him a hearty hug. He patted my back awkwardly.

"I can't believe it! It's so great to see you! We've missed you so much!" I gushed.

"Is that sweet little Summer still here?" asked Becky.

I let out a whoosh of breath. "Oh boy! Sit down. Do I have a lot to tell you!"

I helped myself to a cup of coffee and pulled up a chair to the kitchen table. I'd just started to talk, when Ellen appeared, carrying Kaylie.

"Ma," Kaylie said, holding out her arms to me.

Tears filled my eyes as I took Kaylie into my arms. I twisted around so Becky and Henry could get a better look at her. I proudly brushed back Kaylie's brown hair from her face so they could see her dark eyes and the delicate features of her face. "This is Kaylie Crawford. It's official. She's Brad's and my little girl now."

"Well, isn't that something," said Henry, smiling.

"Yours?" Becky dabbed at her eyes. "I've been praying for something like that for you." She got to her feet and held out her arms. "Here, let me hold her."

I handed Kaylie to her then said, "You remember Ellen, don't you? She's coming to Maine to live." I clucked my tongue. "Oh dear, you don't know that Brad's dad died this summer."

"Aw," said Becky. "I'm sorry, Ellen. He was way too young."

Henry bobbed his head to Ellen. "I'm sorry to hear the news. He seemed like a good man the few times I met him."

"Thank you," said Ellen tearfully, taking a seat at the table. "Like you said, he was a good man. It's still such a shock to realize he's gone."

The sound of crying came through the baby monitor on the kitchen counter.

"Is that Summer?" Becky asked with a hopeful expression.

I smiled. "She's still with us, but we don't know for how long." It pained me to say the words.

"I'll get her," said Ellen, rising and leaving the room.

"Oh my," said Becky. "Such changes. How's that little boy?"

"Silas? He's doing beautifully. He comes with his mother here five days a week."

Becky frowned. "Where's Gracie? And what about Courtney?"

I filled her in on both of them as I fixed Summer's bottle.

Kaylie started to fuss, so I took her from Becky and put her in her highchair. She quieted when I placed a handful of Cheerios on her tray and began to prepare her breakfast.

Ellen came into the kitchen and handed Summer to Becky.

"Thanks." Becky shifted her seat to the rocking chair and began to give Summer her bottle.

I looked out the window as Odelle's car pulled up

"Whew, so many changes," she murmured. "Any more?"

"A few," I said, wondering how Becky would react to this latest piece of news.

CHAPTER THIRTY

Odelle came into the kitchen all smiles, holding Silas. "Sorry, I'm a little late. This young man is real lazy this morning." She stopped. "Oh, hello, everyone."

"Odelle, this is Becky and her husband Henry. They've just come back from a long cruise." I turned to them. "And this is Odelle."

As they exchanged greetings, I took Silas from Odelle. "A lazy boy, are you? Let's give Mommy time to get settled."

"Thanks," said Odelle. "I've brought some special window cleaner with me. Today, I'm finally going to tackle the windows in the sunroom. It looks like they haven't been properly done in some time."

Becky bristled. There was no better way to describe the straightening of her shoulders, the thinning of her lips, the defiant expression that crossed her face. Before she could say anything, I went over to her and whispered, "Don't worry. It's all okay. But we need to talk. Privately."

Silent, she took the empty bottle from Summer's mouth and sat her up in her lap. Rubbing Summer's back, Becky finally nodded her agreement.

Henry looked at me and winked. "So, Marissa, how did the fella do with all the landscaping and such while I was gone?"

"He's reliable like you said, but we really need you to supervise it. "

"Well, now, I can do that."

I turned to Becky. "Let's go into my office to talk. There's so much I want to tell you."

"I'll take the baby," Ellen said, stepping forward to take Silas, sneaking me a worried look. She knew how protective Becky was of the house.

Becky followed me into the office and took a seat in one of the leather chairs. I sat in the other chair, facing her.

"Have you replaced me?" Becky asked. The hurt look on her face made me uneasy.

I reached out and took her hand. "I've just changed things around a bit. I thought it was time to do that. The house is full of babies, and most likely there will be more in the future. We need you to help with them. Odelle is in need of full-time work as part of her rehab recovery. She's taking care of the house and helping with the babies."

"Is she cooking too?"

I shook my head.

Becky let out a sigh of relief. "Good. I'll go back to doing that on my regular schedule. And help with the babies too."

"That would be wonderful. On the weekends I'll take over. But, Becky, it's time for you and Henry to be more like grandparents than people working here. That would mean the world to me."

She studied me. "So you're serious about doing more foster care? I know you've been upset that you haven't been able to adopt Summer. How are you going to handle having more children here? You can't keep them all."

I hid my worry. "Yes, I know. But, hopefully, I can make a difference in their lives for the time they're with us. You know very well how scared I was when Summer was dropped off here. I've learned I can be a good mother. And I believe now that I was given this house for a reason. That's why I've decided to do this."

Becky patted my hand. "You're a good woman, Marissa. I

knew it the moment I met you."

Shaking my head, I said, "Not that good, but I'm working on it. And it's true, I'm going to need your help."

Becky straightened in her chair. "Well, then, I'll do it. It makes me so happy to be with all these babies, don'tcha know."

I gave her a hug. "I do know." Becky was such a good soul. She loved everyone. She'd even taken me under her wing when I first arrived at Briar Cliff and had no idea what I was getting into.

As we rose, relief filled me. I wouldn't want to lose Becky for anything. Becky and I met with Odelle. It took a lot of diplomacy on everyone's part, but the territories of the house were defined as to who controlled what. Odelle, the intuitive person that she was, handled Becky beautifully.

Over the next days, the two of them filled the house with friendly chatter. And when Odelle began to sing as she went about her work, Becky joined in from the kitchen, even after we all grimaced.

The weather turned crisper and cooler as the leaves on the trees turned to red and orange. Ellen helped me pick out two more strollers. When fair weather and the opportunity arose, Odelle, Ellen, and Becky rolled the babies up and down the long private road that connected the driveways to the houses in either direction.

With everyone's help, I was able to concentrate on going over figures for Rivers Papers. The board meeting was coming up, and I wanted to have information ready for Samantha, who was still planning to attend the meeting in my place. She wouldn't be alone. Allison was accompanying her to Riverton to study the paper mill's day care operation.

###

It became even more of a party atmosphere around the house when Brad announced he was returning home with Doris. As he pulled into the driveway, Ellen and I, holding Silas and Kaylie, hurried outside to greet them. Summer was upstairs, still napping.

Brad stepped out of the car and, holding Kaylie, I walked into his open arms. As he kissed me, Kaylie tapped on Brad's arm. "Da, bah".

Laughing, we pulled away from our embrace.

I hugged her to me and handed her over to Brad. "Daddy's home," I prompted.

She ignored me as Brad began to tickle her.

Taking advantage of being free, I hurried around the car to greet Doris. She and Ellen were hugging each other. I waited until they separated before giving Doris a hug. "Welcome! I'm so glad you're here."

She grinned and gave me an extra squeeze. "Me too. It's a long drive."

"Hopefully, the time will come when you won't have to make that trip to see us," I said.

"Have you heard any more from the couple interested in purchasing your house?" Ellen asked Doris as she shifted Silas from one arm to the other.

"They offered too little for it. I told them no. I can't afford to give away the place."

"Something will work out. Brad told me he's looking into a way to make this work," said Ellen. "In the meantime, I can't wait to show you the house I'm going to buy."

"I loved the picture of the house that you sent me," said Doris. "Maybe we can go there tomorrow."

We entered the house together. After Becky and Doris exchanged greetings, I took Doris' elbow and led her into the dining room to Odelle, who was dusting the china cabinet.

"Odelle's taken over the household," I explained to Doris with a grateful smile. "Becky's in charge of the kitchen, as usual."

After we exchanged greetings and pleasantries, I led Doris upstairs to one of the two empty guest rooms. I was pleased to have a full house. I'd been told that when my grandmother was alive, she seldom had guests. This house needed them.

Becky outdid herself making dinner for us. I gave her free rein. Her feelings were bruised enough without my adding to them by telling her what to make. It wasn't a problem. Everyone, especially Brad, loved her cooking.

We set the dining room table with my grandmother's china and silverware, making it a festive occasion. Later, with babies down for the night, we dined on the lemon-stuffed roast chicken and assorted grilled veggies Becky had prepared for us. Following that, no one turned away the apple pie she'd made.

Gazing around the table at Brad and his family, I felt so lucky to have them all here. Losing Jim had made us all more aware of one another.

Later, lying next to Brad in our bed, I sighed with pleasure as his arm came around me. Having him home made everything seemed more doable to me.

"Missed you," he said, drawing me up against his body.

I rolled over to face him. "I missed you too." My stomach suddenly growled.

Brad stared at me. "Are you okay?"

I shook my head and scrambled to my feet. "It must be the rich gravy Becky made." I dashed to the bathroom and promptly got rid of my dinner.

When I returned to the bedroom, Brad gave me a worried look. "Everything okay now?"

I shrugged. "I guess so. I hope I'm not getting the nasty flu Silas had."

Sliding under the sheets, I blew him a kiss, rolled over and closed my eyes.

I awoke to an empty bed, rain falling steadily outside and a deeper chill to the air coming in through the open window. Still feeling a little sick, I lay in bed, listening to the sounds of activity downstairs. I'd decided to stay in bed a while longer when my cell phone rang. I checked caller ID. Alice.

"Hello?" My voice shook at the possibilities behind the call.

"Oh, good, Marissa, you're up," said Alice. "Sorry to bother you so early in the morning, but I just got a call from Cherie. Celeste is going to be released from the program this weekend. She's done well and wants to meet with you today. She specifically asked for you to come alone with Summer. I've made arrangements to have you meet this afternoon at Dr. Smithson's office, in the same place where you met with Eleanor Worthington. Are you able to make it? Say around three o'clock?"

My stomach roiled with nervous anticipation. "Do you know why she wants to meet with me?"

"No, I'm sorry, I don't," said Alice. "Cherie didn't say."

"Of course, I'll come," I said. My nerves vibrated.

"Good. See you there." Alice hung up.

Clicking off the call, I took deep breaths to calm myself. All thoughts of lounging gone, I scrambled to my feet.

Downstairs, I found Ellen and Doris chatting at the kitchen table. Kaylie and Summer were sitting in their high chairs, playing with Cheerios which had been sprinkled on their trays.

"Good morning," said Ellen. "The girls have been fed."

"Good morning and thank you. Has anyone seen my husband?"

"He decided to go to a breakfast meeting in Portland," said Ellen. "He told us he needs to meet with another lawyer there."

Disappointed to find him gone, I fixed myself a cup of coffee and sat down at the table beside them.

"I thought I'd take Doris to Seaside Place to show her my house," said Ellen. "Brad took his new little car. He said I could use the Jeep today." She smiled at me. "Want to come with us?"

"No, thanks. I'd better stay here. I haven't been feeling that well." I didn't mention the upcoming meeting with Celeste. I was afraid sharing that news would add to the fear lurking inside me like a lioness about to spring.

Leaving Doris and Ellen chatting and sipping coffee, I went upstairs to take a shower.

I hurried through the process of getting ready for the day as if by rushing through it I could eliminate the tension-filled hours until I met with Celeste. I left a message for Brad on his phone, but I knew even if he called me back, his encouragement wouldn't get rid of my jitters.

I heard the sounds of activity in the sunroom. When I walked into the room, Doris and Ellen were watching Kaylie pull herself up to the coffee table.

"She'll be walking soon," said Ellen proudly.

Lying on a blanket nearby, Summer easily rolled from back to belly and back again, in preparation for crawling. Seeing them together, they seemed to have a special awareness of each other. My heart clutched at the thought of separating them.

Odelle arrived with Silas as Doris and Ellen headed

upstairs. We placed him in his infant seat in the sunroom where he could watch the girls playing. Sitting quietly, he seemed to take in their every moment before kicking and waving his arms as if he were playing with them.

I took this moment of privacy to ask Odelle how she was doing. She looked great. She'd lost even more weight. But I knew that the greater struggles with recovery were inside one's head.

She sat down on the couch next to me. "It's hard. I've given up the drugs all right, but I still need to work on the reasons why I took them, to begin with." Her eyes welled with tears. "I've been bullied most of my life—for my looks, for being stupid."

I stared at her with surprise. "You mean the kids at school?"

She shook her head. "No, my father."

I sank back into the couch, feeling as if I'd been kicked in the gut. I'd been abused by my step-father because he thought I was pretty. I couldn't imagine how awful it would be to have a father tell his child she was ugly.

"Oh, I'm so sorry," I said, knowing words were inadequate for the pain I felt for her.

"That's why I gained all this weight," said Odelle, patting her stomach. "Eating made me feel better for a short time."

"But you're losing weight now," I said. "And I'm sure I'm not the only one who thinks you're beautiful."

She smiled. "Silas' father thought so too." The smile left her face. "But then he left me."

"But not because of how you looked," I offered.

She shook her head. "No, because he was a lying, cheating bastard."

We laughed, dispelling the gloom that had filled the room.

Odelle rose. "Guess I'd better get going." She stopped and turned to me. "Thanks, Marissa. It felt good to get that out."

"Anytime. You and I might have a lot more in common than you think."

After Odelle left the room, I thought of the damage a parent could do to a child. My gaze turned to Summer. What would her life be like if she left us?

CHAPTER THIRTY-ONE

The babies were sleeping, and I was thinking about taking a nap myself when Brad called.

"Hey, hon, what's up? You wanted to talk to me about something?"

Taking a deep breath, I told him about the forthcoming meeting with Celeste. "What do you think it's about? And don't you think it's odd she wants to meet with me alone?"

"Hmmm. I can't begin to guess what it all means. Do you want me to go with you anyway?"

"No, I don't want to take a chance on annoying Celeste. I'm just scared stiff that she's decided to keep Summer. Alice mentioned she's done really well in the program. Maybe now, she'll be ready to take on the care of a baby." My voice cracked over the last sentence.

"Steady, now," said Brad. "Let's take it step-by-step."

"What are you doing in Portland?" I said, torn between wanting him at my side and worrying about irritating Celeste and getting on her bad side.

"I've been doing some work on getting an office here. Also, in reviewing my father's papers, I found a deed to land that he and Doris owned together. His share was bequeathed to my mother, but Doris still owns her share. I've been in touch with a buddy of mine, a real estate agent in Barnham. He thinks he might have a buyer for the land. If so, and my mother and Doris agree, it could mean a lot of money—enough for Doris to move here. Then Doris could rent her house to the young couple who like it and maybe do a lease-purchase with them."

"That would be wonderful! Does Doris know this?"

"Not yet. I thought it would be a nice surprise for her. Is she there?"

"No, she and your mother are still gallivanting around the area. Listen," I said, "don't bother to come home. Take care of that for them, and I'll let you know how the meeting goes."

"Are you sure?"

"Yes," I said, lying through my teeth.

At ten minutes to three, I pulled up to Dr. Smithson's office, willing my uneasiness away. Through the rearview mirror, I could see Summer in her seat gazing out the window with interest.

Clutching the wheel unnecessarily, I parked the car next to Alice's blue one and sat a moment, trying to gather the emotional strength to take Summer inside.

Unable to avoid the situation, I climbed out of the car and lifted Summer out of her seat. I stood a moment in the parking lot, clutching Summer to me, not knowing if I'd get the chance to hold onto her again.

The same grandmotherly figure who'd greeted me when we'd met with Eleanor stood as I walked inside. After confirming my name, she said, "They're waiting for you in the conference room. Do you remember where it is?"

Not able to speak with the lump in my throat, I nodded.

My surroundings grew dim as I made my way down the hallway to the conference room. Aware of what this meeting might mean for Brad and me, I stopped, and leaned against the wall.

When I walked into the room, Alice rose and came over to me, steadying me with her presence. "You, of course, know

Celeste and Cherie."

The two sisters stood together, their eyes focused on Summer.

"Yes. You both look great," I said, meaning it. Celeste's blond hair was now shoulder-length and sparkling clean. Her eyes sparkled too with a new awareness as she continued to gaze at Summer. Cherie also seemed healthier. The lines of stress that had once marred her facial features were now gone.

"May I hold her?" Celeste asked, holding out her arms.

I wanted to scream "no!" and run away, but I handed Summer to her.

Celeste brought Summer to her child-like chest and, closing her eyes, hugged her tightly.

Observing Celeste's tenderness as she held Summer to her, I was certain she'd decided to keep her. Bile rose in my throat.

"You'd better sit down," Alice said gently. "You look as if you need to."

Silently, I took a seat at the table.

Celeste continued to hug Summer to her body as she paced the room, talking softly to her.

Alice took hold of my arm, diverting my attention. "Cherie has something to say to you."

I turned my gaze to Cherie.

She cleared her throat. "Thank you so much for paying for the last weeks of my schooling." She beamed at me. "I got A's in everything. I have my certificate."

"Nice," I said automatically. "That's so nice. I'm glad you've done so well. Now you can have a career."

"Celeste and I are moving to California. One of the teachers got me a job outside of LA."

I swallowed hard. "Nice," I managed to get out, though the thought of them taking Summer so far away caused tears to form in my eyes.

"I believe Celeste has something to say to you," said Alice. "You'd better stand and face her."

Cold with dread, I forced myself to rise on legs gone weak.

"Here's your baby," mumbled Celeste, her voice shaking.

I tried to grasp what she'd said. When she handed Summer to me, I suddenly understood.

The tears that began to spill down Celeste's cheeks matched my own.

"You mean it? You really do?" I said, sobbing loudly. I hugged Summer to me, never wanting to let her go.

Cherie stood and put her arm around Celeste.

Celeste leaned her head against her sister's shoulder as tears continued to slide down her cheeks.

"Celeste did a really good job of choosing parents for her," said Cherie tearfully. "We know you love her like your own." Her voice broke, but she continued. "And we know you'll give her a good home and all the things we're not able to do."

"Oh, yes! I promise we will!" I rocked Summer in my arms. " I'll be the best mother I can!"

"You already are a wonderful mother," Alice said, dabbing at her eyes.

Summer patted my chest. "Maaa."

Still crying so hard I couldn't speak, I turned to Celeste.

Alice took Summer from me. "Go on. Give Celeste a proper hug for all she's doing for you."

I wrapped my arms around Celeste. "Thank you! Thank you!"

She sniffled. "Someday I want to be a mother like you."

"You will, you will," I said, understanding how much of a true mother she already was for making sure her baby would be well taken care of.

"Time to go," said Cherie, giving her eyes another wipe.

She spoke with a maturity that hadn't been there when I'd first met her. "The termination of rights paperwork is all signed. Alice is taking care of everything."

Celeste and I gave each other another hug, and then Cherie led her sister out of the room.

I collapsed on a chair and let more tears come.

"Are you all right?" Alice said, patting my shaking shoulders.

I lifted my tear-streaked face to her. "I'm just so ... so ... hap ... py ..." I sobbed.

She smiled, and I fought to control myself. Finally, I caught my breath. "Oh! I've got to call Brad. I promised I would."

Alice took Summer outside while I made the phone call. Between sobs, I got the news out. Hearing silence at Brad's end of the phone, I realized he was crying too.

Later, at home in the kitchen, we held a little celebration. Summer was aware of the bright colors of the balloons and stared at the lit candles on the cake Becky had made for her. But she couldn't know the extent of the joy filling our hearts.

Kaylie dug into her slice of cake, smearing vanilla frosting on the tray of her high chair and licking her hands. We laughed at her antics. The celebration was for her too. She had a sister, and we had two sweet girls.

The four of us adults toasted the two of them with a light white wine then raised our glasses to Ellen and Doris. They'd been thrilled when Brad told them about the land deal he was creating. Even now they couldn't stop talking about it.

"Will you help me choose the finishing touches on the décor of my new house?" Doris asked me.

I grinned. "I'd love it!" It was a dream come true for me

that she'd be nearby.

"We've got a lot of time to take care of it," Doris continued. "The builder told me it'll be several months before the house is ready. Maybe by then I'll have sold my house in New York. If not, like Brad says, I'll rent it."

"Until then, Doris can move in with me," said Ellen. She gave her sister-in-law a watery smile. "I really want the company."

"Of course. And my staying with you will give Brad and Marissa some space," Doris said.

Brad and I glanced at each other and grinned. *Time alone? Time for some fooling around?* It sounded like a very good idea.

Samantha called to say plans were set for her trip east to attend the board meeting at Rivers Papers. She and Allison and their kids were going to fly into Portland. Two days later, their husbands would fly in for the reunion. I could hardly wait to see all of them. I'd only viewed pictures of Allison's little daughter Lucy. At my wedding, the twins, Darren and Dawson, had been small toddlers and Samantha's daughter, Renne, and Allison's little Brian just babies.

I made an appointment to get my hair done. Since Summer's arrival, I hadn't made time to pamper myself. Truth be known, I needed a little attention. I'd let myself go.

I drove into Portland and parked the car. Standing outside, glancing at the stores around me, it seemed like ages since I'd been in town to shop or do anything for myself.

Henri, better known as Hank to his friends, was known for giving really good haircuts. I eagerly entered his beauty salon and spa, desperate for his help.

While I was at the check-in desk, Henri approached me.

"It's been a long time, Marissa." He lifted the hair away from my neck and studied it as it fell back. "We'll get a lot of this taken care of. It's really grown out. I see on the books you're going to have a facial too."

I nodded. When I'd told Ellen and Doris about getting my hair done, they'd sweetly suggested I might need a facial. I'd taken a look at myself in the mirror and decided they were right. My skin was uncharacteristically blotchy.

"Well, we'll take care of you," Henri now said sympathetically. "Get changed, have your facial and then come see me. I'll be waiting for you at my chair."

I changed out of my sweater, wondering if Odelle had shrunk it a bit. But then, ever since Becky came back, I'd made a pig of myself over her cooking. We all had.

I lay on the table, listening to the soft music, and felt my body relax as the technician went about giving me a facial.

When she was through, I rose on liquid legs, wondering how long it had been since I'd felt so chilled out.

An attendant led me to Henri.

He greeted me with a hug. "Ready, *ma chere*?"

I smiled. Henri's accent wasn't entirely French, but he was a sweetheart and clever, too.

As I watched in a daze, he performed a miracle with my hair, snipping and thinning and shaping into my familiar, easy style. The natural auburn color of my hair even looked better as he smoothed out the layers.

I thanked him and prepared to leave.

"*Magnifique!*" he declared and turned me over to an assistant who led me to one of the manicurists.

I leaned back in a chair while she worked on my hands, and another woman worked on my toes. The music in the background, the pampering all felt so good, I closed my eyes.

"Marissa? Time to wake up," a voice said close to my ear.

Startled, I opened my eyes to an amused expression on the face of the manicurist.

I sat up. "Have I been asleep long?"

She smiled. "Long enough for us to finish you and let your nails dry completely."

"I'm sorry. I've got two babies at home ..."

She raised a hand to stop me. "You don't have to explain to me. With four kids of my own, I know what it's like—completely exhausting."

I climbed out of the chair and headed back to the dressing area to change out of my robe. Instead of going shopping, I decided to go home. The girls would be getting up from their naps. Doris and Ellen had planned a day of outlet shopping and Becky and Odelle would be leaving soon.

Brad was there when I got home. "Hey, beautiful!" he said, wrapping his arms around me. "All set for the big reunion?"

I grinned. As eager as I was to see everyone else, I was more excited to show off the two little girls who'd become ours.

I was in the kitchen with Kaylie when the sound of the phone caught my attention. I checked caller ID and grinned. Samantha.

"Hi!" I said. "Did you just get in?"

"An hour or so ago. But, Marissa, Allie and I can't wait to see you! Can we come see you and those girls of yours?"

"Yes! What fun! Kaylie's up and Summer is about to get up from her nap. Hurry along. By the time you get here, I'll have them ready." Odelle had left early to attend a special meeting, but Becky was still around if I needed her.

I hung up and lifted Kaylie from the kitchen floor where

she'd been playing with plastic bowls. "C'mon, little girl! We're going to get you dressed up for your aunties."

Her dark eyes lit up.

Whispering baby talk to her, I carried her up the stairs to her room. Passing by Summer's door, I heard her stirring, but didn't stop.

I placed Kaylie on the floor with a book while I quickly looked through her clothes. At almost eleven months, Kaylie was small but wiry and amazingly agile. Like so many girls, she seemed to enjoy being out of play clothes and into a dress. I'd never had dolls growing up, so dressing up the girls was pure pleasure for me.

Together, Kaylie and I chose a white long-sleeved knit shirt with tiny ruffled cuffs to wear under a denim jumper. White tights and pink sneakers completed the casual look. I tied her dark hair up in a pink bow on top of her head.

"So pretty," I exclaimed. Looking at her happy smile, I wondered what would have happened to her if we or another foster family hadn't taken her in. She'd been so scrawny, so withdrawn when she first came to us. Now she was so alive, so bright.

I carried her into Summer's room and let her play while I got Summer changed. I chose a simple navy-blue, plaid dress and green tights for her to wear. The dark colors set off Summer's fair skin and blond hair beautifully. I pulled together what strands of hair I could and clipped on a little green bow.

"There! My girls look pretty!" I exclaimed, swinging Summer up into my arms and reaching for Kaylie.

"Oh, no! What have you done?"

Kaylie's face was streaked with white cream. I glanced at the tube of lotion she was holding and realized she must have opened the bottom drawer of the bureau. The tube must have accidentally fallen into it.

I set Summer down and lifted Kaylie onto the changing table. Gently, I wiped off the lotion from her face. Checking her mouth, I made sure none of it had gotten inside. Though I knew the lotion was food safe, I didn't want any other problems.

"You little imp," I said affectionately. I lifted her down to the floor and discovered Summer was busy shredding a book Kaylie had left there.

"Help!" I cried into the baby monitor.

Moments later I heard Becky as she hurried down the hall to us.

"Oh, thank goodness!" I told her. "I wasn't sure I could get both of them down the stairs and into the kitchen without a disaster. Samantha and Allison are on their way here to see the girls."

Becky picked up Summer. "I've got her."

We walked into the kitchen as Sam and Allie pulled up to the house.

"Let's go outside to greet them," I said to Becky. My heart pounded with happiness at the sight of two of my favorite people in the world.

Sam and Allie opened their car doors, stepped out, and rushed toward us.

"Oh, how cute!" Allie said, sweeping Kaylie into her arms. Kaylie stared solemnly at her.

"I can't believe how much she's grown!" said Samantha, jiggling Summer in her arms.

Summer's face crumpled. She let out a loud wail.

"Oh, dear! I've made her cry." Samantha handed her to me. "Here, Mom. You'd better take her."

In my arms, Summer stopped crying. "I'm sorry," I said. "She's at that awkward stage." I turned so that Summer could see them. "Look, Summer! It's Auntie Sam and Auntie Allie."

"Maaa," said Summer, laying her head against me.

I blinked rapidly, trying to hide the tears that unexpectedly came to my eyes.

Samantha took Kaylie into her arms and turned to me. "Your pictures don't do her justice," she told me, sweeping a strand of dark hair away from Kaylie's face.

Allie gave me a hug, careful not to crush Summer. "I'm so happy for you, Marissa! You have two wonderful little girls."

My throat choked up. I nodded, afraid once more of bursting into emotional tears.

I turned to Becky. "I'm sorry, I've been rude. Allie and Sam, you remember Becky."

"Of course," said Sam. "How are you holding up with all these babies?"

Becky beamed at her. "I love it, don'tcha know."

Allie said, "How was the cruise? I heard you and Henry had a wonderful time."

"Oh, yes, that we did," said Becky. "It's always been a dream of Henry's."

"Come in," I said. "We have some refreshments. And then, if you like, we can take a walk along the beach. There's little wind today so it should be pleasant."

We all went inside. As we walked through the kitchen I saw now the mess that had become natural with the addition of children. I liked it this way. After wondering if and when it would happen, I was thrilled I now faced the challenges of motherhood and all that went with it.

In the sunroom, the girls played around us. We sipped sodas and nibbled on nuts as we chatted, laughing and interrupting each other. It felt good to catch up with one another in a way phone calls never could.

"Are you ready for that walk on the beach?" Samantha

said after a while.

I went to find Becky and grab a light jacket.

When I returned, Allison and Samantha stood by the door on the front porch talking softly. They stopped when they saw me.

"Ready?" I said, curious as to what they'd been talking about.

Giving me impish smiles, they nodded.

CHAPTER THIRTY-TWO

Without an onshore breeze and with bright afternoon sun, the air held a warmth I welcomed. I looped my arms through Samantha's and Allison's. Forming a laughing line, the three of us strolled along the beach. "Ahhh, it feels so good to have some time to myself," said Samantha.

"We're lucky to be able to leave the winery at this time of year. It's a good thing we have good help," said Allison. "After the reunion on Saturday, I'll return to California with Blake and the kids."

"Derek and I are going to spend a couple of extra days with Mom and Dad," said Samantha. "Dad's remarkable for someone his age, but Mom says he's failing."

"That's one reason Blake agreed to come—to see my father." Allison shook her head sadly. "I wanted my kids to at least get to meet him."

"It's sad when the older generation ages and disappears. That's why it's good to keep the family growing," Samantha said, smiling at me.

Allison stopped walking and turned to face me. "So when are you going to tell us?"

I frowned. "Tell you what?"

Allison and Samantha exchanged sly looks.

"She doesn't know," said Samantha, giving me an incredulous look.

"Know what?" I said, more snappishly than I'd wanted.

Grinning, Allison shook her head. "When was your last period?"

"A little tired lately?" Samantha said. "Upset stomach? Emotional? And, like now, a little irritable?"

Their words caught me off balance. I stumbled backward and clapped my hands to my cheeks. "Oh, my God! Do you think ..." I couldn't go on.

Allison came to me and wrapped me in a hug. "Could it be?"

I thought about the symptoms. *Period, no. Tired, yes. Upset stomach, definitely. Emotional? Outrageously so.*

"You really didn't know?" Samantha said, enclosing me in a hug.

"I've been so busy, so tired, so emotional lately, but I thought it was all part of being a mother. And my period. I thought ... never mind what I thought." I suddenly started to laugh, a bit hysterically. "Oh my God! Oh my God!"

As quickly, my laughter turned to sobs. "Brad will be so happy." Tears streamed down my face, warm reminders of all the tears we'd shared recently.

"Oh, I've got to take the test to make sure of it before I say anything to him." I started running toward the house, stopped and called out, "Sorry, I'll catch up with you later."

"Take your time," said Samantha. "We'll take our walk and meet you back at the house."

I dashed up the front porch steps and into the house.

"Everything all right?" asked Becky as I raced by her to get to the stairway.

"I hope so," I answered, taking the stairs two at a time.

At the top of the stairway, I stopped and held my sides. *Be calm! Be calm!*

Walking quickly, I went into my bathroom and opened the drawer that held two pregnancy test kits I'd bought earlier when I thought there was a good chance of getting pregnant.

With shaking hands, I opened one of them and quickly

read through the directions.

Going into the small room containing the toilet, I checked my watch. The result should show up within ten minutes. I closed the door, said a little prayer, and followed the instructions for the test. Afterward, I sat on the toilet seat cover. Not daring to look at the results, I closed my eyes.

After what seemed hours, I opened my eyes and stared at the stick. A big plus sign winked at me.

I held back a scream of joy, jumped to my feet and opened the door.

Brad was just walking into the bedroom. "Are you all right? Becky said she was worried about you."

"You'd better sit down." My voice trembled. "I have something to tell you."

"Are you sick?" Brad's face turned ashen.

"Well, I have been a little nauseous lately, a little tired, a little emotional ..." I couldn't go on. I threw myself into his arms. "I'm pregnant! I'm going to have your baby!"

Brad sat so still I wondered if he'd heard what I'd said. Then I felt his shoulders shaking.

I hugged him hard, crying myself.

The thought of having three babies in one year hit me and I started laughing. "You've always said you wanted a big family. Did you ever think it would happen this way?"

Brad cupped my face in his broad hands. "I love you, Marissa. You're the best mother I know." He placed his hands on my stomach. "Wow! Another baby."

"We won't love this one more or less than the two we have," I said, vowing to make it so.

"You're right. I don't even care what sex this baby is as long as it's healthy." He gazed at me with wonder. "It feels damn good to know my body works."

I grinned and kissed him with all the love I felt.

###

The house rang with children's laughter as Samantha's twin boys and Allison's son raced through the house, chasing each other. Under Odelle's supervision, Samantha's daughter, Renne, sat on the floor in the sunroom with my two girls and Allison's Lucy. Renne was reading to the three younger girls from a picture book that held no words. It didn't matter that the story she told made no sense or that the girls weren't paying attention, what mattered was that the cousins were together at last.

Holding Silas, Brad joined Blake, Derek, and Uncle George on the front porch where a lot of loud talking and teasing were taking place.

Allison, Samantha and their mother Adrienne joined Ellen and Doris and me in the kitchen. Sipping coffee, we chatted together as Becky put the finishing touches on the cake she'd baked especially for the occasion.

I rose quietly and went through the house to the front porch. Brad caught sight of me and nodded at my signal.

"Would you please join Marissa and me in the sunroom?" he asked the men.

Giving him questioning looks, they got to their feet.

I hurried back to the kitchen. "Would you all join Brad and me in the sunroom?" I said.

Allison and Samantha gave me sly looks and rose. We'd sworn them to secrecy.

My pulse racing with excitement, I led the way through the house.

The spacious sunroom seemed almost crowded as everyone gathered around. The children were silent as they stared at the circle of adults.

I went over to Kaylie and picked her up. Brad gave Silas

to his mother and lifted Summer into his arms.

Standing in the middle of the group, I said, "Kaylie has something to tell you." I hoped she remembered what we'd practiced over and over.

"So, Kaylie," I prompted. "What do you have to say?"

Her bright-eyed smile was reassuring. She pointed to my stomach. "Bay Bee."

I watched Ellen's expression change from puzzled to one of surprised understanding.

"We're going to have another baby," said Brad. The pride in his voice was touching.

"A baby!" shrieked Renne. "Can it be mine?"

Everyone laughed, and when Renne clapped her hands, all joined in.

I gazed around the room. Ellen and Doris, their arms linked, were dabbing at their eyes with tissues. Hugging Silas to her, Odelle beamed at me. Clapping like crazy, Becky kept saying "I knew it! Don'tcha' know!" Henry walked into the room and gave me a big smile. Adrienne and George continued to clap enthusiastically while Sam gave me a thumbs-up sign and Allie blew me a kiss. The guys in the group clapped Brad on the back as if he were the only one involved.

Listening to the sound of their applause and seeing their happiness for us, my heart was overjoyed. The family that filled this house would grow and change through the years, but we all would welcome this little one into our lives as we'd done for Summer and Kaylie.

Brad gave me a kiss to louder applause.

We smiled at each other, aware our lives would be filled with more baby talk as little ones of our hearts entered our lives and left, knowing they were loved.

I hope you've enjoyed reading *Baby Talk,* Marissa's journey into motherhood. If you have, please help other readers discover it by leaving a review on Amazon, Goodreads, or your favorite site. It's such a nice thing to for any author.

Enjoy an excerpt from *Finding Me,* Book #1 in the Salty Key Inn Series, which is about the three Sullivan sisters discovering they've inherited a hotel on the Gulf Coast of Florida.

CHAPTER ONE
SHEENA

In early January, Sheena Morelli sat with her two sisters in a conference room of the Boston office of Lowell, Peabody and Wilson, a well-respected law firm, wondering why they'd been ordered to meet to discuss a legal matter with Archibald Wilson himself.

"Do either of you have any idea why we're really here?" said her youngest sister, Regan. "The letter from Mr. Wilson said something about a reading of a will. But that doesn't make sense to me. I didn't even know Gavin Sullivan."

"Me, neither. He's probably some rich uncle leaving us a lot of money," teased Darcy, the typical middle sister, who was always kidding around.

Sheena laughed with her. The three Sullivan sisters had no rich relatives that they knew of in their modest family. They were hard workers who relied on only themselves to make it through life. *Well,* thought Sheena, *maybe Regan wasn't as reliable as she and Darcy.* As the baby of the family, Regan had always been a bit spoiled. At twenty-two and eager to escape her old life in Boston, Regan wasn't about to spend too much time with the family. This time, though, at the formal request of Mr. Wilson, Regan had dutifully left New York City to come to "Bean Town."

As Sheena waited in the conference room for Mr. Wilson to show up, she studied Regan out of the corner of her eye. With her long, black hair, big, violet-blue eyes, and delicate Sullivan features, she was a knockout—a Liz Taylor look-alike.

Darcy sat on the other side of Sheena in a stiff-backed chair. Studying Darcy's blue eyes, red hair, and freckled nose, Sheena thought of her as cute...and funny...and maybe a little annoying, though everyone seemed to love Darcy's sassy attitude. At twenty-six, Darcy claimed she hadn't found her true calling. Whatever that meant.

Sheena had found her calling in a hurry when she got pregnant as she was starting college, where she'd planned to take nursing courses. Ironic as it was, her wanting to become a nurse and getting caught like that, had changed many things for her. Now, at thirty-six and with a sixteen-year-old son and a fourteen-year-old daughter, she still hadn't recovered from losing her dream.

She straightened in her chair as a tall, gray-haired man entered the room carrying a file of papers.

"Good morning, ladies. I'm Archibald Wilson, the lawyer representing Gavin Sullivan. I'm pleased you all could attend this reading of his will," he announced in a bass voice. He looked the three of them over critically. "Which one of you is Sheena Sullivan Morelli?"

She raised her hand. "I'm Sheena. Do you mean the 'Big G' Sullivan?"

Both of her sisters gasped at her. The name "Big G

Sullivan" had been mentioned in the family on rare occasions, and only when her father and his two other brothers had had too many beers. And then it was never kindly.

Mr. Wilson nodded with satisfaction. "Yes, that's my client. Sheena, though all three of you are beneficiaries, I will address you on most of the issues, as it pertains to the specific language of the will."

Sheena sat back in her chair, her mind spinning. This scene seemed so surreal. Their father had broken his relationship with this brother years ago.

"He's left something for us?" said Darcy. "I was only teasing about such a thing."

The lawyer frowned at her, took a seat facing them on the other side of the small conference table, and opened the file he had carried in.

He began to speak: "I, Gavin R. Sullivan, of the State of Florida, being of sound and disposing mind and memory, do make, publish, and declare this to be my Last Will and Testament ..."

Certain words faded in and out of Sheena's shocked state of mind. Though her sisters might have been too young to remember him, she had a clear image of the big, jovial man who'd captivated her with his smile, his belly laughs, and the way her father grew quiet when they were in the same room together. On one particular visit, Uncle Gavin gave her a stuffed monkey that she'd kept on her bed for years. It wasn't until the fur on the monkey was worn off that she'd noticed a seam was tearing. One day, while she was probing the hole, a gold coin fell out.

Sheena showed the coin to her mother, who snatched it away and whispered, "Don't tell anyone about this. It's very valuable. Someday you'll need it. Until then, I'll keep it safe for you. Uncle Gavin loves you very much." As her father walked through the doorway, her mother held a finger to her lips.

Until now, Sheena had forgotten all about the coin.

Archibald Wilson's voice brought her back to the present. "Sheena, you, Darcy, and Regan are now the legal owners of the Salty Key Inn, but you, Sheena, will be in charge of taking over the small hotel in Florida, as your uncle directed in his will. Is that understood by the three of you?"

Sheena and her sisters dutifully bobbed their heads. The bewilderment on her sisters' faces matched her own feelings. How on earth were the three of them going to run a hotel?

"Remember," Mr. Wilson warned them, "the hotel may not be sold for a period of one year. And the three of you must live there together for that entire time if you are to have a share in the rest of his sizeable estate, which will remain undisclosed until the end of your year in Florida. You have just two weeks to prepare. In conversations I had with him in setting up the will, I believe Gavin Sullivan intended for this to be a life lesson for each of you."

"Whoa! Wait a minute! What about the lease on the condo I share with two of my friends? I can't just walk away from that," said Darcy.

"And mine?" said Regan.

The lawyer nodded. "Read over the conditions of the will. Any expenses like that will be taken care of by Gavin's estate. All expenses as you settle in will be handled through me. But, beware, there will be hidden tests for you throughout this entire process. Tests that could make a lot of difference to each of you."

Sheena exchanged worried glances with her sisters. She wished she'd asked their mother for more information about the uncle she was never to mention. And now it was too late. Their mother had died a little over a year ago.

"Live together in Florida for a whole year? Was Uncle Gavin crazy when he set up this deal?" exclaimed Darcy. Her indignation was understandable.

Mr. Wilson stood. "I realize you all have a lot to talk about, a lot to think about. And let me know if you need any further clarification of the terms of the will. You are welcome to continue using this conference room, and please feel free to help yourself to any of the refreshments on the side table." His lips curved with a touch of humor in what had been a mostly expressionless face. "Enjoy the challenge."

After Mr. Wilson left them, Sheena sank back into her chair. Her mind raced at the thought of suddenly leaving Boston to go live with her sisters in Florida for an entire year. How could she do that? It would be difficult for her on many levels. They were sisters, after all, and like sisters everywhere, being together for too long sometimes caused battles to erupt. More than that, she had a family. And her husband, Tony, wouldn't like the idea at all. Her children even less.

"What a joke," said Darcy, shaking her head. "Spending every day with the two of you for an entire year? Running a hotel? No way. And, Sheena, Tony would never allow you to do something like this. You're what he calls 'the Mrs'. And what about the kids?"

At Darcy's dismissive tone of voice, Sheena glared at her. "What did you mean by that 'Mrs.' remark?"

"Don't take it the wrong way," urged Regan. "It's just that your family depends on you for everything. Especially Tony."

Deep in thought, Sheena remained quiet. Tony was a good man who prided himself on always doing the right thing. And he expected her to fulfill what he thought was her proper role.

Though their relationship was still new when she got pregnant, Tony had stepped right up and offered to marry her so all her mother's conservative church friends wouldn't count on their fingers how many days it took for their first baby to appear. It helped that their son, Michael Morelli, had started his life in the outside world a little late. Still, Sheena had always appreciated Tony's consideration.

A worried sigh escaped her. She knew Tony wouldn't support her being away from their family for an entire year. That would be going against his idea of her in the proper role of taking care of their family. And yet, with his business doing poorly recently, it might be an answer to their prayers, though Tony's fragile ego might prevent her from saying so.

"What about you two?" Sheena asked. "You'll have to quit your jobs. What then?"

Regan shrugged. "I don't care. My job is boring—answering phone calls, greeting people and all. They'll just find another receptionist to take my place."

Darcy shook her head. "Receptionist? You were much more than that. More like some kind of hostess with all those special meetings you helped them with. When I visited you in New York, I witnessed how it was—all those guys drooling over you as you served them drinks before they went out to some business dinner."

A blush crept up Regan's cheeks. Her eyes flashed a pretty violet-blue as she stared Darcy down. "It's a decent job, respectable and safe. Those guys can look all they want, but they keep their hands off me. That's the way I set it up, working for this company. Besides they're all old, married men. Why would I want anything to do with men like that?"

"What about you, Darcy?" Sheena asked. "You've got a very good job working in IT."

Darcy grimaced. "Actually, I don't like it very much. Working with numbers and codes all day isn't that exciting. Mom was always so proud of me and my job that I didn't dare tell her I wasn't happy there. But, with her gone, I've been thinking of doing something else." She smiled. "Maybe this whole thing isn't dumb after all. Maybe this will be the beginning of something new for all of us."

Sheena returned her smile. Put this way, it sounded wonderful. If, only ...

About the Author

Judith Keim enjoyed her childhood and young-adult years in Elmira, New York, and now makes her home in Boise, Idaho, with her husband and their two dachshunds, Winston and Wally, and other members of her family.

While growing up, she was drawn to the idea of writing stories from a young age. Books were always present, being read, ready to go back to the library, or about to be discovered. All in her family shared information from the books in general conversation, giving them a wealth of knowledge and vivid imaginations.

A hybrid author who both has a publisher and self-publishes, Ms. Keim writes heart-warming novels about women who face unexpected challenges, meet them with strength, and find love and happiness along the way. Her best-selling books are based, in part, on many of the places she's lived or visited and on the interesting people she's met, creating believable characters and realistic settings her many loyal readers love. Ms. Keim loves to hear from her readers and appreciates their enthusiasm for her stories.

"I hope you've enjoyed this book. If you have, please help other readers discover it by leaving a review on Amazon, Goodreads, or the site of your choice. And please check out my other books:

The Hartwell Women Series
The Beach House Hotel Series
The Fat Fridays Group
The Salty Key Inn Series
Seashell Cottage Books
Chandler Hill Inn Series
Desert Sage Inn Series

ALL THE BOOKS ARE NOW AVAILABLE IN AUDIO on Audible and iTunes! So fun to have these characters come alive!"

Ms. Keim can be reached at **www.judithkeim.com**

And to like her author page on Facebook and keep up with the news, go to: **https://bit.ly/3acs5Qc**

To receive notices about new books, follow her on Book Bub - **http://bit.ly/2pZBDXq**

And here's a link to where you can sign up for her periodic newsletter! **http://bit.ly/2OQsb7s**

She is also on Twitter @judithkeim, LinkedIn, and Goodreads. Come say hello!

Acknowledgements

Writing involves sitting in a room conversing with imaginary people in a world you've created. Without real people, real friends, in a real world, a writer is without balance. I am so appreciative of my real friends who encourage me to continue writing by giving me their support! You know who you are and you know I love you! Thanks!

Made in the USA
Middletown, DE
07 October 2024

62148009R00198